SECRETS
OF THE
UNIFIED FIELD

THE PHILADELPHIA EXPERIMENT,
THE NAZI BELL,
AND THE DISCARDED THEORY

JOSEPH P. FARRELL

Other Books by Joseph Farrell
SS BROTHERHOOD OF THE BELL
REICH OF THE BLACK SUN
THE COSMIC WAR
THE GIZA DEATH STAR
THE GIZA DEATH STAR DEPLOYED
THE GIZA DEATH STAR DESTROYED

SECRETS OF THE UNIFIED FIELD

Adventures Unlimited Press

Secrets of the Unified Field

ISBN 13: 978-1-931882-84-2

Published by:
Adventures Unlimited Press
One Adventure Place
Kempton, Illinois 60946 USA
auphq@frontiernet.net

www.adventuresunlimitedpress.com

SECRETS OF THE UNIFIED FIELD

THE PHILADELPHIA EXPERIMENT, THE NAZI BELL, AND THE DISCARDED THEORY

JOSEPH P. FARRELL

TABLE OF CONTENTS

PART ONE:
THE DISCARDED THEORY

PART TWO:
THE AMERICAN SHIP AND THE ACCIDENTAL DISCOVERY

PART THREE:
THE NAZI BELL AND THE INTENTIONAL WEAPON

BIBLIOGRAPHY

PREFACE

It is perhaps inevitable, having researched so many different aspects of hidden history, of physics, and of the peculiar interplay between the two, that I should turn at last to a consideration of that most famous story within the lore of suppressed science and technology: the story of the Philadelphia Experiment. Ever since starting down this road of research years ago, I knew that inevitably I would have to deal with it. But, if the truth be told, I came to do so not without a great deal of reluctance.

This is not to say that the story did not and does not intrigue me. Indeed, quite the opposite. Ever since I bought Charles Berlitz's and William Moore's *The Philadelphia Experiment: Project Invisibility*, and reading it in one rather breathless and stupefied sitting, the story has captivated me. As it has done for many of its readers, the book left me with a sense of incompleteness and wanting more. Clearly, more needed to be said and done with the story; even Berlitz and Moore implied as much.

But then came a wild and weedy mythological overgrowth to the story. Alleged crew members and participants stepped forward with nonsense about time travel and new lives, with identities so contorted and convoluted that it would take someone with twin PhDs in physics and genealogical research to sort out (and a PhD in psychiatry would probably also help). This tropical overgrowth was not helped any by the grafting of the whole "Montauk Project" mythology onto the Philadelphia Experiment story that included new players. This only added to the jungle, for now the story not only included past lives, altered consciousness, time travel and antigravity, but also bizarre and dark experimentation into consciousness manipulation, induced schizophrenia, Nazi U-boats, and pro-Nazi German "colonists", all of which were concentrated in the unlikely east end of Long Island!

All of this neo-Gnostic nonsense was a strong deterrent to my desire to publish in book form my thoughts, taken over many years and recoded in many notebooks, on the alleged Philadelphia Experiment, since at root I believed the story itself to be true, but true in a way that is simultaneously much more prosaic and less sensational than standard accounts, and yet by dint of that very prosaic character, much more sensational than the weedy and stupid overgrowth that a few have attempted to fasten onto the original story. So much, then, for the Montauk Project and Al Bielek.

However, once the original alleged facts about the story are grasped, then the sensational aspects not only remain, but become even more grim and dark than any Montauk mythology of alleged time-traveling individuals can possibly convey with their stories. This is because the Philadelphia Experiment, born in the cauldron of World War Two, in a strange, cryptic, and almost "synchronous" way is connected to another equally strange story of suppressed science and technology from that war: the story of the Nazi "Bell" device. Accordingly, this book revisits *both* stories, adding to the volume of scientific speculation about them. This book is therefore also a revisiting of the Nazi Bell story, a new look at it, to say the things in the context of the Philadelphia Experiment that could not be said in my previous book on the Bell, *The SS Brotherhood of the Bell,* for there may indeed be a strong connection between the two experiments in theory, or better put, in *a* theory, a *discarded* theory.

As will be seen in the main text, when the two experiments are compared a bizarre and almost ironic set of parallels begins to pop out, and surely one of the strangest of these ironies is that the Americans with their ship, with but a very few exceptions – were not looking for what they found, didn't know what they had found when they found it, and didn't know what to do with it once they had. The Germans with their Bell – and similar devices as we shall discover – conversely not only were looking for what they found, they knew more or less *how* to look, and knew what they wanted to do with it when they found it. They wanted to weaponize it. If there was presumption on their part, it was not in the accidental discovery of unanticipated non-linear effects as it was for the Americans, it was in their confidence that the available technology was sufficient to the task of passing from revolutionary experimental confirmations of theoretical concepts to practical and realizable weapons. Thus, the picture is not one of "bumbling Americans" versus "brilliant Nazis", but more a picture of brilliance on both sides, and a certain presumption and over-confidence as well.

In any case, as will be seen in the main text of this book, the Germans scientists involved with the Bell project, in order to be able to look where they wanted to look, had to "fudge" a bit on Nazi prohibitions of discussions or pursuits of a certain Jewish physicist's ideas and dress them up in the crisply tailored and fine-lined Nazi uniforms. And if that sales pitch failed, they still had other "purely Aryan" alternatives to that Jewish physicist's unfinished theory, alternatives that were *not* based in quantum mechanics, but which were higher dimensional "unified field" theories in their own right. And as we shall also discover, these higher dimensional approaches were the ultimate inspiration for that Jewish physicist to abandon his famous theory of General Relativity and search for something even more complete and theoretically satisfying. He found it, and published it in 1928, and called it the Unified Field Theory, a theory that physics ultimately discarded, and in that, too, lies a story.

This book is thus also about that discarded theory and how it strangely united two of the Second World War's strangest experiments, experiments being conducted by two combatants on opposite sides of the war. It is a story of how that theory arose, why it appeared so promising and, for the Nazis, so weaponizable, and why it disappeared almost completely as a basis for engineering experiments after the war. Indeed, its disappearance as an *electrically engineerable* even if incomplete theory is almost as strange as the experiments themselves, and this raises the specter that maybe someone *wanted* the theory to disappear for reasons *other* than its theoretical "incompleteness". The Philadelphia Experiment and the Nazi Bell are indicators into the possible reasons why someone would have wished its disappearance.

In yet another ironic parallel, the technologies associated with the theory and the two experiments also simply disappeared after the war, and curiously, not a word was ever heard about them again until decades had passed. Not even anything *resembling* these experiments were done for many years, and when they were, the wartime backdrop from which they might have been properly evaluated was long since gone, or, in the case of the Nazis and their Bell device, deliberately buried after the requisite bullets, unmarked mass graves, disappearing SS generals and vanishing massive heavy lift aircraft, all of which is a clear and obvious indicator that someone was desirous of suppressing the science and technology, of expunging it and removing it forever from any potential public scrutiny and analysis.

But what of the American side of this Unified Field equation? How was it buried? Fear, bureaucratic inertia, the promise of other theories, conspiracy…perhaps all of these played a role, and some of them will be explored in this book. In this regard, it is another of those strange ironies surrounding these two experiments that the physical effects named for some of the American scientists allegedly involved in the Philadelphia Experiment were renamed or simply never even mentioned in physics texts in connection with the scientists's names, lest the curious, perhaps, follow things through to their logical conclusions. The scientist's names themselves were almost completely erased, Tesla-like, from mainstream texts. One seldom hears in a university classroom of the Biefeld-Brown Effect, or Kron's tensor analysis of electrical circuits and its implications for that discarded theory. Indeed, with respect to the pioneering work of Kron, one of my attempts to acquire his paper on tensor analysis of rotating electrical machinery through interlibrary loan brought forth a curious response from my librarian: the work was only available for loan from one library, a private corporate library, and would cost $1,200.00 merely to borrow, an effective method of suppression if there ever was one! Finally, one hears little of the deadly and weaponizable potentials of the Philadelphia Experiment and the Nazi Bell device, as if a form of wishful thinking had taken over the alternative research community.

In the latter regard, I have noticed a trend since the appearance of my first books on the Great Pyramid, and more recently my previous book on the Bell, *The SS Brotherhood of the Bell*. The trend, in either case, downplays, or simply outright ignores or pretends not to understand my arguments that these things were conceived as *weapons*. To my continuing surprise, I have received a steady flow of contacts since the first books' appearance. Emails and letters from friends, fans, associates have speculated – often more wildly than I did in the books themselves – on the "time travel" and "dimensional portals" and other possibilities that they represent to them. In this book I hope to dissuade such interpretations by reasserting that at least the Bell and its related cousins in the Nazi black projects arsenal were envisioned as none of these things. It was not even envisioned as a weapons platform, but as a weapon. And given the physics involved, a weapon of mass destruction at that.

Once the physics underlying both projects is in view, and once its frightening and awesome potential is understood, then there simply is no *need* for the monuments of unbridled imagination of the Montauk mythology or split time-traveling identities to provide sensational elements. The physics itself is the story, and it is sensational enough. So if the reader wants more "time-traveling" anecdotes and "fresh revelations" from "new anonymous sources" that have "finally decided to disclose what they know" or "more recovered memories" from hypnotic regression or "channeled messages" from some "spirit guide", then put this book down, pass it by, and go elsewhere.

The science involved in the two projects was not a late night radio talk show game either for the Americans or for the Germans. The harsh realities of World War Two would have prohibited *absolutely* any quests for such nonsense as dimensional portals, time travel, or optical invisibility or teleportation. Both for the Americans and for the Germans it was a matter of life and death priorities of which projects to *fund*. Imagine presenting to those nations' respective scientific research oversight committees requests for funding to make ships invisible, or to open higher dimensional gateways, and one immediately appreciates the ridiculousness and sheer lunacy of some of the speculations surrounding these two experiments. The Americans making such nonsensical proposals would have likely been relegated to the loony farm, and the Germans making them very likely relegated to the slave-labor pools of the concentration camps, or, if the idea were zany enough, becoming researchers for Reichsführer SS Himmler's loony and brutal *Ahnenerbedienst*, the SS' secret occult and esoteric research bureau.

No such things will be offered here. No sound bites, no new revelations, no new recovered memories, no channeled messages, in short, none of the pabulum-puking New Age Gnostic nonsense that so often characterizes alternative research. To be sure, this *is* a book of high speculation, but it is not *ungrounded* speculation. What *is* offered here is a speculation that will require that the reader twist his mind – pun intended – around some difficult mathematical and geometrical concepts that I believe lie at the heart of the Philadelphia Experiment and, more importantly, behind the dreadful doomsday weapon that the Nazis understood their terrible Bell device to be, and *why* they understood it to be such. Accordingly, it is to be emphasized that the technical matter of this book will be difficult, notwithstanding every attempt to present the concepts in a manner condign to a general audience. However, in most of my previous books I have attempted to initiate the reader into a process of scientific speculation gradually and over the course of the book. But here nothing else will do other than to throw him right from the start into the deep end of some very technical concepts whose relevance and importance only becomes manifest as he swims toward the shallow end of their application in these two experiments themselves.

As a result of the speculative scientific analysis, what is also offered here is another look at the possible histories of these experiments based on the scientific model adopted to analyze them. Accordingly, the physics basis for the analysis offered here may indeed be wrong or incorrect – after all the theory on which both projects were in part based was ultimately discarded – but at least it is a basis in the concepts of science and not recovered memories or channeled messages from the sun god Ra. I therefore claim my right to be wrong, and certainly would not argue that the physical model employed here for analysis is the only basis on which to do so. This model merely implies a kind of "provisional history" lies behind both projects.

Indeed, it is difficult if not impossible to reconstruct that science without a reconstruction of those histories. For example, what sorts of considerations actually led to the performance of these experiments? What was going through the scientists' minds as they dreamed them up? What sorts of experimental benchmarks might they have laid down to check their scientific progress and justify their respective governments' funding of their projects? And for that matter, how does one account from the same physics model for the fact the one side found its strange experimental effects by accident, and that the other found them deliberately?

These questions highlight the importance of the histories of both projects, as recounted in the primary sources that broke both stories: for the Bell, Igor Witkowski's superb book on German secret weapons, *The Truth About the Wunderwaffe,* and Nick Cook's vitally important *The Hunt for Zero Point,* and for the Philadelphia Experiment, the book that introduced the story to a wide audience, Charles Berlitz's and William Moore's *The Philadelphia Experiment: Project Invisibility.* The latter book in turn references the crucial book *The Case for the UFOs* by early UFOlogist Dr. Morris Jessup in its "Varo Annotated Edition," a work extraordinarily difficult to come by. Accordingly it is reviewed in some detail here since it is not well-known, even to readers who may be familiar with Berlitz's and Moore's presentation of the story, or with Jessup's work in its non-annotated version.

A final word of thanks is necessary to those who have inspired me to write about the Philadelphia Experiment after so many years of personal demurring on my part and scratching my thoughts in my private notebooks: to my friend Tim Ventura of americanantigravity.com for spending so many hours with me on the phone exchanging and discussing ideas; to my friend Rich Wood and to Zhe Yong for helping me to track down the Varo edition of Jessup's book on the internet. A big word of thanks for Peter Levenda, who graciously allowed me access to the UFO FBI files of agent Guy Bannister, and for the many observations quoted here from his excellent series *Sinister Forces: A Grimoire of American Political Witchcraft.* Also many thanks to Henry Stevens for the excellent material in his most recent and by any reckoning excellent work, *Hitler's Suppressed and Still-Secret Weapons, Science, and Technology,* a book that deservedly ranks at the pinnacle of books about Nazi secret weapons along with Igor Witkowski's *The Truth About the Wunderwaffe.* Finally, thanks as always are due to my publisher David Hatcher Childress, for having the courage to publish it.

Joseph P. Farrell
Rapid City, South Dakota
2007

PART ONE:
THE DISCARDED THEORY

"I discovered that this theory – at least in first approximation – yields the field equations of gravitation and electromagnetism in a very simple and natural manner. Thus it seems possible that this theory will substitute the theory of general relativity in its original form"

Albert Einstein, "New Possibility for Unified Field Theory of Gravitation and Electricity,"
Session Report of the Prussian Academy of Sciences,
June 14, 1928.

1.
TENSORS, TORSION, AND WRINGING AN ALUMINUM CAN

"Then (Marduk) spake with his mouth, and the garment vanished; Again he commanded, and the garment reappeared."
The Babylonian Epic, *Enuma Elish,* Tablet 4[1]

In 1928, in a small paper submitted to the Prussian Academy of Sciences, physics' most famous man included a small little mathematical expression, $\Lambda_{\alpha\beta}{}^{\nu}$, to which he appended a short comment: "this tensor shall be used as a starting point for characterizing a continuum, and not the more complicated Riemannian curvature tensor."[2] The reader's eyes may have glazed over at all of this mathematical jargon, but most assuredly the eyes of the readers of Albert Einstein's latest physics paper did not. And the reason why they did not glaze over is what this book is about, for that little mathematical expression and its related concepts in all likelihood became the conceptual basis for two of the Second World War's most famous and bizarre secret weapons experiments and projects: the Philadelphia Experiment, and the Nazi Bell.

Their eyes did not glaze over because Einstein then followed this pithy and significant statement with three more equations, after which he appended an even shorter comment that he intended to investigate whether "laws with relevance to physics can be derived from this..."[3] By 1930, Einstein had delivered on his promise with the publication of a paper in Germany's prestigious *Mathematische Annalen (Annals of Mathematics)* entitled "Unified Field Theory

---

[1] *Enuma Elish,* ed. L. W. King, M.A., F.S.A., Vol 1 (London: Luzac and Co., 1902) Tablet 4, p. 61.
[2] Albert Einstein, "Riemannian Geometry with Maintaining the Notion of Distant Parallelism," *Session Report of the Prussian Academy of Science (Sitzungsberichte der Pruessischer Akademie der Wissenschaften)* June 7, 1928. For those familiar with more modern tensor notations, it should be noted that on the few occasions that I will refer to Einstein's notations, his older style of notation will be preserved. In this instance the torsion tensor still equates as follows: $\Lambda_{\alpha\beta}{}^{\nu} = \Gamma_{\alpha\beta}{}^{\nu} - \Gamma_{\beta\alpha}{}^{\nu}$.
[3] Ibid.

Based on Riemannian Metrics and Distant Parallelism,"[4] the second paragraph of which, in contrast to the title of the paper, was simplicity itself:

> Since the number of dimensions has no impact on the following considerations, we suppose a *n*-dimensional continuum (sic). To take into account the facts of metrics and gravitation we assume the existence of a Riemann-metric. *In nature there also exist electromagnetic fields, which cannot be described by Riemannian metrics. This arouses the question: How can we complement our Riemannian spaces in a natural, logical way with an additional structure, so that the whole thing has a uniform character?*[5]

Reading closely, one can ascertain what the great physicist was contemplating if we but perform what mathematicians call a simple "substitution," and substitute the word "geometry" for "metric" (even though technically they do not mean *quite* the same thing).

In order to appreciate what Einstein is getting at here, one has to have an understanding of his overall "strategy" in seeking a unified field theory. Some argue that his approach in his Unified Field Theory papers is to be seen as a continuation of the conceptual and geometrical approach he undertook in Special and General Relativity.[6] One of the chief difficulties in the development of the Special Theory of Relativity was its demand for the "existence of an absolute finite limit to the speed of any signal transmission," that is, the velocity of light had a speed limit, and this speed limit was true for any observer in any system.[7] This, of course, necessitated a new theory of gravity since this speed

---

[4] Einstein, *Mathematische Analen,* 102 (1930), pp., 685-697.

[5] Einstein, "Unified Field Theory Based on Riemannian Metrics and Distant Parallelism," trans. A. Unzicker and T. Case, § 1., "The Structure of the Continuum," emphasis added.

[6] Tilman Suaer, "Einstein's Unified Field Theory Program," *Einstein Papers Project,* California Institute of Technology 20-7 (Pasadena, California, April 11, 2007), p. 3.

[7] Ibid.

limit was "violated by Newtonian gravitation theory,"[8] and this new theory of gravitation was the General Theory of Relativity.

The breakthrough came when Einstein considered gravitation as a field, as a geometry, and indeed as a wave. Crucial to this enterprise in General Relativity is the "Equivalence Principle" or "Equivalence Hypothesis," which equates gravitational mass and acceleration with inertial mass and acceleration. This may be more easily understood if one remembers one of Einstein's famous "thought experiments." Imagine one were in a rocket ship, with no windows, and suddenly it accelerates. The acceleration against the mass of your body in the ship produces the familiar sensation of being "pressed back" against the back of the seat. But, said Einstein, this would be no different than if one were falling toward a mass due to its gravitation at more or less the same rate of acceleration. One corollary of this principle for Einstein's formulations is that local variations of gravitational or inertial mass and acceleration are simply not taken into account. In a certain sense, they cannot even exist. However, the gravitational field itself came to be understood as a dynamic system due to this geometrization; the gravitational field could *change.* These concepts, as will be seen subsequently, are quite important.

In any case, in the little quotation from Einstein's 1928 paper, it is clear that he continues his geometrical strategy by describing gravitation as a particular kind of geometry, a "Riemann" geometry.[9] This is the whole principle behind his General Theory of Relativity, which described gravity as a local curvature of the fabric of space-time in the presence of very large masses such as planets and stars. The concept is not as difficult to grasp as it might at first seem, for imagine a trampoline upon which one places a bowling ball. The bowling ball will produce an indentation in the surface of the trampoline – a *local curvature of the two*

---

[8] Ibid. The violation in Newtonian theory occurs because a force of attraction exists instantly between masses regardless of how far apart they are.

[9] Bernhard Riemann was a German mathematician and geometer who formulated the basic mathematical principles for dealing with geometrical objects on curved surfaces and spaces, rather than the conventional flat and rectilinear ones of Euclidean geometry. Riemann also paved the way for techniques to describe geometrical objects in more than three dimensions.

dimensional space surface of the trampoline – that increases as the surface of the trampoline approaches the surface of the bowling ball, until at last the surfaces touch *tangentially* on the bowling ball. Bear that last concept in mind, because it too will assume some importance as we proceed to outline Einstein's ideas and subsequently the physics that may underlie the Philadelphia Experiment and the Bell.

Now obviously our bowling ball analogy breaks down at a crucial point, however, in that the trampoline surface is only *one* surface - a two dimensional one – whereas we know that regardless of where we are on the surface of the earth, when we jump, the force of gravity exerts a pull (or possibly a push), that pulls (or pushes) us back down to the surface. This means that rather than just *one* plane making contact with the curving surface of the Earth or any other large celestial body we might be standing on, we must contend with an infinite number of such "trampoline surfaces" for each point on the Earth's surface. So rather than an two dimensional surface with an indentation caused by a bowling ball, imagine an infinite number of such indentations on an infinite number of planes, each plane of which is arranged to be tangent to one point on the Earth's surface. It is this, more or less, that Einstein meant by the "curvature" of space in the presence of a large mass, and it is this geometrical description of gravity that made his General Theory of Relativity so revolutionary. It was revolutionary because the force of gravity could be explained in the form of geometrical equations. The geometry *was* the force, the force *was* the geometry!

These equations were in turn cast in a difficult mathematical language called "tensor calculus", or, as it is also sometimes known, "the absolute differential calculus." It is an extraordinarily useful mathematical tool in the physicist's arsenal, and more will be said about it in a moment, for it contains a number of crucial concepts that will aid in our interpretation of the Philadelphia Experiment and the Nazi Bell.

Now recall the final sentence from Einstein's statements in his 1928 Unified Field Theory Paper: "in nature there also exist electromagnetic fields, which cannot be described by Riemannian metrics. This arouses the question "How can we complement our

Riemannian spaces in a natural, logical way with an additional structure, so that the whole thing has a uniform character?" Note now that Einstein has pointed out another obvious fact – electromagnetic forces exist – and a not so obvious one: they cannot be described in the same kind of curved surface geometries that constituted Riemann geometries. The not-so-obvious fact becomes obvious, however, once one recalls the shape or geometry of magnetic fields with the very simple experiments one did in school with bar magnets, sheets of paper, and iron filings. As the iron filings were sprinkled on the sheet of paper held over the magnet, the filings aligned themselves along the lines of force – or the *vectors* – of the magnetic field of the bar. When one "considers them all together" – or doing what mathematicians and physicists would call a "sum over all the vectors"- one has the mathematical description of the geometry of the magnetic field, which, like our bowling ball analogy, breaks down, since the sheet of paper is only a two dimensional surface of what is actually a three dimensional phenomenon. If we take that geometry in three dimensions, the magnetic field looks like a "torus" or "doughnut". So there is the difference between gravity and magnetism as *geometrical* objects: one is "spherical" and the other is "toroidal" or "doughnut" shaped.

It is this distinction of basic geometries that led Einstein to his revolutionary proposal: might the "curved surface" geometry of gravity in General Relativity be *supplemented* with an additional geometry that described electromagnetism, and supplemented in such a way that both geometries were *subsets* of a more basic geometry that gravity and electromagnetism both shared? In other words, in this one short quotation, Einstein was announcing the program of his now celebrated, ultimately discarded, and now all but forgotten Unified Field Theory, which was an attempt to find that common geometry of electromagnetism and gravity.

But here an important series of questions occurs: Why was it celebrated? Why was it ultimately discarded and forgotten? And why should we seek to explain these two crucial experiments – The Philadelphia Experiment and the Nazi Bell – in terms of a theory that no modern physicist would accept? The answer to these questions will now preoccupy us, for in answering them we shall discover the significance of the mathematical expression $\Lambda_{\alpha\beta}{}^{\nu}$ that so caught the attention of many of Einstein's contemporaries.

A. A Brief History of the Unified Field Theory Craze of the 1920s and 1930s
1. Kaluza-Klein Theory

Einstein was inspired in his effort to find a "supplemental" or "more basic" geometry to explain both gravity and electromagnetism by what was to go down in the history of physics as the first such attempt to unify gravity and electromagnetism along geometrical lines, the Kaluza-Klein Theory. Named after its first discoverer, Dr. Theodor Franz Eduard Kaluza, the theory is unique in that it "solved" the riddle of a unification of gravity and electromagnetism by the introduction of a new *spatial* dimension in addition to General Relativity's four dimensions, three of space and one of time. Thus, in Kaluza's theory, one has *four* spatial dimensions and one of time.

Kaluza was born in the German city of Oppeln, in Lower Silesia, on November 9, 1885, and died in 1954. During the period when he formulated his now celebrated theory, Kaluza was a *Privat Dozent*[10] of mathematics at the University of Königsberg in Germany's province of East Prussia. These two facts – his connections both with Oppeln and Lower Silesia, and his connection, through his academic post at the University of Königberg – will assume great importance in part three of this book, in our examination of the Nazi Bell experiment.

In 1919 Kaluza wrote Albert Einstein after he concluded a mathematical study of General Relativity and electromagnetism. When Einstein read Kaluza's paper, he was literally stunned. Within a few short lines of his letter to the famous founder of Relativity,

> Kaluza was uniting Einstein's theory of gravity with Maxwell's theory of light by introducing the *fifth* dimension (that is, four dimensions of space and one dimension of time).

---

[10] Basically, the equivalent of an "adjunct instructor" in a modern American university.

In essence, he was resurrecting the old (spatial) "fourth dimension"… and incorporating it into Einstein's theory in a fresh fashion as the fifth dimension. Like Riemann before him, Kaluza assumed that light is a disturbance *caused by the rippling of this higher dimension.* The key difference separating this new work from Riemann's…was that Kaluza was proposing a genuine field theory.

In this short note, Kaluza began, innocently enough, by writing down Einstein's field equations for gravity in five dimensions, not the usual four, (Riemann 's metric tensor, we recall, can be formulated in any number of dimensions.) Then he proceeded to show that these five-dimensional equations contained within them Einstein's earlier four-dimensional theory (which was to be expected) with an additional piece. But what shocked Einstein was that this additional piece was precisely Maxwell's theory of light. In other words, the two greatest field theories known to science, Maxwell's and Einstein's, by mixing them in the fifth dimension.[11]

Dr. Theodor Kaluza at About the Time of his Famous Theory

---

[11] Michio Kaku, *Hyperspace: A Scientific Odyssey through Parallel Universes, Time Warps, and the 10th Dimension* (Oxford University Press, 1994), p. 100, italicized emphasis in the original, bold and italicized emphasis added.

In short, electromagnetic forces were *"emerging as the warping of the geometry of high-dimensional space.* This was the theory that seemed to fulfill Riemann's old dreams of explaining forces as the crumpling of a sheet of paper."[12] The image of crumpling a sheet of paper is an important one, as will be seen subsequently.

The problem with Kaluza's paper was the extra fourth spatial dimension. In fact, the idea initially seemed

> So outlandish to Einstein that he held on to the paper, delaying its publication for two years. However, instinct told Einstein that the mathematics of this theory were so beautiful that it might just be correct.[13]

In fact, after receiving Kaluza's paper, Einstein wrote back to him stating that "the idea of achieving (a unified field theory) by means of a five-dimensional cylinder world never dawned on me... At first glance I like your idea enormously."[14] Still withholding publication, however, Einstein wrote Kaluza again mere weeks later and admitted "The formal unity of your theory is startling."[15]

Formal unity notwithstanding, the problem was still that extra spatial dimension. Clearly, Kaluza had come up with something novel, a basic geometry of the universe that described it in cylindrical terms, and that clearly unified the electromagnetic and gravitational fields by means of a common geometry. But there was no solution of the problem of the extra spatial dimension. Nonetheless, Einstein finally allowed the publication of Kaluza's paper, *Zum Unitätsproblem der Physik* ("Concerning the Unification Problem of Physics") in the prestigious journal *Sitzungsberichte Preussische Akademie der Wissenschaften* (*Sessions Reports of the Prussian Academy of Sciences*) in 1921.

But what had happened to this fifth dimension? Kaluza suggested that it "was different from the other four dimensions because it was 'curled up', like a circle."[16] Finally, in 1926, the

---

[12] Ibid., p. 101, emphasis added.

[13] Michio Kaku and Jennifer Thompson, *Beyond Einstein: The Cosmic Quest for the Theory of the Universe* (Anchor Books, 1995), p. 162.

[14] Albert Einstein, cited in Kaku and Thompson, *Beyond Einstein*, p. 163.

[15] Ibid.

[16] Ibid.

Swedish mathematician Oscar Klein suggested that the size of this circle was so incredibly tiny that this was the reason it was not observable. He even went so far as to calculate its size: the Planck Length, "which is (10^{-33}), or about a hundred billion billion times smaller than the nucleus of an atom."[17] But this too raises its own questions. Why had the extra spatial dimension "curled up" into such a tiny circle, "leaving the other dimensions extending out to infinity?"[18] While these questions are ultimately cosmological and therefore of no immediate concern here, they ultimately spelled the end for the Unified Field Theory craze of the 1920s and 1930s, for the concept of such a tiny added dimension was too much for most physicists to accept, especially as it had no experimental verification. And verification was problematical in any case, since such a tiny dimension would require more energy to probe than the entire planet was then (or now!) capable of producing. Or at least, that was(and to this day remains) the theory…

In any case, Klein's solution to Kaluza's extra curled up dimension, and his calculation of its size, gave to the theory the name by which it is known to this day: the "Kaluza-Klein Theory," physics' first Unified Field Theory of gravitation and electromagnetism.

B. The Torsion Tensor
1. The Meanings of "Torsion"

The problem with the torsion tensor in Einstein's 1928 version of the theory is that, depending on whom one talks to, the meaning changes slightly. Since torsion is, however, a tensor, this means that mathematically it is a real geometrical object, or perhaps better put, a real geometrical effect. Just what all this has to do with Kaluza-Klein, Einstein's 1928 Unified Field Theory, and the Phladelphia and Nazi Bell experiments, will be seen in a moment.

---

[17] Kaku and Thompson, *Beyond Einstein,* pp. 163-164.
[18] Ibid., p. 164.

Bearing this in mind, the following basic meanings of torsion[19] may be noted in the literature, and all of them have something to do with the Philadelphia Experiment and the Nazi Bell:

1) For most authors, torsion means a kind of "twist" or "fold" in space-time, and to a lesser extent, some authors take it to mean the *degree or amount* of that twist. In the next section we will look at a simple analogy to illustrate this point.

2) For some authors, however, torsion is – to overstate things for the purposes of generalization – a mathematical artifact of various Unified Field Theories, including Einstein's 1928 version. It is a mathematical formalism that describes a vector of force undergoing "transport", which, as we have seen, Einstein described by the terminology "distant parallelism." This concept will also become important in the next section and in our understanding of the Philadelphia Experiment and the Nazi Bell.[20]

3) In certain Russian authors, torsion has a slightly different meaning, signifying not so much the "twist" or "fold" in space-time, but rather a kind of "sub-space" to such twists. On this view, torsion means the "stuff" underlying space that would give rise to such twists under certain conditions.[21]

---

[19] We will examine the related concepts of "anholonomity" and contortion in part two, in our survey of the work of the electrical engineers and physicists Corum and Daum on the Philadelphia Experiment.

[20] In this respect torsion resembles the "Zero Point Energy" in quantum mechanics, since some physicists are convinced of its existence, while other argue that it is merely a mathematical artifact of the theory and without actual physical significance.

[21] Regarding the Russian work in torsion, a few words about the work of Dr. Nikolai A. Kozyrev (1908-1983) is necessary. In a recent article in *Nexus* magazine, "The Aether Science of Dr. N. A. Kozyrev" was summarized by researcher David Wilcocks. Noting that Kozyrev bcame "one of the most controversial figures in the history of the Russian scientific community"(*Nexus*, Vol. 14, No. 3, May-June 2007, p. 45) for his work in torsion, Wilcocks points out that controversy notwithstanding, his work and that of his colleagues in the same field was "almost entirely concealed" by the former Soviet Union(p. 45). In Kozyrev's conception of matter, "all physical objects" are viewed" as if they are sponges submerged in water."(p. 45). Accordingly, one can increase or

4) There is also a stream in physics in which "torsion" may be associated, though it is not directly involved with it. This is the stream represented by certain papers of the English mathematical physicist E. T. Whittaker.[22] The effect of these papers was to introduce the idea of electromagnetic vortices in the medium. In Whittaker's analysis electromagnetism possessed a kind of "electrical viscosity" or quasi "fluid"-like behavior. Hence, these "fluid-like" dynamics share certain features with longitudinal pressure waves, being areas of alternating electromagnetc rarefaction and pressure in the medium. Consequently, one implication of Whittaker's paper is that the various forces are but different types or states of vortices.[23]

5) Finally, a consideration of "torsion" in the context of Einstein's Equivalence Principle is in order. When he

---

decrease the volume of water the "sponges" contain by simple mechanical procedures such as heating, spinning, vibrating, cooling and so on(p. 45). In this analogy, the water forms the energy of the medium or physical vacuum itself, a medium or aether that Tesla maintained behaved "as a fluid to solid bodies and as a solid to light and heat." (p. 45) And here enters the idea of torsion, for Kozyrev noticed that life forms in particular demonstrated that they accessed a spiraling form of energy, which he associated with torsion. The idea of torsion came from 1913 and Elie Cartan's work on General Relativity, wherein he demonstrated that space is not only "curved" but possessed a spinning or spiraling motion within itself, which he called torsion(p. 46). Thus, "once you have a spinning source that releases energy in any form, such as the Sun or the centre of the galaxy, and/or a spinning source that has more than one form of movement occurring at the same time, such as a planet that is rotating on its axis and revolving around the Sun at the same time, then dynamic torsion is automatically produced. " (pp. 46-47). Kozyrev also proved – and this is one point at which his work became controversial – that torsion fields, the folds and pleats in space generated by such spinning, traveled at superluminal velocities.(p. 47) But, as we noted in the main text, once Einstein had adopted the torsion tensor in his 1928 version of the Unified Field Theory, he also introduced the possibility that different materials will have a different effect on this field. Kozyrev demonstrated the shielding, reflecting, or amplifying properties of some materials. Sugar, for example, because of the spin in its atoms, shielded from torsion, whereas the oppositely spinning atoms of turpentine amplified them.(p. 47)

[22] For fuller discussions of Whittaker's work, q.v. my *SS Brotherhood of the Bell,* pp. 211-219.

[23] See my *The SS Brotherhood of the Bell,* pp. 211-219.

included the torsion tensor in his 1928 Unified Field Theory, he was in effect proposing that very local "folds" and "twists" in the medium could be possible. Moreover, in General Relativity, there was no consideration of the special properties of various types of matter or, as we saw, of minor local variations of gravitational and inertial acceleration. One corollary of the torsion tensor, however, is that materials properties *might* have local effects on the "folds" and "twists" of torsion itself. Thus, the implications of the inclusion of the torsion tensor were twofold:

a) Variations in local space-time due to materials effects were introduced in theory; and,

b) Variations of local conditions no longer assumed a uniformity of gravity. *Local* significant changes in the geometry of gravity were theoretically possible.

Thus, the inclusion of the torsion tensor now meant that two factors could influence the amount or degree of "folding" or "pleating":

a) the local environment; and,

b) the materials undergoing or inducing torsion.

Einstein had, in effect, almost completely abandoned some of the cardinal principles of his own theory of General Relativity. No wonder his readers' eyes did not glaze over!

But what does all this "torsion talk" actually mean? While the notions of "folding," "pleating" or "twisting" space-time may seem obscure, one has a good grasp on the subject any time one wrings an empty aluminum soda can....

B. Wringing an Aluminum Can

Begin by thinking of a metal pipe which is attached to an absolutely immoveable base:

12

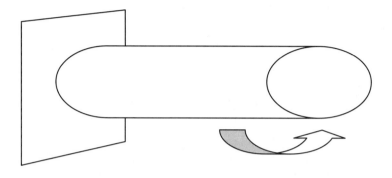

Now imagine grasping and twisting the end of the pipe in the direction of the arrow. With enough force, the pipe will begin to show the effects of the stress; it will begin to show folds and cracks. Now imagine an aluminum can, a cylinder *not* attached to something – an apt comparison given Kaluza-Klein's "cylindrical geometry" in their version of the unified field theory – and wringing that metal can with one's hands. The opposing motion of the twists will produce a similar strain in the cylinder, along the axis of rotation of the wringing motion. In this instance, the opposing motion itself introduces more stress, and consequently, more "folding and pleating" in the cylinder than in our anchored pipe example. The motions of wringing the soda can will introduce *spiraled* folding and pleating, which will increase in intensity toward the center of the can, where the stress is the greatest. Additionally, the ends of the can will draw nearer to each other. If one now understands the soda can to represent the space-time medium itself, and the metallic component of the soda can to represent the brittleness or resistance of ordinary space and time to such folding or pleating, and one has a rough analogy of the effect of torsion in the unified field theories in which it was a component. And note, with enough wringing, our metal pipe or our soda can will eventually break apart or explode violently, precisely near the maximum stress points. Note that this will come *sooner* in the can example than in the pipe example, since more stress is being loaded into the medium by the opposing motions of the wringing.

This is an important concept that will bear much fruit in part three when we turn to examine the Nazi Bell. Finally, note that the concept of torsion itself is intimately related to the idea of a *vortex* or rotation in the medium. It is not the *same* as the rotation; it is rather the folding and pleating of the medium that *results* from that rotation.

3. The Mistake in Unified Field Theories and Their Discarding by Contemporary Physics

As far as contemporary theoretical physics is concerned, the largest mistake in the Unified Field Theory craze of the 1920s and 1930s, the craze initiated by Kaluza's breathtaking 1921 hyper-dimensional paper, was that it sought only to unify the electromagnetic and gravitational forces. The emerging forces of quantum mechanics, the "strong" and "weak" nuclear forces, were not included in the effort to find a common geometry.[24] Hence, for whatever their mathematical beauty or limited success in unification of gravity and electromagnetism, as complete theories, they were, and must remain, a failure. This point must be stressed since, as will be seen in Part Two, Berlitz, Moore, and many others erroneously maintain that Einstein actually secretly *completed* his theory, and that it was on the basis of this secretly completed theory that the Philadelphia Experiment was performed. As will be seen in part two, however, it is not necessary to assume the theory's completion in order to explain the results of the Philadelphia Experiment. Its results can be explained on the basis of torsion and what has already been outlined in this chapter.

Physicist Heinz Pagels put the failure of these theories in the following fashion:

> *After the 1930s, the Kaluza-Klein idea fell out of favor,* and for many years it lay dormant. But recently, as physicists searched out every possible avenue for the unification of gravity with other forces, it has again sprung to prominence. Today, in contrast with the 1920s, physicists are challenged to do more than unify gravity with just

---

[24] For this aspect of the failure of unified field theories to incorporate quantum mechanics adequately, see Michio Kaku, *Hyperspace*, and Kaku and Thompson, *Beyond Einstein*, pp. 32-33, 195-197.

electromagnetism – they want to unify gravity with the week and strong interactions as well. *This requires even more dimensions, beyond the fifth.* [25]

In other words, Kaluza was *so ahead of his time* that his hyper-dimensional approach to the unification of physical fields had to wait until quantum mechanics had progressed sufficiently to be able to indicate the proper number of dimensions that would be needed to confect a correct unified field theory.

But there are other possible explanations for the sudden disappearance of the Unified Field Theory craze, and Pagels provides a significant clue – doubtless inadvertently – Kaluza's idea fell off the radar screen in the 1930s...in the early 1930s, in fact. In other words, when the Nazi regime came to power in Germany, publications of unified field theory papers dropped off significantly. There are two possible explanations. It was, perhaps, due to Nazi ideological prohibitions of Einstein and "Jewish physics." But it is also perhaps *an indicator that the subject matter itself had become a* **Geheime Reichsache**, *a "secret state matter," subject to pre-publication review by the Nazi government.* In other words, someone within the Nazi government had determined that the theories should be classified, and secret research be done to test them. And if it was the case that someone inside Nazi Germany had determined that Unified Field Theories might be practically engineerable theories, one may be reasonably certain that similar conclusions were reached in other countries, especially the United States.

That this observation bears directly on the Nazi Bell experiment will be covered in more detail in part three. For the present moment, however, it is to be noted that Theodor Franz Kaluza, unlike Einstein, *never left Germany during the war,* being appointed a professor of mathematics at the University of Kiel in 1929, and in 1935 a full professor of mathematics at the University of Göttingen where he remained at his post until his death in 1954. Since Kaluza's version of the theory was not "tainted" with having been authored by a Jew, the Nazis had at least *one* version of a unified field theory which was not subject to party ideological

---

[25] Heinz Pagels, cited in Kaku, *Hyperspace,* p. 140, emphasis added.

prohibitions. And as we shall see in Part Three, Kaluza's theory might hold the solution to the involvement of one very mysterious mathematician from the University of Königsberg in the Bell project.

In any case, whether or not the Nazis had decided to forego their own ideological proscriptions of "Jewish physics" and to make very secret use of the 1928 Einstein Unified Field Theory, they nonetheless had a thoroughly "Aryan" version of the theory – the very first one in fact – in Kaluza-Klein theory. It would therefore have been an easy "sell" to the Nazi regime for someone wishing to pursue the practical – and ultimately weaponizable – implications of those theories. All that would have been lacking would be to apply or incorporate the torsion tensor into the Kaluza-Klein version of the theory, and then *to engineer and apply it to electrical machinery.* [26]

4. *...But Some Engineers Took Notice Anyway*

It is this last statement – the application of the torsion tensor to the analysis of electrical machinery – that provides the next significant clue, for notwithstanding the many problems of Kaluza's 1921 or Einstein's 1928 versions of the theory, including its new "fifth dimension," one Hungarian émigré electrical engineer in the United States made an astonishing observation:

---

[26] To my mind, one of the little noticed implications of the torsion tensor within Unified Field Theories, and of torsion theories in general, is that not only can tremendous stresses in the structure of space-time be induced electromagnetically by taking into account the effects of materials on the local system, as in the work of Kozyrev, but also that similar effects probably result in tremendous torsion waves in the medium could be induced by nuclear and thermonuclear detonations. This might account for the fact that in early thermonuclear testing, calculated yields were greatly exceeded, beyond the margins of errors calculated for these tests. The extra energy might thus have come from some hyper-dimensional harmonic or resonance effect such as the induction of torsion waves within the explosion itself. As I have indicated elsewhere (*The Giza Death Star,* p 145) this might be the explanation for the continued testing of nuclear devices by the world's various nuclear powers, as they are attempting to learn the exact scientific laws involved. As I infer there, these laws might be some of the most closely held secrets of those powers, for another force is in play beyond that of nuclear and thermonuclear reactions.

some of the behavior of synchronous electrical machines was explainable on no other basis except extra-dimensionally, and by means of the torsion tensor and its folding and pleating of local space-time.

2.
A LITTLE-KNOWN HUNGARIAN GENIUS AND THE FORGOTTEN VERIFICATION:
GABRIEL KRON AND EINSTEIN'S UNIFIED FIELD THEORY

"You may laugh on hearing that a really scientific analysis of a synchronous machine implies the introduction of such unearthly concepts as nonholonomic reference frames, or multidimensional non-Riemann spaces, or the Riemann-Christoffel curvature tensor... (but) that's where the electrical power engineer must look for new ideas and new inspiration... What's more, he has no other choice!"
Gabriel Kron[1]

A. Introduction

While theoretical physicists were busy firing salvos of mathematical broadsides at the Unified Field Theory for its incompleteness, ultimately sinking it, one Hungarian-born electrical eningeering genius named Gabriel Kron inconveniently applied the very same tensor analysis to electrical circuits to verify *experimentally* the very same incomplete theory. The importance of this point cannot be overestimated, for it was also a demonstration that the theory did not have to be *complete* in order for it to be *engineerable,* [2] nor for it to possess a limited and real world explanatory power.

---

[1] Gabriel Kron, cited in P. Alger, ed., "Gabriel Kron," in *The Life and Times of Gabriel Kron,* Chapter II, Section II (Schenectady, NY: 1969), p. 284, cited in K.L. Corum, J.F. Corum, Ph.D., J.F.X. Daum, Ph.D., "Tesla's Egg of Columbus, Radar Stealth, the Torsion Tensor, and the 'Philadelphia Experiment,'" (1994) Tesla Symposium at Colorado Springs, CO).

[2] The vital importance of this point may best be appreciated by a comparison to the different varieties of string theory, whose verification, until recently, required energies utterly beyond any foreseeable human power production. Recently, "low energy" string theories have been proposed, which might ultimately promise some possible means of verification. But until their advent, string theory – because of this crucial lack of mechanisms of of verification – remained a mathematical formalism more evocative of a metaphysical dogma than a scientific theory. By his formal and experimental

Gabriel Kron

B. A Brief Biography of Gabriel Kron

By any reckoning Gabriel Kron was one of the twentieth century's true "characters," and one of its unsung geniuses. Kron was born in 1901, in the Hungarian town of Nagybanya, deep in the Carpathian Mountains. Kron displayed an early talent for linguistics, mastering Hebrew at an early age – his father was a devout Jewish merchant – and later French and German, and finally, English. Kron earned a place in the *Gymnasium,* a higher school more or less equivalent to the American high school plus first year university classes. There he studied physics, mathematics, and astronomy. Kron talked his older brother Joseph, who had a small pension as a soldier in the First World War, to immigrate with him to the United States to study engineering.

With family backing, Joseph and Gabriel Kron sailed to America, arriving in January of 1921. Eventually, Kron and his

---

verifications of the Unified Field Theory, Kron, in fact pointed to a line of potential technological development that might still prove useful.

older brother applied to the University of Michigan's engineering department and were accepted. Kron described his university experience in the following away, affording a significant insight into his character as a free thinker unwilling to be corralled into a box of standardized "thinking":

> As always happens when a free spirit is obliged to undergo a prescribed routine, I wanted to study everything except what the curriculum called for. How to find time to study what one wishes, and not what the teacher thinks best for one's own good, must be a perennial problem to many an anxious pupil. Finally, I hit on the idea of arranging my schedules so that by Friday noon the classes would be all over. Three full days then each week from Friday noon to Monday morning I was free to pursue my own private schedule of study without the interruptions of regular classwork. The rest of the week I considered as a sacrifice on the altar of mechanized education.[3]

After obtaining his degree, Kron was invited to become an instructor at the University of Michigan but declined, opting ultimately to pursue his dream of traveling the world.

Having become an American citizen in 1926, Kron set off to fulfill his dream, booking passage to Tahiti on a freighter with only $300.00 in his pocket, and a copy of a book on differential equations for his bedtime reading. There he spent several weeks living with a family and spending the afternoon siesta hours, as he often did on his world travel, under a tree and reading his mathematics books. "Having finished his study of differential equations in Fiji, he buried the book in an empty oil can under a large tree, dedicating it to the memory of the early missionaries who had been eaten by the natives."[4]

Shipping from Fiji to Sydney, Australia, Kron took a job in an electrical plant making watt-meters to replenish his exhausted finances. This done, he bought a book on vector analysis, and hitchhiked to Queensland. It was during this period that he began to outline what would become his revolutionary work in tensor analysis of electrical machinery:

---

[3] www.quantum-chemistry-history.com/Kron_Dat/KronGabriel1.htm, p. 7.
[4] Ibid., p. 8.

In those long weary walks through Queensland and later through Asia the outlines of a many-dimensional vector analysis began to take shape in my mind. Under the stimulation of my everyday preoccupations with imaginary maps of unknown territories, an analogous mental picture of engineering structures – such as an electric machine, or a bridge, or an airplane – engraved itself in my mind. They appeared (for purposes of analysis) as a collection of numerous multi-dimensional spaces connected together into one unit is a manner very much as the numerous countries and islands and continents are interlinked by a web of roads and customs and laws.

If communication between the various members disappears, nothing physical is lost, only that intangible something that transforms the forty-eight independent states into a single U.S.A., or the many thousand independent parts into a single airplane. Years later I discovered that mathematicians had already laid a firm foundation under the name *Tensor Analysis* for just such a type of calculus as I attempted to develop.[5]

From Queensland, Australia, Kron then ended up in Angkor Wat, in what is now Cambodia, by way of Manila, Hongkong, and Saigon, having journeyed to the celebrated ancient site by walking from Saigon. From there he walked to Aranha, and from there

Took a train for Bangkok, then joined a caravan that followed the ancient trade route to Cokcrake in Burma. He walked to Rangoon, took a boat to Calcutta, walked on to Agra, where he admired the Taj Mahal. He crossed the Indian desert to Karachi by train, took a boat across the Persian Gulf, and went on by train to Baghdad, stopping to see the ruins of Ur along the way. He spent $5 for a truck ride across the Arabian desert to Damascus, then set out on foot again to Gaza. He hastened on to Cairo by train, saw the Pyramids, sailed from Alexandria to Constantinople and went by train to Bucharest, arriving at midnight at the home of a friend, with just small change left in his pockets.[6]

His friend in Bucharest financed his journey to his home town, where Kron, his shoes now all but ruined, was reunited with his family for the first time since setting out for America. There he stayed for several months, courted his future wife Ann, and

---

[5] www.quantum-chemistry-history/Kron_Dat/KronGabriel1.htm, pp. 8-9, emphasis original.

[6] Ibid., p. 9.

continued to study before returning to the United States and a job with the Lincoln Electric Company in Cleveland, Ohio in 1928.

Two years later, Kron presented the first of many papers, each of which became more and more comprehensive analyses of machines. The basic theme of all his published output was basically the same: *"He thought that all types of electrical machines must be special cases of a generalized machine, and that understanding the general machine would lead to the invention of new types."* [7] Just what tensor analysis had to do with this insight will be seen momentarily.

By an extraordinary fluke of good fortune, Kron was left in the position of being paid a handsome salary in the midst of the depression in a department of Warner Brothers that had no work for him to do, so Kron and his wife returned to his province of Hungary, which had since been ceded to Romania as part of the treaties ending World War One, where they remained for a year while Kron busied himself learning Riemannian geometry and tensor analysis.

This was the turning point for Kron, for "seeing an analogy between these abstruse concepts and the complex interrelations of electric, magnetic, and mechanical forces in machines, he wrote his classic paper on the 'Non-Riemannian Dynamics of Rotating Electrical Machinery,' for which he won the Montefiore Prize from the University of Liege in Belgium in 1935."[8] This is an important point, for the famous Belgian university's Montefiore Prize was a prestigious honor, and one that would inevitably have drawn Kron's writing and concepts to the attentions of the Nazis across the border. This fact, little appreciated or almost never written about, will assume great significance for the speculations presented in part three.

Returning from Romania to the United States, Kron was eventually hired by General Electric in 1934. There he stayed until his retirement from General Electric in 1966. However, it is worth mentioning that Kron did not let his prize-winning paper lie fallow. He followed it up with two significant books, *Tensor Analysis of*

---

[7] www.quantum-chemistry-history.com/Kron_Dat/KronGabriel1.htm, p. 9, emphasis added.

[8] Ibid.

Networks in 1939, and *A Short Course in Tensor Analysis for Electrical Engineers* in 1940.[9] Kron died in 1968.

His output was voluminous, numbering over 100 specialized papers, most of which apply his insight of using tensor analysis on electrical machines. Much of this literature remains obscure, or, as this author discovered in trying to access some of the more sensitive entries in the Kron bibliography, so financially prohibitive, that Kron's work remains virtually unknown to this day, save to a select few in the engineering departments of larger corporations, many of them connected to military research. In any case, Kron's work is almost completely unknown to theoretical physicists and historians of science, a point whose significance will be explored more fully later on in this chapter. Since Kron's work is so scarce, we shall reference the 1959 Dover publication of his book *Tensors for Circuits,* because this book contains many of the central ideas found in his other works, and is more or less accessible to the general public.

C. The Theme of Kron's Work: The Tensor Analysis of Electrical Machines
1. Tensors Before Kron and the Reception of Kron's Work

Before the advent of Kron's work on the application of tensor analysis to electrical machines, the most use tensors had in "practical" physical applications was in the geometry of gravitational fields in the General Theory of Relativity. In that context, tensor analysis seemed to be applicable, not to the laboratory bench, but to the physics of the very large: to planets, stars, and galaxies. Kron's application of the mathematical technique was therefore nothing less than revolutionary, for it brought tensor analysis not only down to earth, but right down to the laboratory bench.

The revolutionary nature of this step cannot genuinely be appreciated without putting it into the context of standard assessments of the development of theoretical physics. To understand why, one need only glance a little further into the

---

[9] www.quantum-chemistry-history.com/Kron_Dat/KronGabriel1.htm, p. 11.

historical and conceptual foundations of the unified field theories. Tilman Sauer, in his article "Einstein's Unified Field Theory Program," states that "there was no compelling reason why the electromagnetic field should be reconceptualized following the example of the relativistic gravitational field."[10] In order words, the geometrical approach that Einstein had successfully adopted for General Relativity lacked any real formal or observational foundations for a Unified Field Theory incorporating electromagnetism. In other words, the success Einstein – or for that matter – Kaluza had achieved in their papers was due *solely* to the mathematical proofs involved. There was – as yet – no sound observational reason that the two fields *should* be related.[11]

In this respect, Kron's work was truly revolutionary, for he took tensor analysis out of the hands of the theoretical physicists

---

[10] Tilman Sauer, "Einstein's Unified Field Theory Program," *Einstein Papers Project,* California Institute of Technology (Pasadena, CA, April 11, 2007), p. 4.

[11] Sauer also observed that "Intrinsic criteria of validation or refutation for attempts at unification were not too sharply defined. They included, first of all, the demand that the known equations for the gravitational and electromagnetic field could be obtained in some limiting cases.... The mathematical representation should assign symmetric roles to the gravitational and the electromagnetic fields in some unspecified sense. In a stricter sense, the representation of the two fields should not be decomposable into two independent sets of equations governing the gravitational and the electromagnetic field. In other words, the unified description should inherently allow for some kind of non-trivial mixing of the two fields. But this mixing might occur on a purely representational level and thus might be principally unobservable. This latter postulate did not, therefore, also entail necessarily the even stronger condition that the unification must also, at least in principle, predict new physical effects." This more or less formalistic approach was the state that the Unified Field Theories were in, and is the approach that, to this day, in standard histories of the development of theoretical physics, remains. That approach, without exception, *completely ignores* the implications of Kron's work, and sees in the unified field theories of the 1920s and 1930s but purely formal and mathematical constructs whose practical implications for technological development were virtually nil. One has to look to the alternative science literature, such as Bearden's work or the paper of the Corums and Daum to find *engineers* examining the same history and reaching radically different conclusions. Michio Kaku, for example, in his histories of string theory, seems to go out of his way to stress the non-testability of the theory, and never once mentions the work of Kron in connection to the history of unified field theories.

with their calculations of gravitational fields of stars and planets, and brought it, and more importantly, tensor transforms such as the torsion tensor, right into the laboratory bench of the electrical engineer. In effect, Kron was saying that Einstein's 1928 Unified Field Theory formed a theoretical basis for explaining certain anomalies often noticed by electrical engineers. Indeed, as the epigraph to this chapter indicates, its conceptions were *the only* way of explaining them. Kron was in effect saying that certain behaviors of electrical machines *verified the theory,* but not only that. If their behavior verified the theory, then *the theory was engineerable once the anomalies were understood.* And the way to understand them was to subject them to the very same tensor analysis as employed to formulate the theory.

Needless to say, it was for this very reason, and for the fact that in seeking a kind of "general theory of electrical machines" by the application of tensor analysis, Kron's work was often dismissed by the engineer as overly complicated when applied to simple engineering problems, and referred to disdainfully – when referred to at all – by the theoretical physics community. To them, Kron's practical and non-rigorous method of presenting his ideas only meant that his ideas lacked rigorous mathematical "proof," and lacking that, they could – so they thought – be dismissed.[12]

Banesh Hoffmann summarizes this dichotomy in his introduction to Kron's *Tensors for Circuits:*

> Why should the work of Kron have excited such general animosity? One reason is, doubtless, its bold originality, for the lot of the innovator is rarely smooth. Another may lie in the very nature of Kron's synthesis, bringing together, as it does, the previously disparate fields of electrical engineering and tensor analysis. In the early days few people were equipped to assay the work of Kron since, for the most part, those who knew electrical engineering did not know tensor analysis and those who knew tensor analysis did not know electrical engineering.... (but) such difficulty as there may be is more than compensated by a superb unification.
>
> But Kron himself is also to blame, for he is far from being a convincing expositor. His primitive concept of rigor, his appeal to

---

[12] Perhaps it is significant that some of the most hostile criticism of Kron's approach came from Germany. Q.v. Banesh Hoffmann, "Introduction," Gabriel Kron, *Tensors for Circuits,* p. vii.

> "generalization postulates" in lieu of proofs, his attempts, fortunately absent from the present book, to impress by a sort of name dropping of impressive-sounding terms like *Riemann-Christoffel curvature tensor* and *Unified Field Theory* – these and other faults have alienated many people.
>
> ....Let us make all other valid complaints against him. There remains nevertheless an impressive corpus of work that stamps Kron as an innovator of major importance.[13]

Note that Hoffmann is dismissive of Kron's use of such terms of tensor analysis as "Riemann-Christoffel Curvature Tensor" and "Unified Field Theory" as a case of Kron "dropping names" in order to "impress." But in doing so, Hoffmann has missed the most significant aspect of Kron's work in general and of his *Tensors for Circuits*, which is but a re-writing of a book Kron had released in the early 1940s, in particular. In short, Kron's analysis of electrical machines was based in part on the very "incomplete" Unified Field Theory of Albert Einstein that the latter had begun to outline in his 1928 paper, the first to include torsion as a principal component. As was observed in the first chapter, that theory was inspired by the "higher dimensional strategy" of Kaluza's five dimensional theory. In short, Kron's work, form his 1934 paper, to his first books in tensor analysis of electrical machines, was maintaining that *only a higher dimensional theory, incorporating some form either of curved geometries or torsion, could account for certain observed and well-known features of electrical machinery, particularly electrical machinery involving rotation, or that was connected in complex networks.* More on what these phenomena were, and how Kron's work helped explain them, in a moment.

As noted above, Kron "thought that all types of electrical machines must be special cases of a generalized machine, and that understanding the general machine would lead to the invention of new types."[14] But what has this to do with tensor analysis?

To answer this question, we must know a little more about tensor calculus, what it does, and how it does it. The basic problem of the tensor analysis is how one type of geometric or physical

---

[13] Banesh Hoffmann, "Introduction," Gabriel Kron, *Tensors for Circuits,* p. viii, emphasis in the original.

[14] www.quantum-chemistry-history.com/Kron_Dat/KronGabriel1.htm, p. 9.

object, described in one system of mathematical coordinates, can be transformed into another object, or alternatively, into the same object, but viewed from a different frame of reference or coordinate system. This is the basic problem tensor analysis was invented to handle, and the process of transforming from one system to another is known as a transformation tensor. The transformation tensor in turn can describe the transformation of an object in, say, five dimensions, to the same object in four dimensions, and so on. This means that any transformation tensor, such as the torsion tensor, is itself a real geometrical thing. Thus, for Kron,

> *A tensor transformation changes, for example, the equations of one electrical machine to those of another electrical machine of different type.* He constructs prototype machines – the primitive machines – from whose equations he obtains those of all other electrical machines by applying appropriate tensor transformations. This in itself is a masterly unification. *But in addition Kron shows how different established theories of a given machine are convertible into one another by tensor transformations.*[15]

Kron had, in other words, not only demonstrated how any electrical machine could be derived from any other electrical machine by means of tensor transformations, but had also shown how the *theory* of one electrical machine was derivable from the theory of any other electrical machine by the same tensor transformations. Thus, his work was not only a unification of the practical with the practical and of the theoretical with the theoretical, but a unification of the practical with the theoretical.

Let us now note what we have:

1) Kron's work explicitly relies – as numerous of his papers attest, on aspects of tensor analysis specifically attributable by Kron to higher dimensional unified field theories of the 1920s and 1930s, and in some instances of this output, specific reference is made to torsion;

---

[15] Banesh Hoffmann, "Introduction," Gabriel Kron, *Tensors for Ciruits,* p. ix.

2) On the basis of a simple method (about which more in a moment), Kron relies on tensor analysis to demonstrate that one may derive any electrical machine from any other electrical machine, and the theory of that machine from the theory of any other electrical machine; and,

3) That the practical and theoretical tensor transformations are themselves unified.

The last point may seem to flow obviously from any notion of a unified field theory – after all, the unification of gravity and electromagnetism was the whole point of such theories. But Kron did something truly revolutionary, for recall from the previous chapter that the first such theory, Theodor Kaluza's, had an extra spatial dimension that was *so small that by any standard theoretical calculation it would have required more energy to probe than was available on the entire planet.* Consequently, by maintaining that certain observable phenomena in electrical machines – particularly rotating and networked machines – could only be explained by a higher dimensional theory incorporating some form of space-time curvarture or warping occurring **locally,** Kron was also saying that the "incomplete theory" was entirely engineerable.

This was the real revolution.

Nor should the timing of Kron's observations be ignored for a moment, for they were made precisely at the time that the war clouds of World War Two were clearly visible to all. The potential combatants in general, and America and Nazi Germany in particular, could not possibly have been oblivious to the enormous implications of Kron's work, for in essence, Kron had opened for them the Pandora's Box of the potential to be able to engineer space-time locally. That in turn would make a technology of vast potential applications possible, technologies that could in theory "bend light" or, alternatively, fold and pleat the very fabric of space in a weapon that would made a thermonuclear bomb look like a firecracker. In this respect, it should be recalled that Einstein emigrated to America, where he spent the rest of his life in pursuit of a successful unified field theory, while Theodor Kaluza, its first inventor, remained behind in Nazi Germany.

It is not coincidental, then, that the two experiments which have every appearance of being designed to test various implications of the different versions of the Unified Field Theory should have been performed in those two eventually warring nations: the American Philadelphia Experiment, and the Nazi Bell. Nor was it coincidental that with the appearance of Kron's 1934 paper for which the University of Liege in Belgium awarded him its Montefiore Prize, and with the accession of the Nazi regime, publications on unified field theory all but ceased in Nazi Germany. Someone, in both countries, had in all likelihood begun to connect the dots between the theory and engineerable military applications, courtesy of Gabriel Kron's tensor road map.

2. Kron's Basic Method of Tensor Analysis of Electrical Machines

For the moment, however, our attention must remain focused on Kron and what he himself states about his method of tensor analysis. For Kron,

> The establishment of symbolic equations is only a stepping-stone toward the final goal of constructing a smooth-running mechanism that automatically unfolds the relatively few symbolic equations to apply to the infinite variety of specific problems with which an industrial civilization confronts the engineer.
> *This mechanism is nothing more than a method of reasoning, a philosophy, that serves as a pathfinder while the engineer cuts his way across the labyrinth of interrelated phenomena.* [16]

Having established that tensor analysis is nothing more than a method of reasoning, of rendering formally explicit the interconnectedness of parts of machines, Kron summarizes his basic approach, which is simplicity itself:

> Let the transient and steady-state performance of an engineering structure, say a turbine-governing system or an electric speed drive, be determined. The steps are as follows:
> 1. Do not analyze the *given* system immediately, since it is complicated. Instead, first set up the equations of *another* related system which is much simpler to analyze (or whose

---

[16] Gabriel Kron, *Tensors for Circuits,* p. xxi, emphasis added.

equations have already been established on a previous occasion).

2. Then change the equations of the simpler system to those of the complex system by a routine procedure.

Tensor analysis supplies the routine rules by which the equations of the simpler (or known) system are changed to those of the given system.

....

> 1. *Break up the complex system into several component systems by removing certain strategically located interconnections so that each component should be easy to analyze. This break-up may be accomplished in several successive steps.*

....

Once the equation of a component part (say, the governor) has been established, there is no more necessity to establish its equation all over again when it is used as a component part of a different engineering system. That is, the results of all investigations in the language of tensors may be stored away for future use in different types of problems just as standardized machine parts are stored away to be reassembled in a variety of structures.

2. In addition to breaking up the complex system into several component systems, *assume new, simpler types of reference frames either in the original or in the broken-up systems.*

For instance, instead of curvilinear axes, assume rectilinear axes if possible; or, instead of brushes at an angle, assume brushes along the main poles; etc. The new axes may be actually existing hypothetical axes (like symmetrical or normal coordinates, for example).

The routine procedure going from the equations of the "primitive system" to the equations of the actual system is usually referred to as "transformation theory" or "transformation of reference frames." This process is the backbone of tensor analysis.[17]

In other words, one simply had to "tear apart" the components of the given system and then analyze the more "primitive" but analogous system.[18] Note too that Kron has also defined Einstein's

---

[17] Kron, *Tensors for Circuits,* pp. xxii-xxiii.

[18] The terminology of "tearing" and "primitive system" and "analogous" system is Kron's. It is to be noted that Kron supplies no formally explicit definition of what an "analogous" system is, nor, for that matter, what formally and explicitly constitutes an analogy in any case. But this is not to his fault, since such formally explicit definitions are lacking in much otherwise formal thought. The construction of a formally explicit calculus of analogies is one of the most difficult tasks, since such a calculus would have to account both for non-quantizable forms of analogies, as well as simpler quantizable or calculable sorts *in the same symbolic language.*

relativistic reference frames *in terms of the electrical system under examination,* another revolutionary step.

3. The Transformation Tensor and Electrical Machines

To see how Kron is able to transform one electrical machine into another via the techniques of tensor analysis, it is necessary to see how he defines the notion of a "transformation tensor" in an engineering context. We will cite Kron himself first and at length, and then unpack the technical language to reveal its meaning:

> *A collection of n-way matrices forms a physical entity, a tensor of valence N" if with the aid of a group of transformation matrices **C** they can be changed into one another.*
> A "tensor of valence 1" like **e** and **i** (represented on each reference frame by a 1-matrix) is called a "vector." A 'tensor of valence 0" like power (P) and energy (T) is called a "scalar". Tensors of other valence have no special names. **Z** is then a "tensor of valence 2," the so-called "impedance tensor."
> A tensor is transformed with the aid of as many **C** (or C_t or C^{-1} or C_t^{-1}) as its valence. Hence **e** and i require one **C**, **Z** requires two **C**'s, P requires no **C**'s. Because of this "chemical" property of a tensor of attracting a different number of **C**'s, the expression "tensor of valence *n*" originated. Many writers, though, still call it "tensor of rank *n*."
> It is often said that *a tensor is a matric with a definite law of transformation.* Actually, a tensor is a physical entity, and its projections are the *n*-way matrices....
> (a) The question now arises: Why is it necessary to say that the **e, i, Z**, etc., matrices of all systems with *n* coils are only different aspects of the physical entities **e, i, Z**?...
> When it is said that the matrices of a particular system are tensors, it automatically follows that *all equations associated with this system are exactly the same in terms of tensors as the equations of a group of physically analogous systems.* [19]

But what does all this technical jargon mean?

Let us recall Kaluza's original insight from the previous chapter. There, he took the four dimensional system of Einstein's General Relativity, and added a new dimension to it, which, as it turned out, incorporated Maxwell's field equations for

---

[19] Kron, *Tensors for Circuits,* p. 40, all distinct font types in the original.

electromagnetism. In tensor calculus, the basic way that Einstein's General Relativity, with its four dimensions – three of space and one of time – is mathematically expressed is by means of a matrix that looks like this:

$$
\begin{matrix}
g_{11} & g_{12} & g_{13} & g_{14} \\
g_{21} & g_{22} & g_{23} & g_{24} \\
g_{31} & g_{32} & g_{33} & g_{34} \\
g_{41} & g_{42} & g_{43} & g_{44}
\end{matrix}
$$

This four by four matrix is the *dimension* or "rank" of the matrix. Each number in a column or row is called an "entry" and each of these entries may, in fact, consist of an entire equation. A tensor is a way of transforming one such matrix into another. Different kinds of tensors describe *how* the entries are transferred from one position in one matrix, to another position in the new matrix. Thus, if this four by four matrix models an object in space, or even space itself, then a transformation of this matrix with a rearrangement of the entries will describe a new kind of object, or a new kind of space.

Recall now what Kaluza did: he simply added an extra spatial dimension to Einstein's four dimensions. In terms of a matrix then, what Kaluza added was an extra row and an extra column, each with new entries:

$$
\begin{matrix}
g_{11} & g_{12} & g_{13} & g_{14} & A_1 \\
g_{21} & g_{22} & g_{23} & g_{24} & A_2 \\
g_{31} & g_{32} & g_{33} & g_{34} & A_3 \\
g_{41} & g_{42} & g_{43} & g_{44} & A_4 \\
A_1 & A_2 & A_3 & A_4 & (\text{Scalar})^{20}
\end{matrix}
$$

---

[20] Q. v. Michio Kaku, *Hyperspace,* pp. 100-103, for a discussion of this diagram and its meaning. The diagram itself is produced on p. 102.

Kaluza's extra row and column are indicated by the entries A_n. Thus, the entries noted by the term "g_{nm}" denote the equations of General Relativity, and the equations of Maxwell by the terms "A_n".

Note that Kron is simply calling by the term "tensor of valence n" what others would call a tensor of rank n, where the "n" denotes the number of dimensions, represented by the number of rows and columns in a matrix. Similarly, when Kron speaks of "n-way" matrices, he simply means a square matrix array of n x n entries, or a tensor of rank n.

The implications of Kron's statements now become obvious, but it is best to state them clearly lest they be missed: *entities such as charge (**e**) impedance (**Z**) and so on are not abstractions, as one normally thinks of them, they **are** the real physical entities and components of the "generalized electrical machine" of which electrical circuits or machines are but its different aspects.* Thus these entities may be transformed by a tensor from one machine into another, one only has to know the particular transformation tensor, denoted by **C** in Kron's notation, that transforms the matrix of one machine into that of another. *Knowing the new arrangement of entries, one knows how the components of the new machine interrelate.*

4. Rotating Machines and Torsion

But what precisely were the observable anomalous phenomena that Kron maintained could only be explained on the basis of a higher dimensional unified field theory and such concepts as torsion and *very localized* space-time curvature? Such phenomena are well-known to electrical engineers, but few today, unless they know Kron's work, might imagine what such simple phenomena actually portend.

Imagine a series of massive electrical generators in a hydroelectric dam, each producing some thousands of kilowatts and all linked to transformers. Let us also suppose, for the purposes of illustration, that each of these generators is propelled by its own sluiceway each with a different liquid, such as water and maple syrup and so on, running out of the dam. The liquids running through the sluiceways will be running at different speeds and pressures, and accordingly each generator will not only be producing different amounts of power, but doing so more or less out of phase or "out of step" with each other.

Since the generators are all coupled together, the anomaly appears, because the total output of the generators, each with its own different rates of spin, and therefore of phase, begins to creep away from what "standard" methods say the system should be outputting. Under some conditions, the system will even output significantly more or less than such calculations state should be the case.

It is here that Kron's tensor analysis now enters the picture in a big way, for Kron would state that such highly anomalous "creeping" in the system is only explainable as a higher dimensional interaction brought about by the geometry of the total circuit. The total system has effected local space-time curvature in such a way that the system is either leaking anomalous power losses into it, or conversely, transducing anomalous amounts of power from it.

If we now inject the notion of torsion into this explanatory analogy, then Kron's work implies that this anomalous loss or gain is the result of the folding or pleating of local space that results when rotating systems are coupled to each other in certain ways.[21] The "spiraling" of the vectors of force that result when torsion occurs means that when torsion is extreme enough, the vectors of normally perpendicular forces, such as electricity and magnetism, may become almost "parallel"; they undergo a kind of "distant parallelism" brought about by such extreme warping of space. Depending upon the amount of torsion, those vectors may not

---

[21] Recall, once again, the work of Russian physicist Nikolai A. Kozyrev in this regard.

necessarily be perpendicular any more, but deviate slightly, or greatly, from such perpendicularity.

This type of phenomenon Kron specifically analyzed in terms of a localized curvature of space-time in the electrical system:

> To establish the invariant form of...equations and thereby to express the phenomena of small oscillations in terms of measurable and visualizable physical quantities, it is necessary to employ such advanced concepts of tensor analysis as the Riemann-Christoffel curvature tensor...[22]

Lest the revolutionary and breathtaking implications of Kron's remark be overlooked it is best to state it succinctly and simply: in the presence of the type of phenomenon illustrated in our crude analogy, *the electrical circuit's geometry is itself an example of an engineered curvature in local space-time.* Under certain extreme conditions then, *it may be possible to induce local distortions of that space time and draw energy from it by virtue of the geometry of the machine.* With this, one is far beyond the tenets of Special Relativity is its non-engineerable local, "flat" space, and once again in the realm of the practical implications of the Unified Field Theories of the late 1920s and early 1930s, as Kron understood them.

D. Summary and Conclusions

We are now in a position to summarize what has been learned thus far:

1) The very first Unified Field Theory was not, in fact, by Einstein but by the German mathematician Theodor Franz Kaluza;
2) Since Kaluza was not Jewish and remained in Germany during World War Two, there would have been no ideological proscription from the Nazi Party to investigate his theory and its practical applications;

---

[22] Kron, *Tensors for Circuits,* p. xxv.

3) Kaluza's theory was a five-dimensional theory – four of space and one of time – in which gravitation and electromagnetism were unified in a common geometrical description of both types of fields and forces;

4) Kaluza's fourth spatial dimension was calculated by the Swedish mathematician Oscar Klein to be of the extraordinarily small size of the Planck Length, requiring more energy to probe than the entire planet could then (or now, or for the foreseeable future) provide;

5) Kaluza was born in Oppeln in Lower Silesia, and submitted his paper on his theory when he was a *Privatdozent* of mathematics at the University of Königsberg, two facts that will acquire significance in Part Three;

6) Einstein's first published version of a "complete" Unified Field Theory incorporated the torsion tensor, and therewith, the idea that under certain conditions of the extreme twisting or folding of space-time, vectors of force ordinarily perpendicular would deviate from that normal pattern to a greater or lesser extent, depending on the degree of torsion. This made the localized bending of light theoretically feasible and engineerable.

7) Notwithstanding the early 1920s Unified Field Theories' "incompleteness" according to the notions of contemporary theoretical physics, and notwithstanding the prodigious amounts of energy to probe Kaluza's "curled up" fourth spatial dimension, Gabriel Kron nonetheless maintained via his tensor analysis of electrical machines that certain anomalous outputs of networked machines could only be explained by higher dimensional geometries incorporating some form of a space-time curvature tensor transformation, such as the Riemmann-Christoffel curvature tensor or the torsion tensor of Einstein.

8) This in turn implied that electrical circuits and machines were themselves, *without exception,* localized space-time curvatures, though in most normal cases no extreme or anomalous effects were observable. Nevertheless, small and observable anomalous behavior was known to most electrical engineers, behavior that could not be accounted for except by the introduction of higher dimensional topologies and space-time curvatures, according to Kron. Thus, these well-known anomalies were for Kron a confirmation of the basic insights of the Unified Field Theories of the late 1920s and early 1930s.

9) Kron's first publication along the lines of tensor analysis of electrical machines in 1934 earned him a prestigious prize from the University of Liege in Belgium, a fact that would inevitably have brought him to the attention of the Nazis, who, putting Kron's and Kaluza's work together – or even Kron's and Einstein's – would have drawn the inescapable conclusion that a doomsday weapon based on such theories was potentially possible;

10) Significantly, at approximately the same time, in the early 1930s, publications on Unified Field Theory began to dwindle in Germany as they did elsewhere. The standard explanation is that it dwindled because of the increasing success of quantum mechanics. While this is certainly true and the most logical explanation, it does not seem to adequately explain the silence in Nazi Germany, which, as noted previously, could not have been unaware of the staggering military implications of Kron's work. It is therefore a possibility that, in so far as Germany is concerned, the silence is due more to active suppression of ideas and techniques that had become classified as a *Geheime Riechssache* or Secret State Matter,[23] and that had become the basis of secret weapons research in the Third Reich;

11) Thus it is theorized that some such basis – a combination of Unified Field Theory in whatever form, Kaluza's or Einstein's – plus the realization of the applicability of tensor analysis to machines would constitute another highly plausible theoretical basis for the Nazi Bell experiment, and therefore a means of analyzing its known operating parameters and effects, a task undertaken in part three;

12) Similarly, Einstein's emigration to the United States, his continued work on Unified Field Theory, and Kron's tensor analysis of electrical machinery would have had a similar effect on the American government and military, and its military implications would have been immediately obvious.

13) Thus, some aspects of unified field theory would have disappeared, like some aspects of quantum mechanics did, from the open literature in the United States just as it did in Nazi Germany, for reasons of national security;

14) Thus, Einstein's 1928 Unified Field Theory with its torsion tensor, plus Kron's tensor analysis of electrical machinery, would have formed the nucleus in a conceptual matrix

---

[23] More or less equivalent to "Top Secret" or "Most Secret" in the American and British classification schemes, respectively.

spanning both the American Philadelphia Experiment and the Nazi Bell. Thus, using Kron's own method, *we may "tear apart" each machine or experiment, and analyze its known parameters and effects, and reconstruct the experiments.* In short, Kron's tensor analysis of machines affords us a method to "reverse engineer" the two experiments to a certain extent, and to reconstruct the machines themselves.

In the preceding conclusions the historical speculation has been advanced that both in Germany and the United States some other motivation was operative in the disappearance of articles in the open scientific literature on Unified Field Theory: national security and highly secret wartime research based on that theory. It is therefore in the years leading up to World War Two that we see what has become a permanent feature in what had hitherto been a more or less open and free discipline, as physics itself split into two branches: that for the masses in a kind of "public consumption" physics intentionally designed to lead to "dead ends", and that for the secret scientists, technicians, and engineers, the wizards in their black projects temples. Before turning to two of those projects and the wizards that wrought them, a further word on the possible physics of doomsday is necessary.

3.

BENCHMARKS:
PRACTICAL CONSIDERATIONS OF THE TWO EXPERIMENTS

"After the war it became evident that the world had avoided a colossal catastrophe by a hair's breath.... This fourth (physics) team worked in a field that was monstrous on a daily basis. And when I say this, I meant thereby that they experimented with things that a well-informed public would to this very day think them to be unthinkable and unbelievable, and thus imaginary. I mean to imply that these specialists worked in conceptions that totally abandoned conventional physical laws." [1]

A. Considerations of the Practical Research Plans in the Philadelphia Experiment and the Bell's "Projekt Kronos"

In the exigencies of war preparations and actual wartime research, it would have been even more imperative both for the Americans and for the Germans to have outlined a basic plan of attack in order to research the extraordinary implications of the various theories outlined in the previous chapter than it would have been in the ordinary course of corporate and/or military research in peacetime circumstances.

This plan of attack would likely have been divided into two distinct phases: phase one: a "proof of concept" phase, where the basic principle is verified through a series of short and small experiments, and phase two, a full scale version, which would have been pursued if the results of phase one were satisfactory enough to warrant the expense of full scale testing.

1. Phase One

Phase One would have been divided more or less into the following steps:

---

[1] Mayer and Mehner, *Day Geheimnis der deutschen Atombombe,* p. 89, my translation. Quotation is also cited in my *Reich of the Black Sun,* p. 96, and *The SS Brotherhood of the Bell,* p. 202.

1) Design of a "Proof of Concept" experiment on a small scale to demonstrate the feasibility – or lack thereof – of the effects or principles to be researched;
2) Design of appropriate measurement devices for the experiment;
3) Award of contracts to various corporations for production of the equipment necessary to the experiment;
4) Recruitment of the appropriate personnel to build, test, and run the experiments of the project.

As will be seen in parts two and three, there is unusual evidence that such proof of concept experiments either were performed (in the case of the Bell), or that such proof of concept experiments can be established in the literature of more modern times, and thus *could have been* performed (in the case of the Philadelphia Experiment).

2. Phase Two

Once experimental results verified the feasibility of the effects and the experimental principles established for phase one, Phase Two would have incorporated more or less the following steps:

1) Scaling up the experiment and incorporation of as many elements to maximize the sought-after effects as possible;
2) Design of the appropriate power plants for the experiment;
3) Production of the experimental and measurement components needed for the full scale experiment and awards of corporate contracts;
4) Selection of appropriately secure test sites and/or "battlefield conditions" under which to conduct scaled up experiments;
5) Assembly of a larger team of researchers, technicians, and laborers to conduct the experiment.

In parts two and three, it will be seen that evidence does exist that all these elements were present in the conception and execution of the Nazi Bell project, and that all elements were present in the Philadelphia Experiment with the exception of item 3, and this item, the award of corporate contracts, can be reasonably guessed at by careful reconsideration of the available data about the experiment.

B. *The Significance of the Basic Methods Previously Outlined*

The significance of this standardized and generalized outline of the normal course of scientific and engineering research may be overlooked, so it is best to draw attention to it before proceeding with the analysis of those two experiments in the subsequent pages. The significance of the outline is simply this: if historical and/or circumstantial evidence can be presented to show that each of the steps were undertaken or *could have been* undertaken at some point, if corporate involvement in the construction of specialized machinery can be documented or reasonably conjectured from available evidence, and if an expansion of the numbers of involved personnel from Phase One to Phase Two can be detected, then the probability increases with each step that the two experiments were actually conducted.

As these steps are examined in the following pages, an additional factor is to be born in mind: if a strong case based on evidence or reasonable conjecture can be reconstructed from available evidence, this would imply in turn that some element of suppression of evidence is therefore involved in both cases. That is, once the case is established that both experiments were actually conducted, then the likelihood increases that someone, somewhere, is suppressing crucial evidence concerning the design of the involved technologies, the underlying theories, and the results of both experiments.

Finally, the implications of unified field theory research in the form of the Philadelphia Experiment and the Nazi Bell – particularly the latter – should not be overlooked. As will be seen in the next section, the Americans were seeking ultimately a form of radar stealth via electromagnetic means in the Philadelphia Experiment. The Germans, as will be seen in part three, were seeking with their Bell device a weapon based upon the manipulation of the local geometry of space-time itself.

41

Consequently, *the underlying theory gives rise to a variety of technologies and applications.*

We turn at last, then, to a consideration of the first of these projects, the Philadelphia Experiment.

PART TWO:
THE AMERICAN SHIP AND THE
ACCIDENTAL DISCOVERY

"My own special interest in the Philadelphia Experiment was connected with the possibility that a shift in the molecular composition of matter, induced by intensified and resonant magnetism, could cause and object to vanish – one possible explanation of some of the disappearances within the Bermuda Triangle."
Charles Berlitz,
The Philadelphia Experiment, p. 10, 1979

"We think that not only can the Philadelphia Experiment be tracked down to statements which Tesla published during World War I, and were grasped by men like (Vannevar) Bush, but that the physics of the experiment can actually be traced back to Tesla's invention of the rotating magnetic field. Furthermore, to us there appears to be a legitimate link between Tesla's rotating fields and the Torsion tensor which appears in Einstein's 1927-29 Unified Field Theory publications. This connection was first identified and published by Gabriel Kron at (General Electric)...during the 1930s."
K.L. Corum, J.F. Corum, Ph.D., and J.F.X. Daum, Ph.D.,
"Tesla's Egg of Columbus, Radar Stealth, the Torsion Tensor, and the 'Philadelphia Experiment'"
1994

4.
FIRST DISCLOSURE:
MORRIS JESSUP AND THE "VARO EDITION" OF *THE CASE FOR THE UFOS*

"The UFOs, whatever they are, seem to create a temporary magnetic vortex, an ionization pattern that can cause ships and planes to disintegrate or disappear. "Jessup, before he died, believed that he was on the verge of discovering the scientific basis for whatever was happening, which he considered explainable according to Einstein's 'unified field theory.'"
Dr. Manson Valentine[1]

While the story of the Philadelphia Experiment first "broke" to a general audience with Charles Berlitz's and William Moore's book of the same name in the late 1970s, the actual history of its gradual emergence to the general public began much earlier. Accordingly, we shall follow the actual basic chronological sequence of its emergence by examining the three books that first brought the experiment to people's attention, first to a small and select circle of U.S. Navy officers in the Pentagon, then to a wider audience with Berlitz's book *The Bermuda Triangle,* and finally to its emergence in full details and view with Berlitz's and Moore's book, *The Philadelphia Experiment: Project Invisibility.* Along the way, the details of the story will gradually emerge.

Were it not for the beginning of the story, moreover, the later books might never have seen the light of day, but the beginning itself was so sensational that it was inevitably bound to reach a wider public. That beginning is found in the "Varo Annotated Edition" of early UFOlogist Morris K. Jessup's book, *The Case for the UFOs.* The book, like the Philadelphia Experiment story itself, is connected with high strangeness at almost every turn. For example, the preface to the Varo Annotated Edition was penned by none other than Gray Barker himself. So a brief history of the Varo Edition and of Gray Barker's own peculiar research interests is in order.

---

[1] Cited in Charles Berlitz, *The Bermuda Triangle* (New York: Avon Books, 1975), p. 148.

A. A Brief History of the Varo Annotated Edition

According to Charles Berlitz and William Moore, the mystery of the Philadelphia Experiment "Begins with a scientist who at first glance appears to have been something of a mystery man in his own right."[2] The mystery man is of course Morris K. Jessup, astronomer, scientist, and early UFOlogist. Born in Rockville, Indiana on March 20, 1900, Jessup's interests included astronomy, astrophysics, mathematics, and even archaeology.[3] After serving in World War One and attaining the rank of sergeant, Jessup obtained a college education that

> Would eventually lead to instructorships in astronomy and mathematics at Drake University, Des Moines, Iowa and the University of Michigan at Ann Arbor. While a doctoral student at Michigan in the late 1920s, he seized an opportunity to travel to the Union of South Africa with a research team assigned to the University of Michigan's Lamont-Hussey Observatory in Bloemfontein, Orange Free State. While working with what was then the largest refracting telescope in the Southern Hemisphere, Jessup perfected a research programme which resulted in the discovery of a number of physical double stars now catalogued by the Royal Astronomical Society in London.[4]

This experience led Jessup to use his data° to seek his PhD in astrophysics, and he published his work in 1933, though "it does not appear that he was ever actually awarded his Ph.D. Even so, many of those who knew him best chose to refer to him as Dr Jessup, and it seems only fitting that we continue to do so."[5] Referring to Jessup as Dr. Jessup has therefore become a custom in alternative literature, and we shall follow Berlitz and Moore's practice, and continue to refer to him occasionally as Dr. Jessup.

During the Depression, Dr. Jessup found employment with the U.S. Department of Agriculture as part of a scientific research team to scout the Brazilian jungle for sources of rubber.[6] After

---

[2] Charles Berlitz and William Moore, *The Philadelphia Experiment: Project Invisibility,* p. 22.

[3] Ibid.

[4] Ibid.

[5] Ibid., p. 23.

[6] Ibid.

returning from Brazil, Dr. Jessup became a photographer for an archeological expedition sponsored by the Carnegie Institute. The expedition was to explore Mayan ruins in Mesoamerica. This, doubtless, is where Jessup acquired his taste for archeology, and for the very radical view of human origins and history he adopted. We shall have occasion to refer to these views extensively later on, but it is worth noting what Berlitz and Moore say about them:

> Jessup...speculated that one possible explanation for these huge stone constructions was that, rather than having been constructed by the Incas, they were built in antediluvian times with the aid of levitating devices operated from sky ships of some sort. This was a rather unusual statement for anyone calling himself a scientist, and, needless to say, one hardly calculated to endear him to his colleagues. It makes Jessup one of the first proponents of what is now, more than three decades later, the well-popularized "Ancient Astronauts" theory.[7]

These are today controversial views, even in the alternative field, and certainly were even more radical in the day Jessup first propounded them. After exploring Central America, Dr. Jessup then continued his explorations of Peru's ancient Incan ruins.

He also made another interesting discovery while investigating the Mayan ruins of Mexico. This was a series of geological formations that,

> Upon closer examination, appeared to be a series of craters of some sort. There were at least ten of these, and they bore, he thought, certain remarkable similarities in structure and size to the mysterious lunar craters Linne and Hyginus N. Again, going off on an unorthodox tangent for a scientist, Jessup, after completing a preliminary study of the matter, offered up his speculation that they had been "made by objects from space." *Commenting still further at a later date, he disclosed that he had discovered that the U.S. Air Force possessed a series of aerial photographs of these craters which had been taken by a reconnaissance plane operating with the permission of the Mexican government, but that these photos and findings concerning them were being kept highly classified.* Wishing to continue his own independent studies of these formations but having run short of money with which to finance the operations, Jessup was forced to return to the United States in 1954 to try and raise the necessary funds.[8]

---

[7] Berlitz and Moore, *The Philadelphia Experiment,* pp. 23-24.
[8] Ibid., p. 24, emphasis added.

We may reasonably speculate that whatever interested the U.S. Air Force in these anomalous crater formations that caused its aerial photographs and findings to be classified was not natural. As we shall see, the Varo Edition corroborates this speculation in a very loose and odd sort of way.

Dr. Jessup also became interested in the UFO flaps that were visited upon America in the late 1940s and early 1950s. And this is where his thought took its most unorthodox turn, for he "began to sense connections between these possible 'space ships' and his ancient ruins and mysterious craters."[9] Jessup moved to Washington D.C. and began to work on a book that would outline the connections that he thought he detected between the UFO phenomenon, his strange Mexican craters, and the ancient ruins of Mesoamerica. Jessup's book was, of course, *The Case for the UFOs,* which was published in early 1955.

The book's publication initiated that strange series of events that would eventually lead to Jessup's involvement with the Philadelphia Experiment story and to the disclosure of the experiment itself to the general public. Jessup's primary interest as a scientist in the study of UFOlogy was in the propulsion technology that they represented to him. "Their means of operation was, he felt, by some as-yet unrecognized principle of antigravity."[10]

> A reliable source of motive power, he believed, was the all-important key to man's development; and until mankind could discover (or *re*discover) something more reliable than the "bully-brute" force of rocket power, he would be tied to the earth like a child to his mother's apron strings. That "something," in Jessup's mind, was the utilization of the universal gravitational field as a source of energy.
>
> Jessup appealed both in print and in lectures to the public for serious research to be undertaken in this area of scientific endeavour, either by the government or by private individuals and corporations.[11]

---

[9] Berlitz and Moore, *The Philadelphia Experiment,* p. 25.
[10] Ibid.
[11] Ibid.

Indeed, as we shall see later, Jessup was not the only scientist to make this plea for research into gravity control through government or corporate financing. More importantly, Jessup specifically connected this quest for gravity control with Einstein's discarded 1928 Unified Field Theory.[12]

In any case, Dr. Jessup's *The Case for the UFOs* with its odd catalogue of theories connecting UFOs and their technology with human prehistory and religion "were to disturb at least one of his readers to such an extent that he began a correspondence wherein purportedly confidential Navy material and apparently bizarre imaginings were intermingled."[13] It was after his book came out in a Bantam paperback edition that Jessup received the first of a series of bizarre letters that came in a package of "fan mail" that his publisher had forwarded to him.

> This particular letter, bearing a Pennsylvania postmark, was written in a rambling, scrawly (sic)hand in several different types and colours of pencil and pen, and in a very odd style. Capitalizations appeared in the midst of sentences, words were oddly used and misspelled, and punctuation, where employed at all, seemed almost to have been thrown in as some sort of afterthought. Entire phrases were frequently underscored in different colours of ink.[14]

The letter which began the short, and very bizarre series of exchanges, was, of course, the famous letter of Carlos Miguel Allende, a name well-known to all who have researched the Philadelphia Experiment story. This initial letter, which began the famous exchange of correspondence between Jessup and Allende, is unfortunately no longer extant.

Our focus here must remain on the role played by the exchange of letters between Jessup and Allende in giving rise to the Varo Edition of Jessup's book. Jessup, like anyone else who has ever read the subsequent Allende letters, was probably perplexed by the radical story it contained. Like everyone else who has read them, Jessup had his interest piqued just enough by its strong "eyewitness character" to send Allende a short response, asking

---

[12] This will be covered in the next chapter.

[13] Berlitz and Moore, *The Philadelphia Experiment,* p. 26.

[14] Ibid., p. 27.

him to supply more details. Months passed without Jessup hearing anything in response from Allende, and Jessup accordingly continued his heavy lecture schedule. Berlitz and Moore reasonably speculate that Allende must have been in the audience and heard one of these lectures, for he was prompted finally to reply to Jessup's postcard:

> On January 3, 1956, exactly one year to the day after his completion of the manuscript for *The Case for the UFOs*, Jessup, now in Miami, was surprised to receive (another letter) from this same Carlos Allende, who now signed his name "Carl M. Allen." While the letter was written in the same odd style and bore the same Pennsylvania return address as had the first letter, the stationary carried the letterhead of the Turner Hotel, Gainesville, Texas, and was postmarked Gainesville.[15]

It is this second letter of Allende to Jessup that actually survived, and it will be examined in more detail in a subsequent chapter.

This second Allende letter was so extremely bizarre in its contents that, according to alternative researcher Vincent Gaddis, Jessup was inclined on first reaction to take it as the ravings of a crackpot, or as a hoax.[16] Nonetheless, there was enough detail in its contents to force Dr. Jessup to pause and reconsider the possibility that its author was merely "giving an exaggerated account of an actual occurrence." The letter, moreover, indicated that the basis of the experiment was Einstein's Unified Field Theory, an assertion that surely must have intrigued an astrophysicist like Jessup.[17] The extreme amount of detail in this second Allende letter finally prompted Jessup to respond to him once again, in another postcard, insisting that Allende supply evidence for the many assertions in the bizarre story his letter recounted.

Once again, many months passed before Dr. Jessup received a response from Allende, once again postmarked from Dubois, Pennsylvania.[18] This letter, like the second, will be examined in more detail in a subsequent chapter. Like the second letter,

---

[15] Berlitz and Moore, *The Philadelphia Experiment*, p. 29.

[16] Ibid., p. 35, citing Vincent Gaddis' *Invisible Horizons,* no page reference given.

[17] Ibid., pp. 35-36, citing Vincent Gaddis' *Invisible Horizons* once again. No page references given.

[18] Ibid., p. 36.

however, its contents were of such a radical nature, written once again in the strange, rambling style and in various colors of ink and pencil, that Jessup probably

> Would have been more than happy to write off the entire matter of these strange letters as the ravings of a crackpot. Several people who knew him agree that in spite of his earlier interest in the matter, he had finally arrived at the very comfortable conclusion that the letters were just too fantastic to put much stock in.[19]

Jessup was, in fact, busy soliciting financial support for another Mexican expedition, and indicated as much in a letter to none other than Gray Barker, who would eventually obtain and republish the Varo Annotated Edition, and supply his own preface to the work!

> Of course, you know of my interest in Mexico, and they have suddenly and unexpectedly come to life: (1) Some commercial interests are probably taking me to Mexico on a preliminary survey for minerals under the meteor craters; and (2) it seems very likely that the government may finance an expedition through the sponsorship of the Univ. of Michigan. On the first, I would leave, probably about Dec. 10, for a five-week trip. On the second, it might materialize about April 1 (1957) and last for at least five months... as (yet) no contracts have been signed.[20]

But it was not to be. For "in spite of Jessup's confident belief that the (Allende) letters were a dead issue, things that he had no immediate way of knowing about or controlling were beginning to take place – a series of extremely curious coincidences."[21] These coincidences would inevitably draw Jessup back into an ever-expanding circle of interest in the letters contents, a circle which would include the U.S. Navy, as Jessup would soon discover.

According to Berlitz and Moore, this aspect of the affair probably began in July or August of 1955, "several months *before* Jessup received the first of his series of perplexing letters from Allende."[22] It began when a manila envelope appeared in the

---

[19] Berlitz and Moore, *The Philadelphia Experiment,* p. 42.
[20] Letter of Morris K. Jessup to Gray Barker, cited in Berlitz and Moore, pp. 42-43.
[21] Ibid., p. 43.
[22] Ibid., p. 44, emphasis added.

51

Pentagon. The envelop was addressed to "Admiral N. Furth, Chief, Office of Naval Research."[23] The envelope was included in the "in box" of Major Darrell L. Ritter who was the United States Marine Corps' Aeronautical Project Officer at the Office of Naval Research.[24] Postmarked from Seminole, Texas, the words "Happy Easter" had been scrawled across the front of the envelope, and inside was the Bantam paperback edition of Jessup's *The Case for the UFO.* [25]

While Admiral Furth most likely never saw the book, Major Ritter apparently regarded its contents with some interest.

> Upon opening the book, Ritter saw that it had been heavily marked up with hand-written annotations and underlinings of a most perplexing sort written in at least thee different colours of ink – annotations which seemed to imply that the writer of them possessed intimate knowledge of UFOs, their means of propulsion, origin, background, and history. The book itself was well worn, and whoever was responsible for this work had apparently spent a great amount of time doing it.[26]

The fantastic details both of Jessup's book and the strange annotations will be dealt with shortly.

For now, however, we remain focused on the Varo Edition's history itself, and how Dr. Jessup became mixed up with it. Berlitz and Moore point out one possible reason that the book apparently intrigued Major Ritter. And intrigue him it did, for he in turn passed the book along to Commander George W. Hoover, the Office of Naval Research's Special Projects Officer, and Captain Sydney Sherby, who had been newly assigned to ONR.[27] Berlitz and Moore maintain that both men were involved with the Navy's Project Vanguard, America's first attempt to launch an earth orbiting satellite, and that both men were interested in antigravity research as well. [28]

Commander Hoover and Captain Sherby were apparently so intrigued by the book's contents and the strange annotations that

---

[23] Berlitz and Moore, *The Philadelphia Experiment,* p. 44.
[24] Ibid.
[25] Ibid.
[26] Ibid.
[27] Ibid., p. 45.
[28] Ibid.

they discussed the matter at some length, and finally issued an invitation to Jessup to come to the Office of Naval Research in Washington "to discuss his book."[29] Jessup arrived and was handed the annotated copy of *The Case for the UFO* that "had fallen into Major Ritter's hands some eighteen months earlier."[30] The Navy officers explained to Jessup that apparently the book had passed back and forth between three different persons, each of whom had his own nickname in the annotations.[31]

Jessup was, of course, mystified by the entire affair as he began to read the marked-up paperback copy of his book.

> Why, he wondered, was the Navy interested in something so obviously the product of a deranged mind? But as to who could possibly have produced such a thing, he couldn't imagine- couldn't, that is, until he happened to notice a certain curious passage which made pointed reference to a secret naval experiment which allegedly occurred in 1943. Realizing that he had encountered such a statement before, Jessup continued to turn pages. Upon finding a few more direct references to the disappearing ship, he was left without a doubt – his erstwhile mysterious correspondent, Carlos Miguel Allende, had to be connected in some strange way with this strange book. Satisfied with his conclusions, Jessup at this point is reported to have looked up and commented that he felt certain that he had at least two letters in his files "from one of the commentators."[32]

According to Berlitz and Moore, Commander Hoover then impressed upon Dr. Jessup the importance that the Navy see the Allende letters, and also informed him that he had taken steps to see that a special limited edition of Jessup's book, complete with the strange annotations, be printed for quiet circulation among

---

[29] Berlitz and Moore, *The Philadelphia Experiment*, p. 45.

[30] Ibid., p. 46.

[31] Berlitz and Moore maintain that this is "an erroneous assumption based on the use of three colours of ink and the impression of several of the annotations gave of being a conversation directed from one person to another. In actuality, there appears to have been no more than one annotator. (*The Philadelphia Experiment*, p. 46,) As we shall see subsequently in this chapter, Gray Barker maintains in his preface to the Varo Edition that there really were three annotators. Either way, it does not affect our analysis of its contents nor the history of how the Varo Edition came to be.

[32] Berlitz and Moore, *The Philadelphia Experiment*, pp. 46-47.

some of "our top people."[33] Commander Hoover also promised that Jessup would receive a copy of this special edition.

And thus originated the Varo Annotated Edition of Jessup's *The Case for the UFO,* for the reproduction of the book was done by the Varo Manufacturing Company in Garland, Texas, outside of Dallas. According to Berlitz and Moore, Varo was heavily involved with 'military research contracts." Moreover, both Commander Hoover and Captain Sherby apparently had some significant relationship with Varo, since "both were later to find employment with the firm."[34] Berlitz and Moore maintain that Varo produced "exactly 127 copies"[35] and that the typing was done by a Miss Michael or Michelle Ann Dunn on a mimeograph machine that belonged to a department of the company known as "Military Assistance."[36] Jessup had apparently complied with the ONR officers' request, for Allende's letters were included as the introduction to the annotated edition. The pages of the special edition were hand-collated and "spiral-bound between pale blue cardboard covers."[37]

Jessup apparently received his promised copies of the book – three in fact – for he then spent a great deal of time going over the annotations in detail.

> Reportedly he was so disturbed at the truly bizarre contents of these annotations that he took the trouble to "reannotate" the book by typing his own comments and reactions on slips of paper and sticking them in approximately every tenth page or so. (This reannotated copy is apparently still in existence but has not been made generally available to researchers by its owner.)[38]

---

[33] Berlitz and Moore, *The Philadelphia Experiment,* p. 47.

[34] Ibid., p. 48.

[35] They also note that "other sources" give the number as much smaller, as being between 12 and 25 (*The Philadelphia Experiment,* p. 48).

[36] Ibid., p. 48. Berlitz and Moore also note that one source maintains that Miss Dunn was *not* the personal secretary of the company's president, but that she was a temporary employee specifically hired to complete the Varo Edition.

[37] Ibid.

[38] Ibid., p. 50.

Both the Navy and Jessup on his own private initiative then attempted to contact the mysterious Carlos Allende at the Pennsylvania address, attempts that were of no avail.[39]

Jessup began to deteriorate after these events, giving up his professorial duties and attempting to write for a living while increasingly delving into "psychic phenomena" and astrology. In 1958, he closed his Miami house and moved back to Indiana. Sometime around Halloween of 1958, Jessup visited one of his closest friends in New York City, the noted UFOlogist and alternative science researcher Ivan T. Sanderson. Sanderson published the events of Jessup's demise in his magazine *Pursuit* in its 4th issue of September 1968.

> Then, in 1958, a whole series of most mysterious events took place.... The most outlandish things then began to happen, which provide ample material for a full-length book in themselves. They ended in a really ghastly tragedy.
>
> On a certain day... Morris Jessup was a guest in my home in New York. There were about a dozen people present off and on, before, during, and after dinner. At one point, Morris asked three of us if we could have a chat in my private office. To this we repaired; and he then handed us the original reannotated copy, and asked us in great sincerity to read it, then lock it up in safekeeping "in case anything should happen to me." This appeared all very dramatic at the time but, after we had read this material, we must admit to having developed a collective feeling of a most unpleasant nature....
>
> Morris was a devoted family man and especially solicitous of the future welfare of his grandchildren. At this our last meeting he was extremely distraught and admitted that, due to an originally pure intellectual interest in natural phenomena, he found that he had been completely sucked into a completely insane world of unreality. He expressed outright terror at the endless stream of "coincidences" that had occurred in his work and in his private life but, beyond this, he was distressed that he might be accused of outright insanity should he mention these aggravations and related matters.
>
> What he actually said to us was in substance: I don't think I'm going balmy but I do believe all this nonsense is actually happening and is not a figment of my imagination. If you read this book you will see why I have been forced to this conclusion. Now, if I am right, I have a feeling that this just can't go on any longer without something unpleasant happening; and, if something does and anybody reads *this* material,

---

[39] Berlitz and Moore, *The Philadelphia Experiment*, p. 50.

> they will immediately say that I obviously went around the bend; and
> once that has even been suggested, you know quite well that the
> average uninvolved citizen will immediately jump to the conclusion
> that there is insanity in my family.[40]

Jessup was clearly in fear of his life, and was worried, if it ended in mysterious circumstances, that he would be made to look like the perpetrator himself, the insane victim and agent of suicide.

Indeed, Jessup's life ended almost exactly as he had feared and predicted, for scheduled to return to Indiana within a couple of days after Sanderson's dinner party, Jessup's family and publisher became concerned when he failed to show up. A month passed, and finally Jessup was located in Florida, the victim of a serious automobile accident. The accident only served to increase his despondency and depression. Then, in mid-April of 1959, Dr. Jessup poured out his soul to another close friend, the celebrated radio talk show host Long John Nebel.[41] On April 20, 1959, Dr. Jessup's "barely breathing body was discovered slumped over the wheel of his station wagon... It is said that he died only moments later, either on the way to the hospital or shortly after having arrived there – a victim of self-inflicted carbon monoxide poisoning by means of a hose which was attached to the exhaust pipe of the car..."[42] Whether or not Jessup committed suicide, or was "suicided" by perpetrators unknown – as his comments to his friend Ivan Sanderson suggested – will never be known. Either way however, almost all who have researched this aspect of the story, including Sanderson himself, agree that it was the strange appearance of the Allende letters and the affair of the Varo Annotated Edition that led to Jessup's demise.

What, then, was so sensational about the contents of Jessup's book and the Varo Edition's annotations? Here is where the plot really begins to thicken...

---

[40] Ivan T. Sanderson, *Pursuit,* No. 4, September 1968, cited in Berlitz and Moore, *The Philadelphia Experiment,* pp. 52-53.

[41] Nebel was more or less the Art Bell of the 1960s and 1970s, devoting much of his talk show to subjects such as UFOs and political conspiracies. The celebrated author and JFK assassination researcher Paris Flammonde was for many years Nebel's producer.

[42] Ibid., pp. 54-56.

B. The Contents of the Varo Annotated Edition

The Varo Annotated Edition, while well-known by name to most informed people familiar with the Philadelphia Experiment story, remains nonetheless an almost inaccessible work, its actual contents almost completely *unknown*. We will therefore reproduce as much of it here as is prudent to do, with a view to try to reconstruct the types of thoughts that might have crossed the mind of an astrophysicist such as Morris K. Jessup. In doing so, a very disturbing picture will emerge, one in which Jessup might have been murdered for any number of *single* concepts expressed in the Varo Edition, much less for the *interconnectedness* of his and his annotators' ideas.

1. Gray Barker:
a. His Preface

The first and most obviously unusual fact about the extant version of the Varo Edition is its source: the now defunct Saucerian Press's Gray Barker. Barker was himself a famous UFOlogist of the 1950s to the 1970s, and as also noted, a close friend of Morris Jessup. Barker had obtained a copy of the Varo Edition, doubtless from their other mutual friend, Ivan T. Sanderson, another famous name of the "classical period" of UFOlogy.[43]

Like Berlitz and Moore, Barker notes that the special edition of Jessup's *The Case for the UFO* had been printed in a "very small run" by "a Garland, Texas manufacturing company which

---

[43] Barker states on p. 6 of his Preface that "We finally acquired one of the rare original copies in 1971 from a friend of Mr. Jessup, to whom he had given one of the few copies supplied him by its publisher." It stands to reason that this friend was none other than Ivan T. Sanderson, and that the copy obtained was one of the copies Jessup had left for Sanderson to lock up in his safe. It should be noted, however, that *one* of the copies Jessup gave Sanderson was his *re*annotated version, and this, to my knowledge, has never surfaced. It is known that on Sanderson's death, his own files and papers were removed from his apartment, and never were seen again. This may have included Jessup's own reannotated version of the Varo Edition.

produced equipment for the military."[44] Barker states that "each page was run through the small office duplicator twice, once with black ink for the regular text of the book, then once again with red ink, the latter reproducing the mysterious annotations by three men who may have been gypsies, hoaxters, or space people living among men."[45] This is classic Barker: provide prosaic details and a wild speculative context all at the same time. Barker then continues, noting that many people disputed that the book ever even existed:

> Because you are now holding a virtually exact facsimile of *The Annotated Edition* in your hands, it is most obvious that the book existed. But the big mystery still remains: why did a Government (sic) contractor go to so much trouble to reprint a book that had been rejected by the scientific community, and further to include mysterious letters to the author and even more bizarre annotations? And with this mystery goes the suspicion that the book may have been printed by the manufacturer at the request of the military, which implies Government interest in some of the weirdest aspects of "Flying Saucer" study.[46]

Note that Barker has leapt to a conclusion, namely, that the government's interest in the annotated Jessup book was due to the UFO mystery itself. And that indeed is an obvious conclusion to make. But it is equally possible that their interest was due to the story of the Philadelphia Experiment contained in the annotations and in Allende's letters. But, as we shall also discover, there are many *other* much less obvious possibilities for the government's interest as well.

In any case, Barker then goes on to outline a brief biography of Jessup's life,[47] before he passes to his real interest: the Allende letters and the annotations themselves. Notwithstanding his leap to view the government's interest in the Varo Edition to be due to its UFO-related contents, Barker nonetheless proves himself to be a

---

[44] Gray Barker, "Preface," in "Varo Edition," *The Case for the UFO, Unidentified Flying Object* (Castelnau-Barbarens, France: The Quantum Future Group), p. 3.
[45] Ibid.
[46] Ibid.
[47] Ibid., pp. 3-4

close observer of Allende's actual letters in at least one significant aspect:

> The mystery of the annotated paperback edition of *The Case for the UFO* was preceded by a series of strange letters from Carlos Miguel Allende addressed to Jessup. Two of these, reproduced as a part of the *Annotated Edition,* appear in the following pages. The letters claimed that as a result of a strange experiment *at sea* utilizing principles of Einstein's Unified Field Theory, a destroyrer and all its crew became invisible during October 1943.[48]

As we shall see subsequently in this chapter, Barker is one of the few who noticed what Allende *actually said* and not what the Philadelphia Experiment legend later maintained, namely, that the experiment was performed *at sea* and *not* while the ship was docked at Philadelphia. This is a significant clue into the nature of the experiment as well as its history, as we shall eventually learn.[49]

Barker also outlines the same details as surveyed by Berlitz and Moore, but once again provides an interesting twist, since he maintains that Admiral Furth, to whom the annotated copy of Jessup's book was originally addressed, actually did thumb through the book and had his interest piqued.[50] This makes more sense, ultimately, than does Berlitz's and Moore's account, since a private and presumably classified special short run publication of the annotated edition by a government contractor would seem more reasonably initiated by someone at command or flag rank. Barker also maintains, in contradistinction to Berlitz and Moore, that there really were *three* annotators, and not just one who was pretending to be three.[51]

---

[48] Ibid., p. 4, emphasis added.

[49] Needless to say, this point is not really appreciated for its full significance by Berlitz and Moore, whose book on the subject gives the distinct impression that the experiment was performed at least in some phases *at a dock* in the Philadelphia Navy Yard.

[50] Barker, "preface," in "Varo Edition," *The Case for the UFO, Unidentified Flying Object,* (Castelnau-Barbarens, France: The Quantum Future Group), p. 4.

[51] Ibid. A comparison between Berlitz's and Moore's account on the one hand, and Barker's account on the other, will reveal that the former authors relied heavily on Barker's account.

However, unlike Berlitz and Moore, Barker is alive to the implications of how the Varo Edition came to be, again, because he is unwilling to dismiss the idea that Admiral Furth himself might have instigated the printing of the book:

> Two theories evolve as to Varo's role in publishing the Annotated Edition:
>
> (1) Top military brass passed this down through the lower echelon, thus avoiding the responsibility should there be any publicity, and it was published surreptitiously by Varo, the personnel of which may have had top military security clearance – avoiding sending it to a government printing source where word might leak out. The Military (sic) was interested in applications of the notes to secret research being carried out by the U.S. After printing, the limited edition could be passed around to interested persons, and distributed to other contactors engaged in secret military development.
>
> (2) Lower echelon officers, such a Sherby, had deep personal interests in the UFO mystery, and wanted copies to give to other Naval (sic) personnel who held similar interests. As a matter of personal interest, they asked the Varo company to make the reprint, knowing that the contractor would comply, as one of the many personal favors they may have extended to military personnel.
>
> The latter of these alternatives is the writer's best guess. No great degree of secrecy seemed to have been employed. Jessup was called in *by Varo* and shown the book, and nothing in his subsequent writings or reported conversations indicates he was requested to maintain secrecy.[52]

Again, note the minor discrepancy between Berlitz and Moore, and Barker. Berlitz and Moore maintain that Jessup received his copy of the Varo Edition from the Navy, while Barker's "best guess" is that he received it directly from Varo. Barker thus makes a significant point: no special secrecy seemed to surround the edition, which is a notion in direct contradiction to Jessup's behavior during his last dinner party with Ivan T. Sanderson. Evidence will be presented later that there was indeed secrecy at the highest level of the project, and thus it stands to reason that there was great secrecy involving the Varo Edition itself, a secrecy

---

[52] Barker, "Preface," in "Varo Edition," *The Case for the UFO, Unidentified Flying Object,* (Castelnau-Barbarens, France: the Quantum Future Group), p. 5, emphasis added.

that might account for Jessup's strange behavior at the end of his life.

b. A Necessary Tangent: Barker's Own Strange Story

Before proceeding further in examination of the Varo Edition, a brief word is necessary about Gray Barker himself. Well-known during his day for his private UFO publishing house, Saucerian Press, Barker is perhaps best remembered today for being the author of a book for which he became famous: *They Knew Too Much About Flying Saucers*, a book which is considered to be the classical treatment of the so-called "Men in Black" sightings that often accompanies UFO incidents. Barker's book is about various people who experienced some UFO sighting, and then who were suddenly and, usually inexplicably, visited and warned by mysterious men, dressed entirely in black, not to discuss the matter any further. Barker's interest in the phenomenon began in 1953, when, as chief investigator for the International Flying Saucer Bureau, he discovered that the entire organization had been suddenly shut down by its founder, a man named Bender, after a visit by the Men In Black. The bureau had published a small magazine of UFO reports called *Space Review,* but after Bender's visit from the Men In Black, all back issues in the organization's possession were confiscated. Barker's book speculates, not implausibly, that the real reasons for such "visits of suppression" are ultimately tied to the suppression of information about new energy sources, and possibly for a terrestrial and subterranean, even Antarctic, origin for UFOs.[53] Barker's conclusions on the place of origin of UFOs are no so different from Jessup's, and his conclusions about the Men in Black "suppression phenomenon" are also related to some of Jessup's ideas as well.

Barker, however, wrote another book, one much closer to the topic at hand, and this was *The Strange Case of Dr. M. K. Jessup.*[54] In that book, Barker reproduces a letter "which Barker claims to have received from an anonymous source known to him only as

---

[53] Gray Barker, *They Knew Too Much About Flying Saucers,* pp. 116-117, 130, 206-207.
[54] Published by Saucerian Press, 1963.

'Colonel B.'"[55] Berlitz and Moore then cite the letter from Barker's book:

> (Jessup) also made a great deal of emphasis on a mimeographed version of one of his books, allegedly circulated in the Armed Services. *He also told me of certain letters he had received purporting to contain information about a secret experiment by the military, involving an application of the Unified Field Theory.*
>
> *I personally feel that too much was made of this by Jessup,* though this can be understandable when one considers it in the light of the sensitivity shown in government circles about the UFO investigation. *It is my educated guess that the allegations contained in (these) [Allende] letters regarding secret experiments were hoaxes of some sort. Yet because this information DID COME CLOSE (emphasis his) to some of the circumstance of ACTUAL experiments (of a much less dramatic nature), it may have been thought that there had been some security leak and this may very likely have been the reason for the great interest by the military.*[56]

This short letter contains a number of important clues which it is best to emphasize, as these elements will become central to our analysis of the Philadelphia Experiment later on in this section of the book:

1) Note that the anonymous author is disinclined to believe the contents of the Allende letters as they stand;
2) The author also notes that he believes Jessup over-estimated the role played by *an application* of the Unified Field Theory;
3) But observe that the letter's anonymous author gives back with the right hand what he has taken with the left, namely, having dismissed the sensational elements of the Allende letters as a "hoax," he nonetheless maintains that "this information *DID COME CLOSE*" to "some of the circumstance of *ACTUAL* experiment *of a much less dramatic nature.*" In other words, Allende either got the results of the experiment wrong while getting the principle

---

[55] Berlitz and Moore, *The Philadelphia Experiment,* p. 82.
[56] Ibid., p. 83. Italicized and capitalized emphasis in the original; italicized, or bold and italicized emphasis added.

right, or the anonymous author of the letter knew what the original purpose of the experiment was, but did not know of the fantastic results reported by Allende, which may indicate that the letter's author did not know of later stages of the experiment or its results. In either case, the author's statement that the actual experiment was of a "much less dramatic nature" is a significant clue as to the probable original goals of the experiment, as will be seen in a later chapter.

4) Finally, note the anonymous author's opinion as to why the Navy had really shown an interest in the annotated edition of Jessup's work: there had been a security leak. This is a highly probable explanation, and its probability increases if Allende's sensational allegations as to the actual results of the experiment are even partially true.

2. The Actual ONR Introduction to the Varo Edition

Back to the Varo Edition. The Office of Naval Research which had commissioned the special version of Jessup's book from the Varo corporation – whether officially or unofficially – provided its own short Introduction to the work. This introduction makes it clear that the *principal* motivation for the publication of the special version was UFOs:

> Notations that imply intimate knowledge of UFOs, their means of motion, their origin, background, history, and habits of beings occupying UFOs provide an interesting subject for investigation. Such notations were found in a copy of the paperback edition of M.K. Jessup's *The Case for the UFO's* (sic). *Because of the importance which we attach to the possibility of discovering clues to the nature of gravity, no possible item, however disreputable from the point of view of classical science, should be overlooked.* [57]

If it be the case that no clue into the nature of gravity should be overlooked, then this is an astonishing admission by ONR, namely,

---

[57] Introduction, "Varo Edition ," *The Case for the UFO, Unidentified Flying Object* (Castelnau-Barbarns, France: The Quantum Future Group), p. 8, emphasis added.

that the military's interest in UFOs conceals a deeper interest in the mystery of gravity itself. If one accepts these statements at face value, then, gravity is the real interest for the ONR's interest in the Varo Annotated Edition. However, if one accepts the anonymous author of the letter to Gray Barker that the Navy's interest was out of a concern for a possible security leak, then these statements should be read with a considerable degree of skepticism. In this case, the statements would be a deep-cover disinformation ploy, designed to deflect attention away from what was the real concern. Throughout the remainder of this chapter, we will analyze the Varo Edition on the basis that the Navy's interest was genuine in the sense expressed in the above statements, and that it was interested not only in the annotations, but also in the main text, of Jessup's book, and in the concepts implied by the relationships *between* the annotations and the main text.

The ONR introduction also indicates that it believes that there really were *three* persons doing the annotations. "The use of three distinct colors of ink – blue, blue-violet, and blue-green – *and the difference in handwriting lead to this conclusion.* This implies that Carlos Allende was only *one* of these three people, a conclusion that the ONR introduction bases on the fact that notes by "Mr. A" on pages 117, 130, and 150 are similar to comments in Allende's letters to Dr. Jessup.

The ONR instruction ends on yet another note, suggesting once again that its interest is in the total content of the Varo Edition, both Jessup's original text and the annotations: "How much truth is there in this? That cannot be answered. It is evident that these men provide some very intriguing explanations; explanations that may be worth consideration."[58] Later on it will be shown that Allende's letters state that it was Einstein's Unified Field Theory that formed the basis of the experiment. If it can be demonstrated that the Navy had an interest during World War Two in the practical engineerability of that incomplete theory for whatever purpose, then its mention in the new context of gravity, UFO propulsion and other odd speculations by Jessup himself in his main texts would impel a similar interest by the Navy in the 1950s. It is as if Jessup

---

[58] Introduction, "Varo Edition," *The Case for the UFO, Unidentified Flying Object* (Castelnau-Barbarens, France: The Quantum Future Group), p. 10.

and his mysterious annotators have pointed out other implications of that theory for the Navy to consider! These implications will be explicitly defined below.

Our examination of Barker's preface and the ONR's introduction is now concluded, and to the main text and its annotators we now turn.

3. *Jessup's Ideas in* The Case for the UFO *and Some Varo Annotations*

An examination of the table of contents of Jessup's *The Case for the UFO* reveals the sweep of his imagination in addressing the problem. Clearly, he saw the UFO as a unifying factor, or rather, sought in it an explanatory paradigm for various "paranormal phenomena."

PART I
The Case for the UFO's

"If it Waddles…"?
UFO's Are Real
There is Intelligence in Space
Short-Cut to Space Travel
The Home of the UFO's
Are UFO's Russian?
Space flights: Common Denominator

PART II
Meteorology Speaks

Falling Ice
Falling Stones
Falling Live Things
Falling Animal and Organic Matter
Falling Shaped Things
Falls of Water
Clouds and Storms
Rubbish in Space

PART III
History Speaks

Disappearing Ships and Crews

PART IV
Astronomy Speaks

While the table of contents clearly reveals that Jessup intended to use the UFO phenomenon as a unifying explanation for various types of Fortean phenomena, and while it may even evoke the response in some that it is a sign of a messy mind, what Jessup's book really is, is an exercise in considered speculation of an hypothesis by an academic willing to think outside the bounds of conventional thought, and who wrote for a non-academic audience in a non-academic way. Thus, his "reasoned speculative hypothesis" style of argument and writing tends to be overlooked by contemporary readers.

Whatever contemporary readers might make of his work, however, the table of contents had already elicited a response from one of the annotators, most likely Allende himself, since the style of the comment is so similar to that of Allende in his two letters to Jessup:

> NOTE:
> Anyone reading this book would have to KNOW that Electron *quatums* Within Molecular structures, are similar in scope of "field" as Planets *orbits*. They Would Have to know that, Electrons in Metal go across, What in planetary Systems, would be BILLIONS OF MILES, Leaving there a Gravitational field. Deadspot or Node, or Vortice or Neutral as *this one thing* is variously called. Realizing this as Dr. Albert Einstein

---

[59] M.K. Jessup, *The Case for the UFO: Varo Annotated Edition*, p. 13.

did, it shows clearly how solids may become Energy or Dissolute AND
How then they May Pass easily out of Visual scope *instantly*. This is
Merely one Clue gleamed from *Einsteins Theory of a Unified Magnetic
Field through all substances* AND throughout Whole inter-Galactic-
Universe. U.S. EXPIERMENTS, 1943 ON ONE PART OF IT
PROVED PLENTY! [60]

Note that when quoting the annotations, all capitalizations,
misspellings, italicization, and underlining will be cited as they are
found in the original. The strange mangled English is typical of the
annotations and of Allende's letters to Jessup.

For all that, one should not be too hasty in dismissing them.
After all, the Office of Naval Research did not dismiss them,
though just what they might have portended for the Navy yet
remains to be seen. This short quotation contains a number of clues
on what may have interested the Navy: it refers to "vortices," to
gravitational neutral points between two masses where the pull
from both masses on an object at that point is equal, and it refers to
Einstein's Unified Field Theory as being a theory principally about
magnetism, an intriguing observation. If one couples the idea of
"vortices" with magnetic fields to get "rotating magnetic fields"
we are a step closer to understanding the experiment and its basis
in the torsion tensor, as will be seen in a later chapter. Finally, note
the last comment, which may be the most significant of all in this
short annotation: the experiment conducted in 1943 was on "one
part of it," namely, on only one aspect or implication of the theory.
This too will be seen to be a very accurate observation for someone
who is merely a "crackpot" or who is perpetrating a hoax. The
observations, in other words, are surprisingly accurate.

A. Jessup and the Antiquity of Man

The Allende letters to Dr. Jessup immediately follow the table
of contents and its annotation in the Varo Edition. As we are
reserving extended commentary on these letters for a later chapter,
we will begin with considerations of Jessup's more interesting
ideas in the main text, and the Varo annotation on some of them.

---

[60] M.K. Jessup, *The Case for the UFO: Varo Annotated Edition,* p. 14.

One of these ideas is the antiquity of man, and an extreme antiquity of civilization. Like another scientist of greater fame and reputation, J. Robert Oppenheimer, Jessup took the indications of human antiquity and technological achievement in extremely ancient times as found in some Sanskrit texts seriously:

> Probably the oldest, and almost surly the most prolific of sources bearing on wingless flight, are the records of the Indian and Tibetan monasteries. These in themselves <u>are almost conclusive</u>. Records of 15,000 years ayo imply wingless flight at least 70,000 years prior to that. Add this to the recorded visit of a space fleet to the court of Thutmose III, approximately 15000 B.C., and we are close to paralleling the sightings of today.[61]

Note that the underlined portion is by one of Jessup's annotators. What is of great importance here is that Jessup believes these ancient epics contain both (1) historical and (2) technological accuracy. And thus Jessup concludes "It is almost an inseparable corollary to our thesis that we admit to an unfathomable antiquity for mankind, or at least intelligence, upon the earth, and its vicinity."[62] While this was certainly a radical proposal in his day, readers of my previous book, *The Cosmic War: Interplanetary Warfare, Modern Physics, and Ancient Texts* will recognize this program for what it really is: Jessup is looking at the technological portions of ancient myths and comparing them to the achievements of modern science, and concluding that the ancient myths were not myths at all, at least, not in the standard sense. In short, Jessup is doing what I have called in my previous books, "paleophysics."[63] He even oddly corroborates the view of the ancient Sumerian, Egyptian, and Hebrew religions that "other intelligences" may have been on earth, and built civilizations, long before mankind arrived on the scene: "So there are two elements of importance in our study of the antiquity of intelligence: the proof that superior beings have been here longer than mankind has been civilized, and

---

[61] M. K. Jessup, *The Case for the UFO: Varo Annotated Edition,* p. 28.
[62] Ibid.
[63] See my books *The Giza Death Star,* pp. 38-110; *The Giza Death Star Deployed,* pp. 60-193, 234-264; *The Giza Death Star Destroyed,* pp. 21-96; 99-245; *Reich of the Black Sun,* pp. 162-180; and *The Cosmic War: Interplanetary Warfare, Modern Physics, and Ancient Texts,* for fuller discussions of this idea.

the demonstration that forces were at work in those millennia, the magnitude and nature of which are only suspected today."[64]

b. Megaliths and Levitation

It is in this context that Jessup then considers the engineering implications of the ancient megalithic marvels such as the pyramids of Giza or the huge stone block walls of Peru. And if the U.S. military was paying attention to these scientists – and it was – it would have noticed Oppenheimer's peculiar quotation of the Hindu epic, the Mahabharata, during the Trinity plutonium atom bomb test in New Mexico in July of 1945. With Jessup one had yet another scientist, also with a background in physics, citing the same texts in reference to the solution to the riddle of controlling gravity, for in the context of considering the antiquity of man or intelligence on the earth, Jessup also states unequivocally that "it is apparent in the innumerable megalithic works of stone which involve masses <u>too huge to be moved by means other than levitation</u> and which have been standing for ages before any written record now available."[65] Again, the annotators have underscored the passage that interested them, and added their own pithy comment: "THE MAN IS CLOSE, *TOO* CLOSE."[66]

C. Jessup and a Varo Annotation Concept:
Interplanetary War and the Exploded Planet Hypothesis

Then follows one of the most amazing passages, to my mind, in Jessup's whole book. With it, a concept is introduced that calls forth from his anonymous annotators various responses throughout the *rest* of the book. This concept is that an ancient interplanetary war was fought in our own solar system, and that one of its results was the asteroid belt, grim remnants of an ancient, deliberately exploded planet:

---

[64] M.K. Jessup, *The Case for the UFO: Varo Annotated Edition,* p. 28.
[65] Ibid.
[66] Ibid.

> As these pieces of the jigsaw puzzle make themselves known, and as we realize fully that this is an old, old problem, we can begin to take comfort. If UFO's have been here for 300,000 years and have not yet chosen to launch a mass attack on humanity, it is scarcely likely that they will do it now – unless they are forced to do something to prevent the world's experimenting militarists and scientists from destroying the earth through ignition of its hydrogen, thus (creating) another nova or a new star in the galaxy, and *(who) may well have done when the fifth planet disintegrated at an incalculable time in the past.* [67]

In mentioning the ignition of the hydrogen in the earth's atmosphere, Jessup is referring to the idea, prevalent in the popular imagination of the 1950s during the era of Soviet and American atmospheric hydrogen mob testing, that these thermonuclear bombs might cause a kind of "fusion chain reaction" and ignite the earth's atmosphere in a continuous thermonuclear fireball like the Sun is thought to be, thus turning the planet Earth into a thermonuclear pyre, and a new star. The real import of this passage is not, however, the then imaginary fears, but Jessup's reference to an idea only seriously revived in modern astronomy by Dr. Tom Van Flandern some decades after Dr. Jessup first mentioned it in connection with UFOs and ancient texts: The Exploded Planet Hypothesis.

First proposed in the late 18th and early 19th centuries, this hypothesis is founded on the Titius-Bode law in astronomy. Based on an exact arithmetic progression, this law successfully predicted the orbits of planets so well that it was used to discover the outer planets of the solar system. There was just one problem. The law also predicted the existence of a planet between Mars and Jupiter, and a planet of large mass at that. Then, with the discovery of the first asteroids in the early 19th century, the law appeared vindicated. And the asteroids provided those astronomers with the clue to what had happened to the missing planet: it had exploded.[68]

---

[67] M.K. Jessup, *The Case for the UFO" Varo Annotated Edition*, p. 28, emphasis added.

[68] See my *Giza Death Star Deployed*, pp. 1-23, *The Giza Death Star Destroyed*, pp. 21-52, and my most recent book *The Cosmic War: Interplanetary Warfare, Modern Physics, and Ancient Texts*, pp. 1-65, for a discussion of the Exploded Planet Hypothesis as propounded by Dr. Van Flandern. Dr. Jessup,

In fact, all of this astronomical history was known to Jessup, who specifically referred to Bode's law in his book.[69] What is of extreme interest is Jessup's suggestion that the missing planet *may have exploded as the result of ancient militarists' experiments gone wrong.* This is but one short step away from maintaining that the explosion of the missing planet occurred as a deliberate act of war. In either case, Jessup's comment carries with it the inevitable implication that he believed there once existed a technology sophisticated enough to explode entire planets – whether accidentally or deliberately. That alone surely would have caught the Navy's attention! The only question that remained was: what *physics* was implied by the existence of this technology?

Surprisingly, the annotators of Jessup's book probably unwittingly drew attention to the implications of Jessup's ideas. Jessup remarks, for example, that an ancient comet impact had possibly wrought the destruction of life on earth, including the destruction of Atlantis, an idea he gleaned from reading the works of celebrated Atlantologist and Congressman Ignatius Donnelly. Donnelly, of course, had maintained that this impact was accidental. But then one of the Varo annotators added the following comment to Jessup's text:

> The Learned Rep Was right, save that it was done by MANY "Comets" in The Great War.

> *Balls* were compressed Earth, Used as Ammo for Force-"Guns" During "The Great War" The success of *that* was so fast, that these were never used.[70]

Were it not for the textual evidence of ancient myths and the physical evidences that I discuss in my previous book *The Cosmic War* for just such a possibility of an ancient interplanetary war fought in our own solar system, I normally would have been disinclined to accept such a comment. As it is, however, it would appear that here as elsewhere in the annotations, Jessup's

---

obviously would not have known of Van Flandern's version, and thus would be referring to its older 19th century version.

[69] M.K. Jessup, *The Case for the UFO: Varo Annotated Edition,* p. 56.
[70] Ibid.

anonymous commentators were very well-informed. One can only hazard a guess at the source of this knowledge, since no indication is given in their annotations of having read or been familiar with the ancient texts that refer to this war.[71]

But what are the "balls" referred to in the above quotation? The annotators underscored a passage in Jessup's text where he refers to spheroid stone balls, called "concretions" by geologists who believe in their origins by natural causes, which were discovered in sandstone layers in California.[72] Both in Jessup's main text and in the annotation, it is clearly implied that the balls were the products of a technology and thus artificial in origin. And for the annotators, the balls were the products of a technology of war.

Jessup puts the implications of his own evidence quite succinctly: "We continue to have a choice between terrestrial antiquity or spatial antiquity. But antiquity we do have, and a race so ancient, on earth, could very well have invented space travel."[73] As for Ignatius Donnelly's accidental ending of Atlantis, or even Colonel James Churchward's accidental ending of his lost Pacific continent of "Mu", the Varo annotators will have none of it:

GREAT BOMBARDMENT.

The great Bombardment Announced the end of Mu.[74]

A subsequent annotation makes it clear that the annotators are not using the phrase "great bombardment" as a metaphor for multiple comet or meteorite impacts on earth, but that it was an act in a vast interplanetary war:

Had Farraday concerned *Himself* With The Mag. FIELD SURROUNDING HIS Elec. Current, Man today would already Have reached the outermost Parts of our Galaxy.

---

[71] The annotators do mention that they are of "Gypsy" ancestry, which may indicate a possible source in the lore and traditions of the Romansch peoples.

[72] M.K. Jessup, *The Case for the UFO: Varo Annotated Edition,* p. 70.

[73] Ibid., p. 71.

[74] Ibid., p. 80.

> There, Jemi, Was given the results of What Would have been possible
> had Dr. Farraday Done as suggested other page. The S-Ms & L-Ms
> FOUGHT *USING* SMALL ASTEROIDS.[75]

The "S-Ms" and "L-Ms" referred to are the annotators' names for
the two types of alien life they believe are involved in the UFO
phenomenon. But note the significant point: asteroids were used as
weapons, and that, in turn, would imply the ability to manipulate
gravity, yet another theme of the annotators' comments.

A final lengthy annotation refers to this ancient interplanetary
war near the very end of Jessup's book:

> If the history of the Great War of the ancients were ever recorded,
> except by the black-tongued ones own tales, it would cause Man to
> stand in awe (or disbelief) that such Huge Satelitic Masses were ever
> deliberately tossed throo this atmosphere in an attempt to Demolish all
> of the "Little Men" Great Works. Fortunately for Mankinds ego only a
> Gypsy will tell another of that catastrophe, and we are a discredited
> peopole (sic) ages ago. HAH! Yes, Man Wonders where "we" came
> from, and I Do Not Believe that they will *ever* know. These folks on
> *this* planet *blind Panic*.[76]

Clearly, the idea of an ancient interplanetary war with its "great
bombardment" was a major theme to the annotators, who imply
that it plays some role in Gypsy lore.

However, it is the context of the above annotation that is
perhaps most revealing, and that probably gave the Navy yet one
more reason to take the annotators of Jessup's book, as well as the
book itself, seriously. For immediately prior to the foregoing
passage, the following intriguing and suggestive annotation occurs:

> WHAT HAPPENS WHEN A BOLT OF LIGHTNING HITS AT A
> POINT WHERE THERE IS A "NODE" SUCH AS A "SWIRL"
> IN THE MAGNETIC SEA *OR WHERE* A MAG. "DEAD SPOT"
> caused by the NEUTRALIZATION OF MAG. SEA contra GRAVITY
> ESPECIALLY, WHAT, WHEN THE NODE & BOLT BOTH ACT
> OVER BRONZE INLAY.

---

[75] M.K. Jessup, *THe Case for the UFO: Varo Annotated Edition,* p. 109.
[76] Ibid., p. 164.

> The Good Doctor is far more aware of committing the cardinal effrontery of Unorthodoxy than he wishes to show, perhaps. Too, He wishes to have More & More & More, a flood of Data, & facts & records of observations that will back-up his Theory. It would seem Much more apropo were he to not ask for further Proof to show to his fellow Professional Deriders *but* Were He To Proceed Himself into the *only* field that *would* convince each and Every one of His fellows; That field of Gravity & Magnetic exploration, as yet Untouched. He THEN could say the Moon is Hollow & *Not* one person would saw a Word. Approach to morals & Ethics of Science, Not New. Newton proved his Theory throo observable phenomena The which *any one* coujld observe & So *has this Man*.[77]

Observe that the annotators offer a rather unusual, and at first glance, seemingly implausible method for achieving the required force to render their "great bombardment" feasible: a "bolt of lightning" has to hit a point where there is a "swirl" in the "magnetic sea" where there is a "dead spot", especially when "the node and bolt both act" over a "bronze inlay."

But reducing this tangle to its basic components reveals something very intriguing, as will be seen in the rest of the book, and particularly in part three in connection with the Nazi Bell. Reducing the tangle to its basic components reveals that what the annotators have in mind is once again a magnetic vortex, this time a vortex that is suddenly and abruptly pulsed or stressed by an enormous electrostatic discharge of almost pure voltage, such as lightning. Moreover, this is to occur over an "inlay" of a metal alloy, in this case, bronze. So we have three elements, according to the Varo annotators, to achieve the control of gravity for their "weaponized asteroids":

1) A magnetic vortex or rotating magnetic field;
2) An abrupt sudden pulse of stress brought about by electrostatic discharge of extremely high voltage into the center of that vortex;
3) A metal alloy closely connected with the magnetic vortex.

---

[77] M.K. Jessup, *The Case for the UFO: Varo Annotated Edition,* p. 163.

These elements will assume great importance as we examine the Philadelphia Experiment later in this section, and even greater importance when we turn to the Nazi Bell in the next.[78]

d. Jessup on the Paleoancient Very High Civilization

In addition to the extreme antiquity of man, or of some other "intelligence", upon the earth, Jessup also subscribed to the view that man, or this other intelligent race, had achieved a very sophisticated level of civilization, and thus he subscribed to the idea of what I called in my *Giza Death Star* trilogy the "paleoancient Very High Civilization." My intentionally redundant term "paleoancient" was meant to convey the extreme antiquity of this civilization, a civilization that pre-dated ancient Egypt, Sumer, India, and China and which was, indeed, their forebear. Jessup subscribed to very similar views:

> All of the centers of civilization and cultural renaissance recognized by present-day anthropologists- India, Peru, Yucatan, Egypt, Babylonia, Greece, China, Rome, England and others – *are but the reviving elements of an empire and civilization which colonized the world a hundred thousand years ago.* They are all "parts," or nuclei, in one great renaissance which has been taking place for, roughly, six to ten thousand years. In it are some traces of the archaic, original, master culture, and, perhaps through India, Tibet, Egypt and Middle America, there are some tenuous links between our immature revival and the parent past. These traces mostly in the form of stone works, and some glyphs, of a singular nature, with very few written records existing mostly in the Orient, and particularly in southern Asia. [79]

The annotators have some intriguing comments to this passage:

LEFT UNAVOIDABLY IN "GREAT WAR."

Above is true, Jemi. They are Written about in Many Writings. So old, as to be nullified by antiquity.[80]

---

[78] For readers of my book *The SS Brotherhood of the Bell* the significance of these three elements will already be apparent.

[79] M.K. Jessup, *The Case for the UFO: Varo Annotated Edition,* p. 103, emphasis added.

[80] Ibid.

In other words, as far as the mysterious annotators were concerned, the fact that there are only traces of that paleoancient Very High Civilization is due to the fact that a great war almost completely wiped it out. Note also, that the annotators appear to be very familiar *with certain ancient texts that tell this story,* texts which, as they observe, are "nullified by antiquity," in other words, no one takes them seriously as containing *real "historical" truth because the texts are so old and the events to which they refer are even older.*

The annotation reveals that Jessup's anonymous commentators, whoever they may have been – and there is little doubt that Allende was one of them – and for whatever faults they may have had as grammarians, were fairly well-informed in areas of paleography that lay far beyond the normal course of reading for any college student, for such texts remained the province of specialists in Sanskrit, Sumerology, or Egyptology, and so on.

e. Jessup's "Invisible Solidities" and the Varo Comment

One of the more interesting concepts in Jessup's main text is that of "invisible solidities." Noting that a number of airplane accidents were not really explicable by any known and popularly accepted natural mechanism, Jessup speculated that some crashes were caused when airplanes seemed "to hit something which crushed them or tears them apart, which is nevertheless invisible, and which strikes with such suddenness that the pilots do not have time to make an outcry via their ever-live radios."[81] He continues with his idea:

> From such an analysis we come by easy steps to conceive of a force, ray, or focal point. In some force-field either unknown to us, or at least not understood, which produces rigidity in a localized or sharply delimited volume of air, *or possibly in space itself...* (An) example might be the passage of a limited but powerful magnetic field through a scattering of iron filings or iron powder. Before the approach of the magnetic flux enters it, invisibly and imperceptibly to the senses of man, this docile powder becomes rigid, tenacious, coherent, and at least

---

[81] M.K. Jessup, *THE Case for the UFO: Varo Annotated Edition,* pp. 33-34.

semisolid. Do the space dwellers have a force which produces this temporary rigidity in the air, or even possibly in the gravitation field itself? Or do they create "local" concentrations of the gravitational field as we are able to do with the magnetic field?[82]

Thus far, what Jessup is describing sounds very similar to Nikola Tesla's "standing waves". And given the explorations of the torsion tensor surveyed in part one, the answer to Jessup's final question would have to be a tentative yes. A localized "fold" or "pleat" in space-time, such as encoded in the torsion tensor, if extreme enough, could conceivably create the "invisible solidities" and temporary "rigidity" that could do what Jessup describes. Moreover, as a scientist, Jessup most likely knew this hidden implication of a localized variation of gravity and electromagnetic fields implied by Einstein's torsion tensor.

He expands further on his idea:

> Such a thing would be invisible, would have many of the physical attributes of a solid body, *but very small mass.* For example, its movement through the air would be wavelike, and would not involve translation of the medium any more than the spot of the searchlight would require the movement of the cloud which enables the beam to attain visibility. In moving, this island would simply "freeze" on the advancing edge and "thaw" on the trailing edge. In this way it could have almost infinite velocity and also acceleration… In this manner it would appear to be free of mass, and actually it would be free of mass, because only the force beam would move, not the air. Yet in resisting the impringement of a bird, a plane, or perhaps a meteor, it would have mass, and a very destructive mass at that.[83]

In other words, imagine a particular kind of "fold" or "pleat" in space-time, a pure wave of stress in the medium. Under certain conditions, this stress might so configure air or space itself as a solid object, as a kind of "virtual mass" to other objects it would encounter. The result, as Jessup outlines, would be destructive. The weaponizability of such an idea would doubtless have drawn the attention of the Navy officers he encountered. Equally important to notice, however, is Jessup's suggestion that this type of wave would also be massless; i.e., a means possibly of achieving control

---

[82] M.K. Jessup, *The Case for the UFO: Varo Annotated Edition,* p. 34.
[83] Ibid., p. 35.

of gravity locally. Consequently, whether Jessup actually states it explicitly or not, he is thinking in terms of the implied concepts of the torsion tensor. *Jessup, in other words, has in view the specific 1928 version of Einstein's theory.*

He goes yet further, and connects these ideas to basic concepts of plasma physics, a perfect non-linear medium for possibly achieving many of the types of effects that he proposes, under extreme conditions:

> If such a force island were formed in the upper atmosphere, it might be very possible for it to have many of the physical characteristics of a solid body, and yet in matters of illumination it could behave exactly as any other auroral phenomena. In this connection we must remember that <u>auroral phenomena are magnetic</u> and may be caused by streams of electrons from the sun which are, in effect, <u>precisely the type </u>of force beam upon which we are speculating.[84]

The annotators underlined portions of this passage, and commented as follows:

> <u>Yes, He is close, but doesn't think of Mag. Inductors *or* of Gravity as "air" Or thought of in Jet propulsion. He doesn't know gravity & Magnetizm (sic) can be drawn into a ship, built up to High power, While being converted & used as a Force-Propulsive HE MAY KNOW OF FORCE-SHIELDS of Primitive Ancient type.</u>[85]

---

[84] M.K. Jessup, *The Cazse for the UFO: Varo Annotated Edition,* p. 35. Readers familiar with the various uses proposed by the Eastland patents which lie behind the HAARP project – uses that include the formation of a defense shield – will recognize some of these concepts. Jessup, it would appear, was some thirty years ahead of the game, at least in this respect. Insofar as HAARP is concerned, the shield is designed to be a weak shield that would be similar to a perpetual electro-magnetic pulse. Any object with sensitive electronics passing through such a shield would have its electronics hopelessly scrambled or fried. Jessup is simply taking the concept to the next stage and suggesting - again most likely based on some aspects suggested to him by Einstein's Unified Field Theory of 1928 – that electromagnetic means might be able to achieve gravitational effects with the creation of "invisible solidities." Any object smashing into them would accordingly be crushed or obliterated.

[85] Ibid., p. 35.

As if this were not enough, Jessup goes even further, and suggests that *interferometry* would be the method of choice to achieve the "invisible solidity" effect:

> It seems obvious that a single beam could not have the effect which we have suggested, else the freeze would take effect along the entire length of the beam. However, it is possible that the three-dimensional volume enclosed within the intersection of two beams might create such a congealed island.[86]

The annotators have one principal disagreement with Jessup at this point. Whereas Jessup is thinking in terms of electromagnetic interferometry, the annotators are thinking in terms of purely magnetic interferometry. And again, they do so in the context of their alleged inside knowledge of details of the Philadelphia Experiment.

In any case, these passages clearly indicate why the Navy would have expressed an interest in the annotated Jessup book, for from one and the same approach three applications are being described both in the main text and in the annotators' comments: 1) weaponry of virtually unlimited power, 2) a means of propulsion, and 3) the very alteration of matter itself by means of ripples or interfered waves in space-time, in a new kind of materials science.

f. The Artificiality of Mars' Satellite Phobos

Jessup was, if nothing else, unhesitating in his proposals of radical explanations for known phenomena that dogged modern science's dogmas. In the case of proposing the artificiality of Mars' satellite Phobos, Jessup voiced the view that this object was perhaps artificial, long before Soviet scientists would propose similar views:

> It has been pointed out that this inner body is too close to Mars to be in adjustment with any known postulate of the natural distribution of

---

[86] M.K. Jessup, *The Case for the UFO: Varo Annotated Edition,* p. 35.

satellites relative to their parent body. This may be an indication that Mars' inner satellite is artificial.[87]

Given that the Navy's ONR officers Commander Hoover and Captain Sherby were both connected to American's first artificial satellite project, Project Vanguard, Jessup's remark once again would have aroused curiosity and interest from the military. His remarks implied a hidden reason for mankind to undertake space missions: there was a recoverable technology out there.

g. Soviet "Scalar" Research

As Lt. Col. Tom Bearden (US Army, Ret) has often pointed out,[88] the ability to engineer space-time locally implies two further abilities: 1) the ability to suddenly put energy into a target area, and 2) the ability to suddenly extract energy from a target area in a kind of "cold bomb." Bearden also maintains, on the basis of a rather carefully constructed circumstantial case, that much of the research into these types of applications of this physics was conducted after World War Two in the former Soviet Union.

Here again, Jessup appeared to be hot on the scent long before contemporary researchers, noting that one alleged accomplishment of Russian physics "was said to be a method of freezing large areas of ground to subzero temperatures, killing everything therein."[89]

h. Close Proximate Origin of UFOs

One of the most interesting concepts that Jessup entertains is his speculation concerning the point of origin of UFOs. Already in the 1950s, with the advances in technology and optical telescopy available to astronomy, Earth's neighboring planets increasingly looked to be hostile environments to any form of intelligent life such as we know. This fact led those with an interest in UFOlogy to push the point of their alleged origin farther and farther away

---

[87] M.K. Jessup, *The Case for the UFO: Varo Annotated Edition*, p. 37.

[88] See my *SS Brotherhood of the Bell*, pp. 207-241 for a summary of Bearden's historical reconstruction of scalar physics.

[89] M.K. Jessup, *The Case for the UFO: Varo Annotated Edition*, p. 44.

from the Earth to points outside the solar system. Unwittingly, however, as they did so, they compounded the physics problem UFOs represented, for the *observed* flight characteristics of UFOs, while exotic and beyond human technological capabilities, *were not exotic **enough** to indicate a potential for practical interstellar travel.* In short, the physics signatures of UFOs – at least the ones that could be reasonably identified to craft of *some* sort – while extraordinary, were not extraordinary enough to imply a physics sufficient to the task of interstellar travel.

Jessup swam upstream against this tendency in UFOlogy that was already beginning to emerge in his day. He chose to assign their point of origin much *closer* to the Earth, and in the process of doing so, fleshed out his theory of the paleoancient civilization he believed that they represented, its extent, and its possible relation to the exploded fifth planet:

> It is hard to discourage the innate feeling that there has recently been a great surge of activity on the part of UFO's as if in preparation for something big. One does not have to look far for a motive. These entities have probably been living in the solar system long enough to have seen the fifth planet explode, destroying itself and perhaps jeopardizing life throughout the system. *They may have originated on that planet... It is no longer necessary to explain them as visitors from Mars, Venus, or Alpha Centauri. They are part of our own immediate family – a part of the earth-moon, binary-planet system.*[90]

For Jessup the scientist, it was not only the insufficiency of the physics signature of UFOs to indicate an interstellar origin for the phenomena, but also the totality of *other* evidences – the astronomical data of the Exploded Planet plus the ancient texts themselves – that pointed to a close proximate origin for the phenomenon. To these ideas the Varo annotators add their own comment, and pose a question: "<u>Matches our own thoughts</u>" and "<u>He *Knows* Something but *How* Does He Know</u>."[91] The answer lies in the fact that Jessup made no secret of his knowledge of the ancient texts that referred to the ancient interplanetary war, for

---

[90] M.K. Jessup, *The Case for the UFO: Varo Annotated Edition,* pp. 46-47, emphasis added.
[91] Ibid., p. 47.

those texts implied a similar point of origin for the "gods" that fought that war.

i. The Philadelphia Experiment Itself, and its Withdrawal

And so finally we arrive at the centerpiece of the annotations, the Philadelphia Experiment itself. Here, of course, we abandon Jessup's main text, which never refers to it, and take up the annotators who, referring to the experiment, notice one of Jessup's cases of ships that disappear for no apparent reason or good natural explanation:

> Tried that with XXXX[92] & I on XXXXXXXXXXXXXX[92] and he XXXXXXX[92] was drunk enough to slip out of the "freeze" & He Made them know it *in No uncertain terms*. They put us down & *Then* unfroze the crew who to this day Do Not remember of it. *THEY CAN'T*, (Mr. M. was Chief Mate, "Hatteras" 1943).

> Perhaps they detected "FIELD" activity of NAVY D-E WHICH WAS CLOSE BY, (BEFORE) TESTING AN *INVISIBILITY* EXPIERMENTAL (sic) "gadget."[93]

Needless to say, such statements would have stimulated the ONR's interest, for there is a clear reference to a destroyer escort (DE), and to the testing of "an invisibility gadget." One can imagine the consternation this must have immediately produced in the ONR officers who received the paperback annotated copy of Dr. Jessup's book, for what had invisibility to do with gravity and UFOs?

The annotators themselves provided a clue toward answering this question, though it would seem that the Navy's Varo Edition editors missed the point initially:

> Einsteins Theory of Unified Field throughout all Space & atmosphere WAS SO WELL PROVEN that upon realizing Mans Misanthropic emotionality He Withdrew it. 1927. [94]

---

[92] This word was crossed out by Jemi (Varo Editions own editorial note).

[93] M.K. Jessup, *The Case for the UFO: Varo Annotated Edition*, p. 94.

[94] Ibid., p. 31.

This is one of the most important statements in the Varo annotations, for clearly the annotators believe that the theory was actually *proven,* but with such horrible implications for mankind's stunted spiritual character that Einstein allegedly withdrew it, the implication being that he feared what man might do with it.

Of course, the year of the theory is wrong – 1927 as opposed to 1928 – and most likely the annotators meant to refer to the 1928 version of the theory, the one which first incorporated the torsion tensor. As for Allende's explanation for its withdrawal, nothing could be father from the truth, for the real reason Einstein withdrew it was that he was still unsatisfied with it, and set off to pursue yet a different strategy of geometric unification of forces in his post-1928 papers.

Nonetheless, the annotators are insistent: the 1928 theory was "well proven." Yet this comment is not so strange if viewed from the perspective of Gabriel Kron's work on tensor analysis of electrical machines, for that work also indicated that Einstein's 1928 theory was engineerable, and therefore to that extent also "proven."

So again, the annotators' syntax and diction notwithstanding, they have not stated anything scientifically implausible.

C. Conclusions

So what really piqued the Navy's Office of Naval Research's interest to the extent that it went to the expense and trouble of reprinting a copy of the annotated version of Jessup's book? As has been seen, it most likely was a combination of several factors:

1) At the top of the list is the concern that security may have been breached;

2) But also at the top of the list is the Varo Edition's own Introduction which states that "any clue" into the nature of gravity and its control is "worth pursuing." Furthermore, given that

   a) two of the ONR's officers that were connected with the Varo Edition were also connected with the Navy's

Project Vanguard, America's first attempt to orbit a satellite around the Earth; and

b) Given the many references both in Jessup's main text and in the annotations to various means and results of controlling gravity waves of stresses in the medium of space-time were also connected to Einstein's 1928 Unified Field Theory, the Navy would have had reason on these bases alone to pursue such a publication.

3) But as was also seen, Jessup's ideas and the annotations also occur in a much wider speculative context, a context which includes ancient technology, an artificial satellite around Mars, an interplanetary war, the close proximate origin to the Earth of UFOs, and an exploded planet whose destruction was brought about by technological means. All of this implied an ancient technology (some of which, like Mars' artificial moon Phobos, was still in existence, according to Jessup). For a nation taking the first faltering steps into space, and in a race with its superpower rival the Soviet Union, these factors would have constituted an inevitable second tier of interest for the Navy.

4) Finally, as a result of the considerations examined in connection with point 3) above, a common physics with a potential threefold application was outlined:

a) for weaponry of tremendous destructive power reliant on stress in the fabric of space-time itself;

b) for propulsion and energy sources that would free mankind from what Jessup called the "brute force" approach of rockets; and,

c) for a new materials science based on the manipulations of matter by imprinted force fields – Lt. Col. Tom Bearden would call them "templates of action" – an imprinting that Jessup believed would lead to his "invisible solidities."

There is much in the Varo Annotated Edition, in other words, that would have caught the Navy's attention beyond UFOs or even the Philadelphia Experiment itself, for as the edition's existence itself attests, Jessup's whole "paleophysical approach" to various phenomena was well-known to at least one branch of the U.S. military, and has been known to it for almost five decades. This has obvious implications for the basic scenario concerning paleophysics and its probable covert development by the world's various military powers, a case that I have outlined in my previous books.[95]

But what about the centerpiece in all this, the Philadelphia Experiment itself? The next stage of that unfolding story was first broached to a wide audience in Charles Berlitz's book, *The Bermuda Triangle,* which contains some significant and often overlooked clues...

---

[95] See my *Giza Death Star, Giza Death Star Deployed, Giza Death Star Destroyed, Reich of the Black Sun, The SS Brotherhood of the Bell,* and most importantly, my most recent book *The Cosmic War: Interplanetary Warfare, Modern Phsyics, and Ancient Texts*, all published by Adventures Unlimited Press.

5.

SECOND DISCLOSURE:
CHARLES BERLITZ AND *THE BERMUDA TRIANGLE*

"Jessup told me that he thought that the U.S. Navy had inadvertently stumbled on this in a wartime experiment carried out on a destroyer which has been called 'the Philadelphia Experiment.'"
Dr. Manson Valentine[1]

The famous alternative researcher and language school owner, the late Charles Berlitz, did not come to write about the Philadelphia Experiment by a direct route. It was, rather, a story that he learned of while researching another phenomenon, the so-called Bermuda Triangle. It was while investigating this story and the strange events associated with the region – including several UFO sightings – that Berlitz learned of the Philadelphia Experiment. And the connection between the stories was, not surprisingly, the late Dr. Morris K. Jessup.

Berlitz learned of Jessup's interest in the Bermuda Triangle and its many UFO sightings, and interviewed a friend of Dr. Jessup, Dr. Manson Valentine. Berlitz incorporated the transcript of his interview in his best-selling book *The Bermuda Triangle*. Since this interview contains the first real mention of the Philadelphia Experiment in the literature available to a wide audience, we shall spend some time going through it and noting its details and some of the significant clues it contains.

A. The Interview with Jessup's Friend, Dr. Manson Valentine
1. Jessup on "Controlled Magnetism" and Optical Invisibility

According to Berlitz, Dr. Jessup, after investigating reports of UFOs in the Triangle, "became convinced that a covert censorship was smothering many important reports and developments."[2] But there was more. Berlitz also learned that Jessup was interested in a very unusual topic for a scientist, for "he was also preoccupied

---

[1] Cited in Charles Berlitz, *The Bermuda Triangle,* p. 148.
[2] Ibid., p. 141.

with the question of how controlled magnetism could produce invisibility, an outgrowth of Einstein's 'unified field theory,' which Jessup considered the key both to the sudden appearance and disappearance of UFOs and the disappearance of ships and planes."[3] This strange idea led Berlitz to contact one of Jessup's friends in Florida, Dr. Manson Valentine, where Jessup maintained his second house.

As Berlitz was soon to learn from Dr. Valentine, he had in fact invited Jessup to dinner "on the evening of April 20 (1959)." Jessup accepted the invitation but never showed up.[4] Jessup had, of course, apparently committed suicide on April 29, just nine days later, though as Berlitz points out, there are those who consider Jessup's death very suspicious, and "that the incident is an indication of the dangers of too close research" into the field of UFOlogy.[5] In any case, Dr. Valentine was one of the last people ever to talk to Jessup, and according to him, Jessup was "in a depressed state of mind."[6]

2. Valentine as the Source for Berlitz's Knowledge of Jessup's Ideas on Controlled Magnetism

As already indicated, Jessup was interested in the idea of "controlled magnetism" for the possibility of invisibility, and as a mechanism of explaining the mysterious disappearances of ships and airplanes in the Triangle region. Jessup's friend, Dr. Manson Valentine – a zoologist, archaeologist and oceanographer[7] – had studied the Triangle for years, and doubtless was the source that first clued Berlitz into Jessup's interest in magnetism and Einstein's 1928 Unified Field Theory.

---

[3] Charles Berlitz, *The Bermuda Triangle*, p. 141.
[4] Ibid.
[5] Ibid.
[6] Ibid.
[7] Ibid.

3. Valentine on Jessup's "Invisible Solidities"

After some preliminary questions to Dr. Valentine concerning the relationship of UFO sightings to the Triangle, Berlitz came to the subject of Jessup:

> *Did Dr. Jessup think there was a connection between the UFOs and the Bermuda Triangle?*

Valentine's response to the question is intriguing:

> He had a theory that the power of magnetic fields could transform and transport matter from one dimension to another... That UFOs could come into our dimension and get out again taking human or other samples with them. He further thought that some of the accidents were caused by the UFOs' cathode rays creating a vacuum which disintegrated planes when they entered this field.[8]

This answer requires some unpacking.

First, on the basis of Jessup's own thoughts surveyed in the previous chapter, and in connection with the Varo Edition of his book *The Case for the UFO,* we can be reasonably certain that Jessup did not talk about cathode rays except perhaps as an analogy to illustrate his point with his oceanographer friend. This brings us to the second point: the real clue lies in the first sentence of the answer, where Valentine refers to Jessup's idea that magnetic fields can "transport matter." From the previous chapter's examination of the Varo Edition, we know that Jessup used this idea *as an analogy* to explain his concept of how electromagnetic waves, properly interfered on a region, could imprint matter with a field and create an "invisible solidity" which, though massless in itself, would be a kind of *"virtual"* mass to any object running into it. Thus, while it would appear that Valentine somewhat misunderstood his friend, he nonetheless has accurately conveyed Jessup's *basic* idea, though in a very general manner.

Valentine goes on to volunteer the following information about Jessup's opinions:

---

[8] Berlitz, *The Bermuda Triangle,* p. 147.

> The UFOs, whatever they are, seem to create a temporary magnetic vortex, an ionization pattern that can cause ships and planes to disintegrate or disappear.
>
> Jessup, before he died, believed that he was on the verge of discovering the scientific basis for whatever was happening, which he considered explainable according to Einstein's "unified field theory."[9]

Note again the accuracy of Valentine's comments, for ideas of magnetic vortices were, indeed, found in Jessup's book. However – and this is quite the crucial point – it will be recalled from the previous chapter that the idea of magnetic vortices was *not* found in Jessup's main text, but stemmed rather from the mysterious annotators of the Varo Edition of his book. This means that Jessup had related to Valentine ideas deriving from the annotations. This means in turn that Jessup had begun to think deeply about their possible scientific foundation.

This places Valentine's last comment into a unique perspective, for having pondered the implications of the annotations, Dr. Jessup had concluded that the only possible or scientifically feasible basis to accomplish his "invisible solidities" or, for that matter, to accomplish the sudden disappearances and reappearances associated with some UFO sightings, was through some sort of manipulation of the fabric of space-time itself. Hence, Jessup has settled on Einstein's Unified Field Theory as a foundation for further speculation. From what we already know of the history of that theory, we know it was also probably the 1928 version with its torsion tensor and the local folding and pleating of space-time that Jessup most likely had in mind. He was, in other words, already thinking of the possibilities and implications of torsion, and hence his interest in "controlled" magnetic vortices.

Berlitz then follows this question up logically:

Can you give a simplified explanation of the unified field theory?

---

[9] Berlitz, *The Bermuda Triangle,* p. 148.

Recall once again thet Berlitz is asking this question of an oceanographer and archaeologist, and thus, Valentine's answer is likely to be based on what he recalled and learned from Jessup:

> The basis of it is that all our compartmentalized concepts of time-space and matter-energy are not separate entities but are transmutable under the same conditions of electromagnetic disturbance.

Reading between the lines once again, Jessup had probably concluded, as did Gabriel Kron before him, that while the 1928 version of the Unified Field Theory was incomplete as a theory, it was nonetheless an *engineerable* theory, and that under certain conditions, it might be possible to observe various effects – alterations of the states of matter, gravitational anomalies and so on – *locally, to engineer them.* Valentine continues:

> Actually the unified field theory offers yet another explanation of how UFOs could materialize and disappear so suddenly.
>
> In practice it concerns electric and magnetic fields as follows: An electric field created in a coil induces a magnetic field at right angles to the first, each of these fields represents one plane of space. But since there are three planes of space, there must be a third field, perhaps a gravitational one. By hooking up electromagnetic generators so as to produce a magnetic pulse, it might be possible to produce this third field through the principle of resonance. Jessup told me that he thought the U.S. Navy had *inadvertently* stumbled on this in a wartime experiment carried out on a destroyer which has been called the Philadelphia Experiment.[10]

Note that Valentine explicitly states that Jessup informed him that he believed the Navy had *inadvertently* stumbled on to something, in other words, that the designed purpose of the experiment and its actual achieved results were two different things. We shall later see how the scientific principles involved corroborate this view, and thus corroborate Valentine's testimony and character as a reliable witness.

Thus, the story has finally broken open.

Note also from the tone of Valentine's remarks that he once again is trying to recall the basic concepts Jessup had told him.

---

[10] Berlitz, *The Bermuda Triangle,* p. 148, emphasis added.

Jessup would have known that trying to explain the effects of torsion – or for that matter any other type of tensor transformation – to his oceanographer friend might have been too difficult for him to grasp, so in all likelihood, he resorted to the standard expedient of arguing from the "right hand rule" of electromagnetism, to demonstrate to his friend how that third plane or field might be induced through resonance between the other two basic fields. It would have been an analogy that his oceanographer friend would have understood more readily based on his probable exposure to basic concepts of classical electromagnetic theory. Valentine is relaying an analogy that Jessup most likely employed to explain his concepts to him.

But keep in mind that first point that Jessup had concluded that the U.S. Navy had stumbled upon something very significant by accident. In other words, it had been looking for one thing, and found something either quite different in kind from what it was looking for, or had found something different in degree than what it was looking for. This point will become very crucial in a couple of chapters. Moreover, this clue is significant for another reason, because it indicates that Jessup had pondered the details and implications of the Varo Edition of his book, and of the two Allende letters, *quite deeply*. His insistence on the role of magnetism thus emerges as a significant clue of where his thought was heading, and as we shall eventually learn, he most definitely was on the right track.

4. Valentine's Account of Jessup's Version of the Philadelphia Experiment

The story thus broken, Berlitz naturally follows up once again with the next logical question:

What was the Philadelphia Experiment?

According to Jessup the Philadelphia Experiment was a secret experiment conducted by the U.S. Navy in 1943 *at Philadelphia and at sea.* Its purpose was to test out the effect of a strong magnetic field on a manned surface craft. This was to be accomplished by means of magnetic generators (degaussers). *Both pulsating and non-pulsating generators were operated to create a tremendous magnetic field on and around a docked vessel.* The results were as astonishing as they were important, although with unfortunate aftereffects on the crew. When the experiment first began to take effect, a hazy green light became evident, something like the reports we have from survivors of incidents in the Triangle who tell of a luminous greenish mist. Soon the whole ship was full of this green haze and the craft, together with its personnel, began disappearing from sight of those *on the dock until only its waterline was visible. The destroyer was subsequently reported to have appeared and disappeared at Norfolk, Virginia, which may have been the result of a trial invisibility run, involving a related time-warp phenomenon.*

It was reported by a former crew member that the experiment was successful at sea, with an effective field of invisibility or spheroid shape extending one hundred yards from each beam, which showed the depression made by the ship in the water, but not the ship itself. As the force field intensified, some crew members began disappearing and had to be rediscovered by tactual contact and restored to visibility by a sort of laying-on-of-hands technique. Certain others became so far removed from their original material dimensions that they could only be detected and brought back to normalcy by a specially designed electronic device. For such cases, when a shipmate could neither be seen nor felt, the crew had a quaint expression: Being "stuck in molasses." Actually it was a state of suspended animation from which full recovery could be a serious problem. It was rumored that many were hospitalized, some died, others were adversely affected mentally. Psychic ability seemed to have been generally sharpened while many retained the effects of transmutation from the experiment, temporarily disappearing and reappearing, either at home, walking on the street, or sitting in bars or restaurants, to the consternation of onlookers and waitresses. *Twice the ship's binnacle suddenly burst into flames while being taken ashore, with disastrous results to the carrier.* [11]

And with that one has the first widely publicized account of the Philadelphia Experiment in open literature.

There are a number of significant points in this quotation that must be highlighted.

1) Observe that right at the outset Dr. Valentine begins with the words "According to Jessup...." In other words, the whole story that follows is Valentine's recollection of Jessup's version of the story, a version that Jessup had no doubt pieced together from the Varo Edition annotations, Allende's letters, and his own personal investigations.

---

[11] Berlitz, *The Bermuda Triangle,* pp. 148-150.

2) Notice also the highly important statement that the experiment was conducted in 1943 *both in Philadelphia and at sea*. As we shall see in subsequent chapters, this is a conclusion that Jessup could not have drawn either from the Varo Edition's annotations – it made no mention of the experiment having been conducted in Philadelphia – nor from Allende's letters. These, as will eventually be seen, do not mention any experiment in the Philadelphia naval dockyards at all (or any other dockyard for that matter). They refer only to an experiment conducted at sea. This means either of two things: Jessup either independently learned of one stage of the experiment that was conducted at Philadelphia, or he conjectured on its occurrence and location based on other factors.

This requires some further explanation. As we outlined at the end of Part One, the normal procedure for scientific and engineering projects such as the Philadelphia Experiment or the Nazi Bell would have been to recruit a team, and design a "proof of concept" experiment. If successful, a full-scale experiment would then have been designed and conducted. It is not only possible, then, but highly likely that Dr. Jessup, as a scientist realized that a full scale "invisibility" experiment conducted at sea was some later stage of whatever project the experiment represented. He would have known a similar experiment or series of experiments would have been conducted on a smaller scale, very likely at a naval dockyard, and very likely using some of the metal and wooden model ships that the Navy produced to test its designs in advance of building a full-sized ship.[12] Thus, while the evidence remains merely conjectural, the Navy would have conducted a proof of concept experiment somewhere on land, perhaps using some of its model ships and testing tanks to do so. The evidence for this type of earlier version of the experiment is speculative, admittedly, but it is in line with the normal process of scientific experimentation as outlined at the end of part one. And as we shall see in a subsequent chapter, this "proof of concept" experiment is a crucial clue into the viability and validity of the Philadelphia Experiment story.

---

[12] One such small scale model is the battleship U.S.S. South Dakota, on display at the battleship South Dakota memorial in Sioux Falls, South Dakota.

3) And this brings us to the third point. As Valentine's recounting of Jessup's version of the story makes clear, the experiment consisted of using ship-borne magnetic degaussing coils and their associated generators. But more importantly, there is a detail that occurs in Valentine's recounting of Jessup's version, which appears nowhere else in the literature of the story. This detail is also significant, for Valentine states that the generators were designed usuing two modes of operation: *non-pulsed* and *pulsed.* This is another clue, and one which, if true, connects the Philadelphia Experiment's conceptual basis to the Nazi Bell. It is this detail that place's Jessup's version, as recounted by Valentine, at variance with the known conceptual foundations for the experiment related elsewhere.

4) Valentine also indicated that the results "were as astonishing as they were important," another indicator that the results, detailed in Valentine's following remarks, were not anticipated by the American scientists conducting the experiment *in its full scale version.* These results included disappearing crew members and the complete optical invisibility of the experimental test ship itself. *In other words, invisibility of the ship and crew were **not** what the experiment was originally designed to accomplish.* The following questions are therefore inevitably raised by Valentine's account: What *was* the original objective of the experiment? And were the stated "astonishing results" different in kind from the original objective, or only degree? As already noted, these "details" no doubt were related to Valentine by Jessup himself, who in turn probably gleaned them from the Varo Edition's annotations, Allende's letters, and a process of reasoning and extrapolation similar to our own. Seeking a conceptual and theoretical basis for the experiment and its "astonishing results", Jessup concluded that the best candidate to explain it was Einstein's Unified Field Theory of 1928, the one incorporating the torsion tensor, since this mathematical transform came the closest to embodying the notions of vortices that the annotations and Allende letters spoke about. Jessup was not, therefore, engaged in wild speculation, but rather, hot on the trail.

5) Note also that Valentine relates that the field of invisibility was spheroid in shape, extending some one hundred yards from

each beam of the test ship, and that the depression of the ship's hull could be clearly seen in the water, "but not the ship itself." Only with the apparent intensification of the field around the ship did the crew members disappear from each other's sight. They could, as Valentine stated, only be made visible again by "a sort of laying on of hands technique." When stuck in the "invisibility field" the crew called it "being stuck in molasses." These details could only have come from Jessup himself, since they are clearly enumerated in Allende's letters to Jessup.

6) Finally, Valentine recounts the fact that the test ship's crew members were apparently capable of disappearing in full view of other people, in ordinary circumstances, long after the experiment was over. This once again is a detail that could only have come to Valentine from Allende's letters, via Jessup.

All these details taken together constitute the first Berlitz version of the Philadelphia Experiment.

But what of the interview itself? Having learned all these wild and truly spectacular allegations from a credentialed scientist, Berlitz once again displayed his skill as an interviewer and asked the next logical question:

Did Jessup witness these incidents?

Observe Valentine's answer carefully:

> I don't know how much he personally witnessed of the things he told me *but he researched it pretty thoroughly.* You must remember that he was not a "crank" writer but a distinguished and famous scientist and astronomer. He had been in charge of the largest refracting telescope in the Southern Hemisphere, directed several eclipse projects, was the discoverer of double stars, and had a brilliant scientific record. The reason that he became involved with the Philadelphia Experiment was that a man who claimed to have been a survivor of the experiment named Carlos Allende (or Carl Allen), wrote to Jessup in 1956 about his book *The Case for the UFOs* because of the similarity to the basic theory.[13]

---

[13] Berlitz, *The Bermuda Triangle,* p. 150.

The similarity of the basic theory to *what?* Valentine appears not to have noticed that he left the last sentence dangling with no obvious referent or answer. We are allowed to answer the question based on what he had already told Berlitz, namely, that the theory referred to was probably the 1928 version of Einstein's Unified Field Theory. He continues:

> Allende started a correspondence with Jessup, who naturally answered like any author answering fan mail. Some time after this correspondence began, Jessup was requested to come to Washington by the ONR (Office of Naval Research). Remember that censorship had covered up the Philadelphia Experiment *except for one brief article in a Philadelphia newspaper.* [14]

So far Valentine's version of the events squares neatly with the version outlined in the Varo Edition. But notice the new detail: only one article appeared in a Philadelphia newspaper that gave any indication of the performance of the experiment, though Valentine does not indicate what the contents of the article were, nor how it was connected to the experiment. Once again, Valentine is simply relaying what Jessup had told him, and thus may not have known the contents of the article.

The article doubtless refers to the story, circulated subsequently in Berlitz and Moore's *The Philadelphia Experiment,* that a small column-filler article ran in a Philadelphia newspaper describing a drunken brawl in a bar, during which a waitress observed some of the participants totally disappearing.

Dr. Valentine then continues by outlining the sequence of events that led to the publication of the short run Varo Annotated Edition of Jessup's book, and Jessup's involvement with the Office of Naval Research, adding the significant detail that the Navy and Jessup had both failed to track Allende down, and that they had been unsuccessful in identifying the other two commentators in the Varo Edition.

Finally, Berlitz addresses the problem of Jessup's death:

Why did Jessup kill himself?

---

[14] Berlitz, *The Bermuda Triangle,* p.150, emphasis added.

> *If* he committed suicide, it was probably due to extreme depression. **He had been approached by the Navy to continue working on the Philadelphia Experiment or similar projects but had declined – he was worried about its dangerous ramifications.** He was also despondent over the criticism directed against his books by the scientific and academic world. [15]

This is yet another peculiar detail that is found nowhere else in the literature on the experiment that had appeared up to that point. Berlitz breaks it here for the first time in *The Bermuda Triangle*, namely, that Jessup had been approached by the Navy, presumably the Office of Naval Research itself, to continue work on the Philadelphia Experiment.

This admission, doubtless again a detail provided to Valentine by Dr. Jessup himself, raises a whole host of new problems and questions, for why would the Navy, the very branch that had allegedly conducted the experiment in the first place, now behave as if it knew nothing about it, much less seek outside assistance from Jessup to continue work on an experiment it knew nothing about?!? There are a few possibilities, two of which seem worth mentioning:

1) The Navy knew full well that such an experiment had been conducted, and, sensing Jessup was getting close to piecing together the actual history of the experiment, based on his hypothesis that it had involved the 1928 Unified Field Theory, decided to keep him under close observation by "involving" him in an ongoing "project;" or,
2) The Navy, or at least the ONR, had at some point and for whatever reason, *lost track of and perhaps even lost control over* the project and its records, and was anxiously searching for a way to quietly reconstruct the experiment. Jessup and his ideas therefore presented themselves as a logical place to start.

These two possibilities should be borne in mind as we consider Berlitz's penultimate question and Dr. Valentine's answer:

---

[15] Berlitz, *The Bermuda Triangle,* pp. 150-151, italicized emphasis original, bold face emphasis added.

You said, "If he committed suicide." Is there reason to believe that he was killed?

There were comments – some people have thought so – perhaps he could have been saved. He was still alive when he was found.... Perhaps he was allowed to die. His theories were very advanced and perhaps there were people or influences that wished to prevent their spread. It is curious that Jessup's own edition of the annotated Navy book as well as a copy that he had given to Briant Reeves (another writer on UFOs) disappeared from the mail when they were sent to other people.[16]

Valentine thus remained suspicious of Jessup's "suicide", and speculates that "people" wished to prevent the spread of Jessup's "advanced theories."

If this be so, then it would appear that Jessup's death – on this view a murder – was yet another event in a string of events that sidelined the various Unified Field Theories into a backwater of "incomplete theories." Moreover, if it is true as Valentine suggests that Jessup's mail was being intercepted, then this points the finger to the government as being the most likely interceptor since it was one of few entities both with the means and motivations to do so.

Viewed in this light, the two possibilities mentioned above – that the Navy had either lost control of the experiment and was attempting to reconstruct it, or that it was merely keeping an eye on Jessup because he was getting "close" – take on a new significance. Jessup, it will be recalled, had refused to work on the Experiment any further. If this be the case, then perhaps it decided that he had become too much of a security risk, as attested by his mailings of his own reannotated copy of the Varo Edition to his friends, and decided to eliminate him. The other possibility would indicate that someone, somewhere, who had co-opted the experiment, did not want to risk that the Navy would be able to reconstruct the experiment on the basis of such clues as Jessup could provide. And there was always the risk, in both possibilities, that Jessup would go public with his knowledge and publish his findings. In either case, he would have been seen as a loose

[16] Berlitz, *Tge Bermuda Triangle,* pp. 151-152.

cannon, and therefore had to be silenced. In this respect, it is worth recalling that Jessup indicated as much in his remarks to his friend Ivan Sanderson.

B. The Clues and Their Implications

A review of the clues and their implications from Berlitz's *The Bermuda Triangle* is now in order, not the least of which is the most obvious one. It has been left unstated until now: What possible relationship would Jessup have seen between the Triangle, UFOs, and the Philadelphia Experiment story as he had learned of it from the Varo Edition of his book, and Carlos Miguel Allende's letters?

Surprisingly, the answer lies in Jessup's own speculation that all these disaprarate phenomena were related by the 1928 version of Einstein's Unified Field Theory with its torsion tensor. Let us recall from part one that this mathematical transform was one of the most significant components of that theory, if not the most significant. In that theory, as was seen, Einstein had for all intentions and purposes *abandoned* General Relativity in pursuit of the geometric unification of gravity and electromagnetism, in which the torsion tensor played a central role. But what does *this* mean?

In General Relativity, *gravity* and *inertia* were treated as equivalent phenomena since, geometrically, they were indistinguishable by observers. Physicists call this idea the "equivalence principle," as was seen. But as was also seen earlier, one corollary of this principle is that the gravitational acceleration of large masses does not vary with any significance locally, that is, on the surface of a star or planet.

However, when Einstein had *coupled* gravity and electromagnetism in a more fundamental geometry that included *torsion,* a local space-time curvature, he in effect allowed the theoretical possibility of local variations of gravitational acceleration and mass on the surface of a large planetary mass. In effect, Einstein had allowed the possibility for anomalous regions of magnetic and gravitational disturbances – such as the Bermuda Triangle – to exist. He had provided a theoretical framework for explaining such anomalous regions on the surface of a large mass such as the Earth. More importantly, he had allowed the theoretical possibility that gravitational and intertial effects could be locally engineered by electromagnetic means. No wonder when scientists read Einstein's 1928 paper, that their eyes did not glaze over! Anything but!

So in pinpointing this theory as a possible means for a unified explanation of the Triangle, the Philadelphia Experiment, and some types of UFO phenomena, Jessup was working out what he considered to be the theory's explanatory power. There were also other clues. Jessup had, for example, connected "controlled magnetism" with the idea of "optical invisibility." This, too, must be viewed in the context of what Jessup believed about the theory's explanatory power. Jessup had conveyed to Valentine that the results of the experiment were accidental, and thus the implication is that the theory could possibly account not only for its conceptual foundations but also its accidental results.

Additionally, Valentine implied that Jessup was exploring his concept of "invisible solidities" in relation to the "invisibility" results of the Philadelphia Experiment and in relation to the Unified Field Theory itself.

And finally, we encountered new details concerning the Experiment that appeared for the first time in Berlitz's book. These are:

1) that the experiment involved both pulsed and non-pulsed modes of operation;

2) that the experiment involved a "time-warp" phenomenon, that the ship's binnacle suddenly burst into flames when it was taken ashore, and that some aspect of the experiment apparently appeared in a local Philadelphia newpaper;

3) that Jessup's death may not have been a suicide but a murder, indicating at a minimum that someone, somewhere, was continuing the line of development that the Experiment represented, and was taking "active measures" to prevent its scientific conceptualization from reaching a wider public, as it surely would have had Jessup lived and continued to research and publish;

4) that the experiment itself was conducted both in a "dockyard" during the "proof of concept" phase, and at sea, in the actual full-scale version. It is during operation of the latter experiment that the accidental results were observed.

From all the previous considerations, often overlooked in examinations of the Philadelphia Experiment that often focus too exclusively on his book of the same name, Berlitz's *Bermuda Triangle* is nevertheless an important component to the overall story, for it allows us a crucial insight into the possible thought processes of Dr. Morris K. Jessup, who may very well have been murdered for thinking as he did.

6.
THIRD DISCLOSURE:
CHARLES BERLITZ, WILLIAM MOORE, AND
THE PHILADELPHIA EXPERIMENT: PROJECT INVISIBILITY

*"My own special interest in the Philadelphia Experiment was connected with
the possibility that a shift in the molecular composition of matter, induced by
intensified and resonant magnetism, could cause an object to vanish – one
possible explanation of some of the disappearances within the Bermuda
Triangle."*
Charles Berlitz[1]

With the above epigram, researcher Charles Berlitz
acknowledged how he had come to know the Philadelphia
Experiment story; as was seen in the previous chapter, he had more
or less bumped into it, like one of Morris Jessup's "invisible
solidities," while researching his book *The Bermuda Triangle.*
Having thus registered in a brief sentence his own initial exposure
to the story, Berlitz records that a rather interesting thing occurred
whenever he mentioned the experiment in any of his many
lectures in the United States: "Occasionally there appeared a
'witness,' who usually had a passion for anonymity."[2]

During one such lecture at a college, Berlitz recounts that he
met an English professor, "an author with a flair for research."

> His obsessive interest in the Philadelphia story has taken him to various
> parts of the country, and his dedication has helped him to overcome
> official denials, to locate conveniently missing documents, to renew the
> memory of forgetful witnesses, and even to find certain key scientists
> whose proximity to and familiarity with this experiment "which never
> took place" had impelled them to live quietly in an extremely isolated
> area, perhaps for reasons of health (or survival).[3]

---

[1] From the Introduction in Charles Berlitz and William Moore, *The
Philadelphia Experiment: Project Invisibility* (London: Souvenir Press, 1979), p.
10.

[2] Ibid.

[3] Ibid.

This researcher was eventually to be Berlitz's co-author of *The Philadelphia Experiment: Project Invisibility*: William Moore.

The story itself, as outlined in the "first public version" in Berlitz's *The Bermuda Triangle* was extraordinary, for if the experiment was carried on as indicated, "we once stood, and perhaps still stand, at the edge of the discovery of how to make objects and people, others and ourselves, invisible – one of the oldest dreams of man."[4] But then, as he often does, he tosses out one of those revelations that he never comments any further upon throughout the remainder of the book:

> But this (dream of invisibility) and other ancient dreams no longer seem so unattainable, especially since 1945, when a dream of supreme and explosive power first became an actuality at Alamogordo. Coincidentally, at least two other projects more properly reserved to the domain of science fiction were reportedly under way at a time (1943) when America was seeking usual aids for protection and survival. *One of these was concerned with antigravity* and the other with invisibility, but work on these was reportedly suspended with the evident success of the atom bomb.[5]

Clearly the Philadelphia Experiment was the project that concerned invisibility, but what was the unnamed project that concerned antigravity? Berlitz and his co-author William Moore never refer to it again.

This author has combed both through his memory and his files trying to discover some recollection of a wartime American antigravity project, but can recall and find none, which implies an important question: what did Berlitz and Moore know? Whatever it was, they were not talking. However, we are permitted a speculation: if, as has been suggested, Dr. Jessup hit upon the scientific conceptual foundation behind the Philadelphia Experiment with the 1928 version of Einstein's Unified Field Theory, and sought in this theory a basis for his conjectures concerning the propulsion of UFOs, it stands to reason that perhaps, somewhere in America's burgeoning defense establishment during the Second World War, someone proposed

---

[4] Berlitz and Moore, *The Philadelphia Experiment,* pp. 10-11.
[5] Ibid., p. 11, emphasis added.

the idea of a project to control gravity. That would have indeed been the grand prize, for to control gravity would open doors to many other technologies, and more importantly, provide a basis for tremendous weapons platforms and weapons of awesome destructive power. Consequently, their allegation is not as farfetched as it might at first glance seem. Whatever the source of motivations for their remarks, however, they must be left behind to consider the Experiment itself.[6]

A. General Observations

It is crucial to establish the accuracy of Berlitz and Moore's recounting of the story at the outset, since some have called it into question on a variety of bases, some alleging that Berlitz cannot be trusted because of his alleged intelligence background and connections, others alleging that the occasional historical inaccuracies or unsubstantiated statement call into question their handling of the evidence. What will be argued here is that in the main, Berlitz and Moore's recounting is accurate, though they occasionally miss subtle points. Moreover, as will eventually be seen, some of these subtle points form the basis for an accurate scientific appraisal and assessment of the story, as well as a basis for its historical reconstruction.

We may begin with Berlitz's and Moore's summary of the Varo Edition annotations:

> The annotations seemed to be explanations of the mysterious disappearances of ships, planes, and people, discussed in Jessup's books, many of the incidents taking place within the area of the mysterious "Bermuda Triangle." Further, they elaborated, sometimes in considerable detail, upon the origin of the many "odd storms and clouds, objects falling from the sky, strange marks and footprints, and

---

[6] Berlitz and Moore do, of course, connect the physicist Thomas Townsend Brown to the Philadelphia Experiment, as will be seen later in this chapter. Brown, well-known to alternative researchers for his interest in "electro-gravity", was seriously committed throughout his lifetime to gravitational research and the means to control gravity. But there is no evidence that Brown was involved during the war with any project to control gravity or achieve antigravity capabilities. Such projects in his case had to wait until after the war.

other matters" which Jessup had written about. Mentioned also was the construction of undersea cities in connection with two groups of presumably extraterrestrial creatures referred to as "the L-Ms" and "the S-Ms", only one of which (the "L-M's") was to be regarded as friendly. In addition, odd terms – mothership, home ship, dead ship, great ark, great bombardment, great return, great war, little-men, force fields, gravity fields, sheets of diamond, cosmic rays, force cutters, inlay work, clear talk, telepathing nodes, vortices, magnetic net – were found throughout the various handwritten annotations.[7]

As can readily be ascertained from this thorough list, in comparison with our own previous survey of the Varo Edition, Berlitz and Moore stay very close to the considerable textual evidence. One cannot reasonably maintain that their treatment is intentionally inaccurate. Likewise, Berlitz and Moore report accurately on the number of copies of and the manner of production of the Varo Edition.[8]

In a very few instances, however, their analytical skills seem to desert them. For example, Berlitz and Moore state that "if in fact the Navy did somehow succeed, either by accident or design, in creating force-field invisibility…then…might not the results of such experiments also offer some clues towards explaining the strange series of events and disappearances that seem to plague the area popularly known as the Bermuda Triangle…?"[9] As will be seen from a close examination of their own book and of the Allende letters, the preponderance of the evidence suggests that the Navy's test results, when run in its full-scale experimental version, were unanticipated and accidental, though the results were within the conceptual foundation of the experiment. The results were different in *degree,* not in *kind*, from what the experiment was designed to achieve. This characteristic of the experiment was already guessed at by Dr. Jessup, as we have seen in the two previous chapters.

However, this being stated, it is only fair to point out that Berlitz and Moore were certainly alive to the implications of the Experiment, whether accidental or not: "Did it reveal clues to a

---

[7] Berlitz and Moore, *The Philadelphia Experiment,* p. 45.
[8] Ibid., pp. 48-50.
[9] Ibid., p. 59.

new and cheap way of travel or energy production, not to mention the fact that in such a fantastic discovery might lie the key to the ultimate secret weapon?" The possibilities are, as they conclude, "both endless and staggering!"[10]

B. An Additional Detail Concerning Jessup's Alleged Suicide

Berlitz and Moore also provide an additional detail about Dr. Jessup's alleged suicide in their book:

> Toward the middle of April, 1959, Jessup told Valentine that he had reached what he considered to be some definite conclusions about the series of reactions implied by the Philadelphia Experiment and had *prepared a rough draft he wished to discuss.... No notes or manuscript were mentioned in the police report, nor, according to a statement by a witness later given to Dr. Valentine, were any found inside the car.* [11]

If this allegation is true, and there is no reason to doubt Dr. Valentine's veracity, then the likelihood of Jessup being murdered increases.

C. The Strange Meeting in Colorado Springs

Berlitz and Moore begin their book by recounting an episode in Colorado Springs that occurred on a late summer evening in 1970. Two airmen, James Davis from Maryland, and Allen Huse from Texas[12] decided to use their leave time to take photographs of the War Memorial Park. Davis and Huse were approached by "a rather strange-looking man" whom Davis had earlier observed around the monument, "a short, balding, somewhat unkempt fellow."[13] Striking up a conversation with Davis, the stranger removed his wallet and showed him an old outdated Navy ID card.[14] The man had claimed to be a naval officer during World War Two, and

---

[10] Berlitz and Moore, *The Philadelphia Experiment,* p. 45.

[11] Ibid, p. 91, emphasis in the original, citing Charles Berlitz, *Without a Trace*, no page number cited.

[12] Ibid., p. 13.

[13] Ibid.

[14] Ibid., p. 14.

claimed that the Navy had "done things" to him, finally forcing him to retire, claiming that he was "crazy."[15] The man volunteered to Davis the reason he had gone "crazy": "It was the experiment that did it."[16]

> Davis was curious. "Experiment?" he said. "Just what sort of an experiment are you talking about?"
>
> The answer stunned him.
>
> "Invisibility," said the man. "It was when they were trying to make a ship invisible. It would have been perfect camouflage if it had worked. And it did, too! With the ship, that is. But those of us on board... well, it didn't work too well on us. We couldn't stand the effects of the energy field they were using. It did things to us. I should never have taken that assignment up to Philadelphia. It was Top Secret...."
>
> Davis was beginning to wonder whether he was hearing what he thought he was.
>
> "Just what are you talking about?" he wanted to know. "Are you saying that the Navy tried to make you invisible, in some sort of experiment, or what?"
>
> "Electronic camouflage," came the answer. "Some sort of electrical camouflage produced by pulsating energy fields. I don't know exactly what sort of energy they were using, but there was sure a lot of it. We couldn't take it – none of us. Though it affected us in different ways. Some only saw double, others began to laugh and stagger like they were drunk, and a few passed out.... And in some cases the effects weren't temporary. I was told later that several had died. Anyhow, I never saw them again. But as for the rest of us – those of us who survived – well, they just let us go. Disability, they called it. Discharged as mentally unbalanced and unfit for service. Pensioned off!" he said bitterly.[17]

At this point, Davis' companion, airman Huse, overhearing occasional bits of the conversation, joined the other two men. After introductions Davis continued the conversation with the strange ex-Navy man.

> "You mean," he said, "that the Navy discharged all these men as mental incompetents because the experiment failed?"
>
> "That's correct," said their mysterious companion. "That's exactly what they did. Of course, they put us away for a few months before

[15] Berlitz and Moore, *The Philadelphia Experiment,* p. 14
[16] Ibid.
[17] Ibid., pp. 14-15.

107

they did it. To 'rest up.' They said. Also, to try to convince us that it had never happened, I think. Anyway, in the end they swore us to secrecy – even though nobody's likely to believe such a story anyway. How about you? You're in the Air Force; do you believe it? Do you believe what I'm telling you?"

"I don't know," Davis replied. "I certainly agree that it's a fantastic story. Almost too fantastic. I just don't know."

"Well, it's true just the same. Every damn word of it. Of course, that's exactly why they discharged us as mentally unfit. In case anybody ever thought about believing it, I mean. That way, if the Navy ever got questioned about it, they could just chalk it up as a story cooked up by a bunch of nuts. Who's going to believe a certified nut? Anyway, that's my story."[18]

After some more conversation with the stranger for approximately another hour, the two airmen returned to their base. [19]

The two airmen eventually forgot the incident until 1978, when Berlitz's book *The Bermuda Triangle* was published and the story of the Philadelphia Experiment was first broken to a wide audience. Davis contacted William Moore, co-author of *The Philadelphia Experiment* with Berlitz, and outlined the strange event.[20] What interests us here is that Berlitz and Moore, examining the Varo Edition's annotations, maintain that in all likelihood there was but one person behind all the annotations, rather than three as the ONR personnel involved with the Varo Edition's "Introduction" maintained.[21]

Here is an instance where Berlitz's and Moore's otherwise finely honed analytical skills seemed to have abandoned them, for later in their book they relate the following:

> The possibility that (Carlos Miguel) Allende himself might have been the strange little man who related the bizarre story to airmen Davis and Huse in a Colorado Springs park in 1970... seems to be without foundation. In their interviews, both men stated with certainty that they felt they would be able to recognize the man they had met if they were

---

[18] Berlitz and Moore, *The Philadelphia Experiment,* pp. 15-16.
[19] Ibid., p. 16.
[20] Ibid., pp. 16-17.
[21] Ibid., p.

ever to see him again, yet neither of them was able to identify the photograph of Allende as the character in question.[22]

It does not seem to have occurred to Berlitz or to Moore that perhaps the strange man Davis and Huse encountered in Colorado Springs might have been one of the *other* annotators of the Varo Edition's marginal comments. The only thing arguing against this possibility is that the stranger's diction does not seem to be of the same wild, scrambled sort as found in those annotations.

Carlos Miguel Allende[23]

---

[22] Ibid., p. 76.
[23] Picture was taken by APRO.

D. Einstein
1. His Wartime Employment by the U.S. Navy

Berlitz and Moore are more thorough on the matter of Einstein's employment by the U.S. Navy during World War Two. This point is an important one, since Allende alleged in his letters to Jessup that part of the conceptual basis of the Experiment involved Einstein's Unified Field Theory, and that Einstein himself was actually involved, though Allende never indicates how nor in what capacity. Establishing a connection between Einstein and the Navy would thus corroborate some of Allende's assertions.

> In 1943, during the time Allende states he witnessed a manifestation of the Philadelphia Experiment at sea, Dr. Einstein was employed by the U.S. Navy as a scientific consultant, ostensibly for the Bureau of Ordnance. Records of the Office of the General Services Administration in St. Louis show that Einstein was employed "intermittently in a Special Services Contract of the Department of the Navy, Washington D.C. as a *scientist* from May 31, 1943 to June 30, 1944.[24]

Additionally, Berlitz and Moore cite a letter from Dr. Einstein to his friend Gustav Buckley indicating that the famous physicist had developed "closer relations to the Navy Office of Scientific Research and Development."[25] Moreover, Einstein indicated that the science "tsar" of the Roosevelt and Truman Administrations, Dr. Vannevar Bush, had placed Einstein in "a committee where it seemed... his particular skills would be most likely to be of service."[26]

---

[24] Berlitz and Moore, *The Philadelphia Experiment,* p. 96, emphasis in the original.

[25] Ibid.

[26] Ibid., pp. 96-97.

Dr. Einstein and US Navy Officers, July 24, 1943[27]

2. Einstein's Unified Field Theory of 1928

The centerpiece of Allende's allegations in his letters regarding Einstein and his association with the Philadelphia Experiment, however, is his insistence that the whole experiment was designed to test aspects of Einstein's Unified Field Theory. Accordingly it is crucial to see how Berlitz and Moore understand Einstein's famous and incomplete theory, in order to assess their own reconstruction of the Experiment.

As will be seen later in this chapter when we examine the Allende letters themselves, Allende maintained that Einstein actually *completed* his theory, and then withdrew it on the basis of moral qualms of what might be done with it. Of course, it is well-known that Einstein worked on the theory for most of the rest of his life, trying various approaches toward his sought-after

---

[27] This picture from the National Archives also appears in the photo section of Berlitz and Moore's *The Philadelphia Experiment.*

unification of gravity and electromagnetism. Berlitz and Moore comment as follows:

> Dr. Einstein did indeed complete *a* version of his "Unified Field Theory for Gravitation and Electricity" in the period 1925-27. The results, published in German, appeared in Prussian scientific journals for 1925 and 1927.[28]

This is another minor inaccuracy, for Einstein's first "full" version of the theory – as was seen in part one – was in fact published in 1928, not 1927. And it is this version which first included the torsion tensor as a component of the geometry of unification in Einstein's paper. As also noted in part one, Einstein followed this paper up in 1930 with a much fuller one, relying on the idea of "distant parallelism" as a geometric basis for unification. And as was also noted there, Einstein was inspired to pursue such a theory by the earlier "hyper-dimensional" Unified Field Theory of German mathematician Theodor Kaluza.

However, it is important to note that Berlitz and Moore have confirmed what essentially has remained a process of reasoning thus far, namely, that it was the 1928 version of Einstein's theory that was involved with the Experiment, though they do not offer any substantiation or reason why it was this version of the theory, and not the later 1930s "distant parallelism" version, that formed the conceptual foundation for the Experiment. We have implied that it was the incorporation of the torsion tensor *in conjunction with a Kron-like tensor analysis of rotating electrical machinery* that formed the basic concepts that underwrote the Experiment, since torsion also played an important role in some of Kron's analysis.

Thus the assertions in Allende's letters to Jessup depart on one crucial point from the standard history of the Unified Field Theories. The standard history maintains that Einstein proposed, and then withdrew, several versions of a Unified Field Theory right up to the time of his death, withdrawing each in their turn for their incompleteness. Allende, on the other hand, maintains that

---

[28] Berlitz and Moore, *The Philadelphia Experiment,* p. 94.

Einstein withdrew the 1928 version for reasons of moral scruples. Berlitz and Moore propose that the idea of Einstein withdrawing the theories for moral reasons may not be so far-fetched, since the physicist's post-war pacifism and horror at the atom bomb are well known. Perhaps, they maintain, Einstein had similar private fears about his Unified Field Theory.[29]

However plausible this might seem as a moral reason for their withdrawal, it nonetheless remains absolutely the case that the versions of the theory which Einstein proffered were simply theoretically incomplete due to their lack of incorporation of the strong and weak forces of quantum mechanics. The theories were, as theories, incomplete, and there is no getting around this fact. Nonetheless, some were less incomplete than others, and this is the case with the 1928 version with its bold outlines. So a different explanation is in order for Allende's assertions concerning the theory's "completeness".

Allende was not a scientist, and therefore, could not be expected to understand the difference between a *complete* theory and an *engineerable* one. As I have implied throughout the argument thus far, the "completeness" of the theory was really not provided by Einstein, but by Kron, who employed tensor transforms as a means of explaining the anomalous "creep" and energy outputs of rotating electrical and synchronous machines and systems.[30] It is in this sense of engineerability that one must look for Allende's allegations of the "completion" of the theory.

But in any case, Berlitz and Moore point out that two years prior to his death, Dr. Einstein

> announced to the world what he referred to as 'highly convincing' results in his quest to find a mathematical proof of the connection

---

[29] Berlitz and Moore, *The Philadelphia Experiment,* p. 95.

[30] To my knowledge, no evidence exists tying Gabriel Kron to the Philadelphia Experiment *directly*. But anyone with an engineering and mathematical background would almost certainly have appreciated the significance of his work and, moreover, have seen in it a key to many wartime research possibilities. The case being argued, in other words, is a logical and scientific one, not an evidentiary one. This will remain the case in the next chapter, Corum and Daum assert that Kron was involved, but without providing any substantiation.

between the forces of electromagnetism and gravity. Keeping in mind Allende's statements concerning the completeness of Einstein's Unified Field Theory in 1925,[31] it is significant to note that this last theory was really a very close cousin to that earlier version which Allende says was "withdrawn" for reasons of "humantics."[32]

"Humantics" is the peculiar term that Allende used to indicate Einstein's moral qualms about releasing his full theory publicly.

One effect of this 1928 version of the theory is that "a pure gravitational field can exist without an electromagnetic field, but a pure electromagnetic field cannot exist without an accompanying gravitational field."[33] To put it differently, one effect of the torsion tensor's incorporation into the 1928 version is that electromagnetic fields of enough intensity can induce the folding, pleating, and spiraling of the fabric of space-time normally experienced in strong gravitational fields.

There is a final item of interest in Berlitz's and Moore's exposition of the Unified Field Theory.

> Possibly of interest at this point, however, is a tiny "filler" item from an April, 1956 edition of *The New York Times,* which reported that a Dr. Parvis Marat, physicist from the University of Maryland, had "partly confirmed the late Dr. Albert Einstein's famous Unified Field Theory," and that "Einstein's newest and most radical theory had come through one stage of critical tests with flying colours." The nature of those "critical tests" remained undisclosed.[34]

----

[31] Here again, Berlitz and Moore's analytical skills seem to have deserted them. The paper Einstein published in 1925 was hardly to even the degree of completeness of the 1928 version of the theory. Indeed, in the 1925 paper, Einstein was only attempting to outline possible strategies for approaching a unified field theory. The 1925 paper is thus an "exploratory" paper, and in reading it, one can sense this quality almost immediately. Berlitz and Moore's comment here thus raises an important question, since Allende's letters *never* refer to a specific version of Einstein's theory. While the most likely candidate is the 1928 version, since this would have been understood as an engineerable theory by anyone who had also absorbed the implications of Kron's papers, Berlitz and Moore do not themselves ever explore nor argue the case why they think it is the 1928 version.

[32] Berlitz and Moore, *The Philadelphia Experiment,* p. 101.

[33] Ibid.

[34] Ibid, p. 102.

Indeed, one looks in vain for any mention of this item in any contemporary history of the development of theoretical physics. Either the theory ultimately failed in later tests, or the results were deliberately concealed.

We have now reached the point where our survey of the background history of the Philadelphia Experiment is complete, and we may at last get down to the details of the Experiment itself. In examining them as they are contained in Berlitz's and Moore's book, we will concentrate on four areas:

1) the history of the test ship, the U.S.S. Edlridge, DE 173;
2) The Moore-"Rinehart" Interview;
3) the Thomas Townsend Brown Connection; and finally and most importantly,
4) The Carlos Miguel Allende Letters to Dr. Morris K. Jessup.

In following this outline, we shall concentrate on pulling out the details that will be tested for their possible scientific accuracy in the light of the 1928 Unified Field Theory, as well as for their accuracy in the *process* of establishing a series of experiments to begin with. We will therefore search for indications of a "proof of concept" experiment or series of experiments, and then for a full-scale version. Accordingly, we shall also be looking for the original conceptual foundations of the experiment in order to ascertain why Allende asserted that the results were not what the Navy expected, though they were different in degree and not in kind from what was anticipated.

E. The History of the U.S.S. Eldridge, DE 173

The U.S.S. *Eldridge*, DE 173, the alleged test ship for the Philadelphia Experiment, was laid down in February of 1943, and launched later that year in July. She was commissioned, according to Berlitz and Moore, on August 27, 1943 in New York, when her skipper Lieutenant Charles R. Hamilton assumed command.[35] According to her official service records, she served in the Atlantic

---

[35] Berlitz and Moore, *The Philadelphia Experiment,* p. 106.

until the end of the European war, and was transferred to the Pacific theater where she served until the end of the war there. The *Eldridge* was decommissioned on June 17, 1946, and remained in the naval reserve until 1951 when she was finally sold to Greece as part of the Mutual Defense Assistance Program, where she was renamed the *Leon* (Lion).[36]

However, as Berlitz and Moore observe, when this story is viewed "in the light Allende's story, this neat, *official* history of the *Eldridge* shows signs of considerable patching and doctoring."[37] Allende, whom they had tracked down to being a crew member of the merchant ship *S.S. Andrew Furuseth,* had made it clear that he had observed the Experiment while both ships were at sea in 1943. So in other words:

> If the *Eldridge* and the S.S. *Furuseth* could be shown to have been in the same place on even as little as one single date during the period that Carl M. Allen was a crew member of the *Furuseth*, then at the very least an air of possibility is added to his story. On the other hand, if no such similarity of positions can be shown, then Allende's tale is seriously (and perhaps fatally) damaged.[38]

The neat and tidy history of the U.S.S. *Eldridge* began to unravel when co-author William Moore decided to acquire the logs of the two ships.

What resulted from this search was a clear indicator that "all was not as it should be" with the official story, for Moore discovered that

> (1) the deck logs of the *Eldridge* for the date of commission (August 27, 1943) through December 1, 1943, were "missing and therefore unavailable"; and (2) the logbooks of the *Furuseth* had been *"destroyed by executive order"* and thus no longer exist.[39]

If the logbooks of the two ships had indeed been destroyed "by executive order", then clearly the cover-up of the experiment went

---

[36] Berlitz and Moore, *The Philadelphia Experiment,* p. 107.
[37] Ibid.
[38] Ibid.
[39] Ibid., pp. 107-108, emphasis added,

very high and very deep, implying the involvement of the Oval Office of the White House and Franklin Delano Roosevelt himself! Clearly, whatever had happened during this period that involved these two ships was truly extraordinary, and beyond even the standard classification requirements of normal wartime operations, otherwise the White House would not have been directly involved.

According to the *Furuseth's* parent company, the Matson Navigation Company, she made "two complete voyages to North Africa in this time period," one voyage beginning August 13, 1943, when she sailed from New York to Norfolk and then participated in a convoy to North Africa in support of the American landings there. The second voyage began on October 25, 1943, when she sailed from Virginia once again to the French port of Oran in Algeria.[40]

And this is where there is a discrepancy between the official stories of both ships, for

> According to the Navy Department's official history of the *Eldridge*, that ship was launched July 25, 1943, at Newark, New Jersey, and commissioned August 27, 1943, at New York Navy Yard. Her shakedown cruise began early in September, took place in the area of Bermuda, British West Indies, and lasted until December 28. These same records indicate that her first overseas voyage began on January 4, 1944, and ended on February 15 with her arrival in New York Harbour.[41]

Thus, if one accepts the official histories of these two ships at face value, they were never anywhere near each other in 1943, and as a consequence, the veracity of Allende's story is called into serious question.

However, as Berlitz and Moore point out, "the mysterious unavailability of the ships' logbooks casts certain doubts" upon the official histories of the two ships.[42]

> The first missing piece that fitted into the puzzle came quite unexpectedly with the uncovering of a previously classified bit of information about the Eldridge which seemed to discredit the official

---

[40] Berlitz and Moore, *The Philadelphia Experiment,* p. 108.
[41] Ibid.
[42] Ibid., 109.

histories completely. The document in question was a report on Antisubmarine Action by Surface Ship filed by the commander of the *Eldridge* on December 14, 1943, in accordance with the fleet regulations, and concerned an action which took place on November 20 in the North Atlantic. According to official histories, the *Eldridge* was operating on a shakedown cruise in the vicinity of Bermuda from early September until late December 1943, and her first overseas voyage began on January 4, 1944. According to the action report filed by ship's commander, Lieutenant C.R. Hamilton, the *Eldridge* dropped seven depth charges against a suspected enemy submarine shortly after 1:30 P.M. local time on the afternoon of November 20, 1943, while steaming *westward* (towards the United State) in escort of convoy UGS 23. The position of the *Eldridge* as listed in the report was latitude 34° 03' north and longitude 08° 57' west – *a position which places the ship barely 200 miles off the coast of Casablanca, North Africa, and some 3,000 miles from Bermuda!* [43]

In other words, the official history of the *Eldridge* attempted to conceal its shakedown cruise in Bermuda, while the *Furuseth* and Carlos Miguel Allende were thousands of miles away. This official story, even with these discoveries, will come even further into question as we shall see in a subsequent chapter.

At this juncture however, a new bit of information surfaced that completely altered the official history once again: the engineer's logs of the *Eldridge*. These logs contained the records for the *Eldridge's* positions

For the dates in question, which were missing from the deck-log file. This and other documentation which came to light at about the same time showed that the *Eldridge* had indeed steamed out of port (Brooklyn) on November 2 to round up stragglers from convoy GUS 22 which had been knocked out of line by a late-season hurricane blowing up from the south in last days of October. This was a valuable piece of information indeed, *since the convoy in question was none other than the S.S. Furuseth's convoy, which had left Norfolk-Lynhaven Roads on October 25!* And more important, the *Furuseth*, steaming along in the last rank of the convoy, is almost certain to have caught sight of the DE 173 as it mothered stragglers back into line. Furthermore, the *Eldridge's* reported position off Casablanca on November 20 seems to indicate that the *Eldridge* accompanied the

---

[43] Berlitz and Moore, *The Philadelphia Experiment,* p. 109, emphasis added.

118

Furuseth and her GUS convoy all the way to North Africa (the convoy arrived there on November 12, remember), and was on her return trip home escorting UGS 23 when she encountered the submarine mentioned in the action report. Were it not for the discovery of this action report, which had been kept secret some thirty-four years, none of this would ever have come to light.[44]

Note what we have: missing deck logs from the *Eldridge*, logs from the *Furuseth* destroyed "by executive order," and an action report and engineer's logs from the *Eldridge* totally in contradiction with the tidy official history of both ships, which does indeed place both ships in close proximity to each other.

This raises a pertinent question, and Berlitz and Moore are quick to point it out: if there is one such major contradiction between the official histories and the action reports and engineer's log of the *Eldridge,* might there be others?[45] But there are also other questions. For example, is it likely that the U.S. Navy would "risk attempting such a dangerous, daring, and obviously Top Secret experiment as electromagnetic invisibility under such circumstances and in full view of an entire convoy? It certainly doesn't seem likely."[46] But it is unlikely *only* if the original aim of the Experiment was invisibility, and not something else. As we have argued all along, and as the stranger who confronted airmen Huse and Davis in Colorado Springs indicated, the results of the experiment were unexpected and accidental. So if the Navy indeed conducted an experiment during the convoy run, whatever results were achieved were not really expected to be observed by the other ships. In other words, contrary to the impression created to a certain extent by Berlitz and Moore themselves, *invisibility was not the goal to begin with.*

But there is more to the problems raised by these discoveries than this.

> ...Allende seems to indicate explicitly that the experiments took place at dockside in Philadelphia and "at sea" – presumably off the coast of the mainland. His dates – the latter part of October – coincide with the

---

[44] Berlitz and Moore, *The Philadelphia Experiment,* p. 110, emphasis added.
[45] Ibid.
[46] Ibid.

convoy operation, but the other circumstances do not; especially since the *Eldridge* steamed out of Brooklyn, not Philadelphia, to join GUS 22. In fact, nowhere in the ship's records for the period in question does it indicate that the *Eldridge* was ever even in or near the Philadelphia area – except during the time she was under construction at Newark.[47]

There were other facts that emerged besides the fact that the *Eldridge* never appeared to have been anywhere near Philadelphia at the times mentioned by Allende for the experiment.

Berlitz's co-author William Moore received a letter from a former ship commander who indicted that during the war, "he recalled the *Eldridge* putting in to Bermuda immediately following the *first* hurricane of the season in 1943 – a date which he feels would have had to have been in late July or early August of that year!"[48] The former skipper recalled the incident because the *Eldridge* flew no signal flags nor did she attempt to contact any of the other ships in the area.[49] If this is so, then the DE 173 appeared in Bermuda mere days after its launch in Newark, during a period when a ship's construction is normally completed, and "fully a month before the ship was even assigned a crew!"[50]

The implications were clear if the former skipper's testimony was true: the *Eldridge* had to have been launched earlier than the official history maintained.[51] Then Berlitz and Moore discovered records of the Greek navy, which eventually purchased the destroyer-escort after the war, that indicated that the DE 173 had actually been launched on June 25th, and not July 25th, of 1943! And there was something else in the Greek records that proved to be highly significant. According to the Greek records, the *Eldridge* displaced 1900 tons fully loaded, not 1520 tons! As they correctly observe, "the only way for a ship to gain 380 tons of buoyancy is for something of that weight to have been removed from that ship before the time of its sale to the Greeks."[52] What was it? Berlitz

---

[47] Berlitz and Moore, *The Philadelphia Experiment,* pp. 110-111.
[48] Ibid., p. 111.
[49] Ibid. p. 112.
[50] Ibid.
[51] Ibid.
[52] Ibid.

and Moore supply the obvious answer: "Electronics equipment, perhaps?"[53] Thus the conclusion is inescapable that the official history of the U.S.S. *Eldridge* for the period from her launch to January 1933 is almost certainly contrived, and not the genuine history of the vessel at all.[54]

The U.S.S. Eldridge, DE 173, in September 1943

At this point, Moore decided to confront one of his contacts in the Navy which had been helpful, but who was suspected of knowing more than he was telling, with the discrepancy between the actual and official histories of the DE 173. His contact agreed to speak but only on conditions of anonymity.

When asked how one might have acquired a ship for experimental purposes during the war, Moore's contact, who held the rank of commander in the Navy, indicated that the best time would have been between the ship's actual completion and prior to her commissioning, for once commissioned, she immediately

---

[53] Berlitz and Moore, *The Philadelphia Experiment,* p. 112.
[54] Ibid.

became operational and therefore part of naval planning.[55] This appears actually to have been the case from the history Berlitz and Moore uncovered. The commander went on to state that it was his belief that the Navy "did succeed in getting a ship out of Philadelphia or Newark for a limited time, probably not more than two or three weeks..."[56]

As for the Experiment itself, Moore's contact believed that tests were done along the Delaware River and along the mid-Atlantic coast. These tests apparently involved

> *The effects of a strong magnetic force field on radar detection apparatus.* I can't tell you much else about it or about what the results ultimately were because I don't know. My guess, and I would emphasize *guess*, would be that every kind of receiving equipment possible was put aboard other vessels and along the shoreline to check on what would happen on the "other side" when both radio and low- and high-frequency radar were projected through the field. Undoubtedly observations would have also been made as to any effects that field might have had on light in the visual range. *In any event, I do know that there was a great deal of work being done on total absorption as well as refraction, and this would certainly seem to tie in with such an experiment as this.*[57]

This is the first real indicator of what the original purpose of the experiment was: *the Experiment was designed to test the possibilities of radar refraction or even total absorption – in other words, radar stealth – and optical invisibility was **not** the purpose.* From the scientific standpoint, as will be seen in the next chapter, this is not only possible but in all likelihood the *plausible* original conceptual foundation of the Experiment.

But note also what the anonymous commander also states: the Navy was doing "a great deal of work" on "total absorption as well as refraction." The Philadelphia Experiment was, in other words, part of a larger, and apparently quite extensive project or series of projects. Implausible as this sounds, it is really not that difficult to

---

[55] Berlitz and Moore, *The Philadelphia Experiment,* p. 113.

[56] Ibid., p. 114.

[57] Ibid., p. 115, italicized emphasis in the original, bold and italicized emphasis added.

understand if one places it into the context of the war at that time. Both the United States and Germany were expending tremendous resources to research and achieve practical radar stealth properties, both refraction and absorption, the Germans to counter the increasing Allied dominance of the seas and the air, and the United States to prepare for the coming invasion of the European mainland. In the United States' case, the allocation of a recently launched destroyer escort would have been seen as a very small investment in an experiment that could provide great dividends and savings in lives and materiel during the coming invasion. If "proof of concept" experiments had been successful – and they must have been in order for the Experiment to reach this stage of testing – then the investment of the DE 173 into its realization was a small price to pay. The Navy's actions are eminently justifiable and logical.

However, Moore's anonymous Navy contact then volunteers an additional piece of information:

> One thing I can tell you: It is highly unlikely that any experimental work of such a nature as this would have taken place aboard a ship after it was commissioned and had a crew. Such a thing just wouldn't have been done – especially not at sea while on convoy duty. Absolutely no one doing research of this type in '43 would have dared to risk placing several hundred tons of valuable electronics equipment at the mercy of some German submarine commander in the middle of the Atlantic.[58]

Observe then that according to the anonymous Naval officer, not only did the "at sea" Experiment take place close to the coast of the United States, but moreover the Navy would never have risked performing it while on convoy duty, which clearly contradicts Allende's story. So, if Allende's allegations are correct, and the Navy officer's story is as well – and we have seen that at least as far as his scientific information goes, it is not only plausible, but actually enhances his credibility – then how does one explain what happened "at sea" and what Allende saw? What was the Navy doing?

One possibility that is often overlooked by investigators of the story is that the experiments with the *Eldridge* along the coastline

---

[58] Berlitz and Moore, *The Philadelphia Experiment*, p. 115.

may have been quite successful with radar refraction and perhaps even a degree of absorption. Perhaps the experiments were not run at full power and none of the deleterious effects that Allende and airmen Davis' and Huse's mysterious stranger reported occurred during these trials. Moreover, being under close supervision by scientists might also have mitigated any potential health hazards from the experiment. In this instance, with scaled up "proof of concept" experiments successfully completed, the *Eldridge* was released to convoy duty with her radar deflection equipment still in place. Thus, during the encounter with the German submarine, the captain of the *Eldridge* may have decided to give his ship the extra measure of protection that its special equipment afforded him, and switched it on. But for whatever reason – lack of close scientific supervision or the presence of other unknown factors – the Experiment now "ran away", not only achieving radar absorption but actual optical invisibility, with all the dire effects on the crew reported. Or perhaps, with the experiment successfully completed in its scaled up "proof of concept" stage, the Navy decided to test the concept at full power and under combat conditions. But in any case, we now have the first indications of what the original conceptual foundations of the Experiment were: it had been designed to test the effect of strong magnetic fields on radar refraction and absorption, two very significant clues, and we shall have more to say about these sorts of possibilities and these clues in the next chapter.

F. The Moore-"Rinehart" Interview

A great deal of corroborating evidence for these views is provided in the interview William Moore conducted with a source known pseudonymously as "Dr. Rinehart." Berlitz and Moore tracked down this source, whom Allende had referred to under the pseudonym of "Dr Franklin Reno,"[59] and since Allende indicated in his letters that Einstein's 1928 Unified Field Theory had undergone a "complete (group math) recheck…with a view to any

---

[59] For the full story of this curious pseudonym, see Berlitz and Moore, *The Philadelphia Experiment,* pp. 117-121.

and every possible quick use of it...in a very short time,"[60] it became imperative for them to do so. William Moore finally did so, and the reasons for "Dr. Rinehart's" pseudonymous existence became clear, for Rinehart,

> When he began to suspect he knew too much for his own good (and perhaps for his survival), chose to hide himself away from the segments of society that seemed to threaten him most. Those years had seen him abandon a brilliant and promising scientific career to install himself in a neat little bungalow nestled between the hills half a continent away and content with living the life of a hermit – venturing out only occasionally for supplies, or even more occasionally to visit an old friend or former colleague.[61]

Like Dr. Jessup before him, Dr. Rinehart suspected that foul play might befall him if he maintained too high a profile.

After some months of negotiations and preparations,[62] "Dr. Rinehart" agreed to an interview with William Moore. Unlike the other interviews conducted by Berlitz and Moore, "Dr. Rinehart's" interview is more that of a story-telling session, with Moore interrupting for questions but very few times. The interview has the characteristic of a lecture, in fact, with "Dr. Rinehart" trying carefully to reveal as much as he could, and yet discretely trying to avoid going too far.

The following excerpts, then, are crucial to the case we are building. They will be cited in full, and then brief commentary will be given after each.

"Dr. Rinehart" begins by outlining how the Experiment came to be:

> I have impressions of wartime conferences in which I recall the participation of naval officers. In relation to the project in which you are interested, *my memory persistently suggests an inception distinctly earlier than 1943, perhaps as early as 1939 or 1940* when Einstein was concerned with ideas in physical theory brought to him by physicists and others who had military applications in mind....
>
> ...I think I can say with some degree of certainty that *the proposal initiators were Einstein and (Rudolph) Ladenburg.* I do not know who

---

[60] Berlitz and Moore, *The Philadelphia Experiment*, p. 117.

[61] Ibid., p. 120.

[62] Ibid., p. 121.

should be named first; and if the initiators were "Blank," Einstein, and Ladenburg, then I cannot now recall Blank's identity.[63]

This revelation rings quite true on two accounts.

First, as we outlined in part one, any Experiment such as the Nazi Bell or the Philadelphia Experiment would have had an initial stage designed to test a concept in various scaled down "proof of concept" experiments. Given that the time frame for the known and alleged facts of the Philadelphia Experiment occurs during the summer of 1943, "Dr. Rinehart's" time estimation is accurate and logical, for these proof of concept experiments would have had to have been designed and in place and performed *at least* one to two years prior to the actual fuller scale experiments.

However the second and more significant point is the mention of Einstein and Rudolf Ladenburg (1882-1952). Ladenburg had earned his doctorate in physics at the University of Heidelberg studying under the direction of the famous Dr. Wilhelm Röntgen, discoverer of the X-ray. After spending a brief period in the physics department of the University of Breslau, Ladenburg became chief of the physics division of the prestigious Kaiser Wilhelm Institute in Berlin. His specialty was the detection of dispersion lines in atomic spectrographs.

However, during the First World War, during which Ladenburg actually served in the German military, he founded an artillery test commission in Berlin, which explored all possible means – optical, acoustic, seismographic, and electromagnetic – for determining the positions of enemy artillery pieces, with an acoustic method of detection eventually being introduced for front line use.[64] Emigrating to the U.S. during the pre-war Nazi era, Ladenburg also worked for the American military in the field of preventive measures against mines and torpedoes. He also worked with Dr. John von Neumann and Einstein himself on the development of a "air reflection effect." According to the article in the online encyclopedia, Wikipedia, Ladenburg was consulted sometime in

---

[63] Berlitz and Moore, *The Philadelphia Experiment,* p. 123, emphasis added.

[64] 4.233.197.104/translate_c?hl=en&sl=de&u=http://de.wikipedia.org/wiki/oRufolf_Ladenburg

1940 for computations designed to show the needed strength of a field designed to curve light![65] Recalling what was stated earlier - that one sought result from the Philadelphia Experiment was a field that would not only refract radar but possibly be strong enough to deflect projectiles just enough from their targets – and knowing this about the man, Ladenburg would have been an *extremely* logical choice for just such a project!

Moreover, "Dr. Rinehart's" mention of Ladenburg *in connection with Einstein* is once again yet another indicator that the Unified Field Theory version that is in view is the 1928 version, with its space-time twisting torsion tensor. *Someone* in the USA was thinking precisely along the lines of Gabriel Kron's tensor analysis of electrical machines, and what military applications might be possible from it!

The mention of Dr. John von Neumann in the Wikipedia article is also significant, for "Dr Rinehart" goes on to reveal *his* role in the emerging story:

> On some proposal, very possibly the one at hand, von Neumann was asked by the Navy brass whether he was talking about this war or the next...
>
> Anyway, it was von Neumann who talked to Dr. Albrecht[66] on this proposal, and it was one or the other of them who obtained an indication of future cooperation on it from the Naval Research Laboratory. The proposal partly overlapped ideas developed by the physicist R.H. Kent (Robert Harrington Kent, 1886-1961, noted American theoretical and research physicist) many years before, during, the course of design and experimental work with the solenoid chronograph. If you think about the principle of the solenoid chronograph, you will see why work with it would suggest all kinds of ideas bout detection and defence against missiles by the use of electromagnetic fields.[67]

At this point Moore quips that "Rinehart evidently assumed that I knew what a solenoid chronograph was. I didn't, but an interruption at this point didn't seem in order."[68] But apparently

---

[65] 4.233.197.104/translate_c?hl=en&sl=de&u=http://de.wikipedia.org/wiki/Rudolf_Ladenburg

[66] Dr. Albrecht is another pseudonym, used by "Rinehart".

[67] Berlitz and Moore, *The Philadelphia Experiment*, p. 125.

[68] Ibid.

Moore never found out either, for no mention of it ever appears again in Berlitz's and Moore's book. Neither, for that matter, is the significant clue given by the mention of Robert Harrington Kent.

So again, a pause is in order so that these two fresh clues may be briefly considered. The solenoid chronograph was a device designed by the military's ordnance bureaus to test and prove the accuracy of cannon barrels at their proving grounds. It is nothing but a special kind of solenoid – a magnetic bar passed through a coil of wires connected to a circuit. As everyone knows, when one does this, an electrical current is generated. A solenoid chronograph was simply a special adaptation of this principle. Prior to being loaded into a cannon for proving, a projectile would be lightly magnetized. The cannon would then shoot it through a series of "screens" consisting of these coils, which would then measure its passage through them and its angle of deflection. By such minute measurements, barrel accuracy could be adjusted to great precision. It is a short step from this principle to see how one might expand on it and come up with the idea that in a strong enough electromagnetic field a projectile might possibly be deflected enough from its target to miss it completely. Alternatively, the idea would also have occurred to physicists and engineers pursuing this line of thinking that such a field could be used to alter the ballistic properties of the atmosphere itself in such a way as to adversely affect the accuracy of projectiles.[69]

But what of Robert Harrington Kent? Interestingly enough, Kent supposedly came up with the idea of "using the principles of resonance to generate a sufficient magnetic field to bend light."[70] Again, these are clues that American scientists, no less than their German counterparts, were taking seriously as full a set of the implications of torsion in the Unified Field Theory as was to them practically feasible. And it is an indicator of something else: *long*

---

[69] For those paying attention, this is similar, if not identical, in concept to the principles that some allege are really behind the military's HAARP (High Altitude Auroral Research Project) antenna array in Alaska.

[70] Byron Weber, "The Philadelphia Experiment and Johnny von Neumann," September 26, 2004, www.unexplained-mysteries.com/viewcolumn.php?id=21, p. 2. Q.v. also Berlitz and Moore, pp. 124-125.

before President Ronald Reagan's "Strategic Defense Initiative" speeches of the early 1980s, indeed from the crucible of World War Two, the American military was researching the conceptual and technological foundations for the means to "bend and twist" the medium, whether the atmosphere or space-time itself, as a means both of camouflage and of missile defense. As we shall shortly see, "Rinehart" eventually confirms this conclusion.

The next revelations from "Dr. Rinehart" are bombshells:

> Now that I think about it, I feel confident that the idea of producing the necessary electromagnetic field for experimental purposes by means of the principles of resonance was also initially suggested by Kent.... I recall some computations about this in relation to a model experiment (i.e., *an experiment conducted using scale models rather than real ships)* which was in view at the time... I have the impression that the Navy "took hold" not long after.... *It also seems likely to me that "foiling radar" was discussed at some later point in relation* to this project. I recall this vaguely in relation to some conference.[71]

"Dr. Rinehart" corroborates a notion introduced in part one, namely, that in establishing the overall outline of such an experimental project, benchmarks would have been laid down to test proof of concept experiments on a smaller scale, perhaps even using some of the scale models of navy ships in testing tanks. Moveover, while Dr. Rinehart indicates that "foiling radar" was not part of the initial design concept of the experiment, the context of his remarks indicate that it entered into the conceptual foundations close to the inception of the project at "some conference" that occurred later. He has not yet mentioned optical invisibility as a goal of the project.

But this follows shortly afterward with a revelation of what the project's real initial conceptual goal was:

> From its beginning this was strictly a defensive-measures type project rather than any attempt at creating offensive capabilities. *The initial idea seems to have been aimed at using strong electromagnetic fields to deflect incoming projectiles, especially torpedoes, away from a ship by means of creating an intense electromagnetic field around that ship.*

---

[71] Berlitz and Moore, *The Philadelphia Experiment,* p. 126, emphasis added.

This was later extended to include a study of the idea of producing optical invisibility by means of a similar field in the air rather than in the water.[72]

And there it is: the original goal was *deflection of projectiles* by means *of the impression of a field on a physical medium in order to distort the normal ballistic performance of the projectiles.* This, it should be noted, is quite similar to Jessup's ideas concerning "invisible solidities." Moreover, the creation of such a field would inevitably have involved large amounts of power and precisely calculated interferometry and resonance effects resulting from it. Accordingly, as "Rinehart" indicates, the discussions of the conceptual foundations of the project logically and inevitably branched out to include ideas of radar refraction, absorption, and ultimately, optical invisibility. The deflection of incoming projectiles is President Ronald Reagan's "Strategic Defensive Initiative", 1940s style.

"Rinehart" then discloses something else:

> What Albrecht wanted to do was to find out enough to verify the strength of the field and the practical probability of bending light sufficiently to get *the desired "mirage" effect. God knows they had no idea what the final results would be. If they had, it would have ended there. But, of course, they didn't.* [73]

In other words, once the idea of bending or refracting radar occurred to the scientists in the project, it immediately followed that trying to refract waves in the optical spectrum might be possible as well. Additionally, however, "Rinehart" discloses that "God knows they had no idea what the final results would be," in other words, the Experiment at some point achieved completely unexpected results. What the project ultimately issued in was an *accidental* discovery. The final results were unexpected.

---

[72] Berlitz and Moore, *The Philadelphia Experiment,* p. 128, emphasis added.

[73] Ibid., p. 130, emphasis added.

Later on, "Dr. Rinehart" would attend a conference where the scientists were trying to ascertain some of the obvious side effects that would occur as the result of a full-scale experiment on a ship:

> Among these would be a "boiling" of the water, ionization of the surrounding air, and even a "Zeemanizing" of the atoms; all of which would tend to create extremely unsettled conditions. *No one at this point had ever considered the possibility of interdimensional effects or mass displacement.* [74]

"Rinehart" has now let slip other important sets of revelations. The first of these concerns what the scientists *expected* to be the normal side effects of the experiment: ionization of the air, a "boiling" of the water surrounding the ship, and "Zeemanizing" of the atoms. Zeemanizing is simply the induction of a split in the excitation states of atomic particles and atoms. But the other set of disclosures is "Rinehart's" revelation that one unanticipated result of the experiment was an "interdimensional" effect or a mass displacement effect, i.e., an antigravity or even "teleportational" effect. In other words, Rinehart has disclosed or confirmed the sensational details of the Experiment without confirming outright, so to speak. He has indicated that the achieved results were wildly beyond what was expected. They were different in degree, not in kind, from the original purposes of the Experiment. And as for the first set of *expected* side effects, these, as will be seen later in this chapter, exactly match the descriptions of Allende's letters.

Finally, "Rinehart" discloses two more things. The first is that some of these Experiments took place at the Navy's Taylor Model Basin, located in Bethesda, Maryland. [75] Again, Rinehart has confirmed our basic outline of the benchmarks and stages of the project, since he has strongly implied that proof of concept experiments were done – presumably on the Navy's model ships – at the extraordinarily tight security of the model basin's facility. The final disclosure is even more interesting:

---

[74] Berlitz and Moore, *The Philadelphia Experiment,* p. 131, emphasis added.

[75] Ibid., p. 132.

> There were, for example, numerous instances when we were more
> successful in prevailing upon the U.S.M.C. to allow us to place
> experimental equipment on board merchant ships for trials than we
> were in persuading the Navy to allow us to use their ships.[76]

"Rinehart" has suggested, in other words, that there was more than
one test ship, and that they were merchant ships and not connected
to the Navy at all!

G. The Thomas Townsend Brown Connection

Berlitz and Moore include a whole chapter devoted to the
American physicist most often connected in alternative literature
with the subject of antigravity: Thomas Townsend Brown. Some
controversy has risen in the alternative community concerning this
inclusion of Brown in connection with the Philadelphia
Experiment, with some adhering to the viewpoint of Berlitz and
Moore, and others maintaining that there is little physics
connection between the ideas of Brown and those conceptual
foundations likely to have formed a basis for the Experiment. This
author takes the latter view, though is not strongly committed to it.
However, for the sake of thoroughness and completeness in our
survey of Berlitz's and Moore's now classic work on the
Experiment, we will review their presentation of material on
Brown, and offer some of our own observations regarding more
recent reception of his work.

Brown exhibited an interest and curiousity in physics as a
youth, and in fact during his teenage years he managed to find an
ex-ray tube and designed an experiment to test what he thought
might be a means of spaceflight. Mounting the tube on an
extremely sensitive balance, Brown thought he might detect a
small force exerted by the x-rays. However, no matter what
direction he aligned the tube, no such force was detectable.

---

[76] Berlitz and Moore, *The Philadelphia Experiment,* p. 133.

NICAP Photo of Thomas Townsend Brown. Brown was a founding member of this famous UFO Investigative Body

What he did discover, however, was a principle that would preoccupy the rest of his life's scientific work. "Each time it was turned on, the tube seemed to exhibit a motion of its own – a 'thrust' of some sort, just as if the apparatus was trying to move!"[77] After further investigation Brown discovered that it was the high voltage that was producing the brief motion.[78] Brown expanded his investigations. He produced a device from Bakelite, a "brick" about one foot long and 4 inches square, that "he optimistically

---

[77] Berlitz and Moore, *The Philadelphia Experiment,* p. 139.
[78] Ibid.

chose to call a 'gravitor.'"[79] When connected to a 100 kilovolt power supply, it would lose or gain about 1 percent of its normal weight, depending on the polarity used.[80] There were even a few newspaper accounts of his work, and even though Brown had not yet even graduated high school, no scientist expressed any interest in it.[81]

Brown entered the California Institute of Technology in 1922 at Pasadena, and there studied with Nobel laureate Dr. Robert A. Millikan. However, Brown was unsuccessful in interesting his professors in his discovery, so in 1923 he transferred to Kenyon college in Gambier, Ohio, where he studied with a physics classmate of Albert Einstein, Dr. Paul Alfred Biefeld. Unlike the California professors, Biefeld was genuinely interested not only in Brown's discovery, but in Brown's explanations for the behavior of his "gravitor," for Brown speculated that some sort of coupling effect between electromagnetism and gravity was being exhibited. Biefeld decided to cooperate with his student in designing a series of experiments using high voltage capacitors to test the "weight loss" or antigravitational effects of these capacitors.[82] They discovered an effect which would eventually – at least for a short period of time – be called the Biefeld-Brown Effect, which is that a highly charged capacitor seems to exhibit motion toward its positive pole.[83]

Following college, Brown signed on for four years at the Swazey Observatory in Ohio where he also married. Then, in 1930, he left the observatory and joined the staff of the Naval Research Laboratory as a "specialist in radiation, field physics, and spectroscopy."[84] Consequently, there is a loose connection between Brown and the Experiment, for he is clearly connected with the Navy doing research in the same general area of physics as the Experiment itself represented. In any case, during this period

---

[79] Berlitz and Moore, *The Philadelphia Experiment,* p. 139.
[80] Ibid., p. 140.
[81] Ibid.
[82] Ibid.
[83] Ibid., p. 141.
[84] Ibid.

Brown continued to perfect his "gravitors" and continued experimenting with them. By 1939 Brown was a lieutenant in the naval reserve and had moved to Maryland where he joined the engineering staff of Glenn L. Martin Company in Baltimore.[85] Brown was only at Martin a few months, for as the war clouds in Europe gathered, the Navy recalled him to begin work on magnetic and acoustics minesweeping, i.e., on techniques for the safe sweeping of German acoustic and magnetically homing mines.

> It was shortly after receiving this appointment that Brown came into contact with the early development stages of the project that may have become the Philadelphia Experiment. According to Dr. Rinehart:
> "I believe that when he (Brown) was brought back from Martin into the Bureau of Ships as officer in charge of acoustic and magnetic minesweeping, all projects that Ross Gunn, then director of the Naval Research Laboratory, thought interesting were brought up to him because of his background in physics. This is where he got involved in your 'project' – this is his beginning point."[86]

"Rinehart" even confirms Brown's presence at "several conferences" during which the Philadelphia Experiment was discussed.[87]

Notwithstanding Rinehart's accuracy on other points however, Berlitz and Moore acknowledge that "it is questionable whether Brown was really ever very heavily involved in the Philadelphia Experiment project."[88] One reason – from a purely scientific standpoint as we shall see – is that many scientists debated Brown's own conclusions on what the motive force being displayed in his gravitors was. However, even if some other alternative mechanism was in fact at work and not a "coupling effect" between electromagnetism and gravity, as Brown believed, Brown's inclusion in the project at some point seems likely, since Brown's own explanations for the Biefeld-Brown Effect would have been totally in line with the conceptual foundations of the

---

[85] Berlitz and Moore, *The Philadelphia Experiment,* p. 141. The Glenn L Martin Company later became Martin Aerospace.

[86] Ibid., p. 142.

[87] Ibid.

[88] Ibid., pp. 142-143.

project, based as they were in the 1928 version of Einstein's Unified Field Theory.

After Pearl Harbor, Brown was promoted to the rank of lieutenant commander and transferred to the Atlantic Fleet's Radar School in Norfolk, Virginia, where he became the school's head.[89] This too, is significant, for as has been argued, the initial concepts of the project most likely were to achieve radar refraction, and if possible, absorption, along with projectile deflection. This would, again, have been a likely basis for Brown's involvement with the project, for as head of the radar school, he would have been in the best position to know just what could, and could not, be done with the radar available in the early 1940s.

Berlitz and Moore confirm this assessment of things, for one of their other contacts told them that it was during this assignment that Brown apparently proposed to the Navy that electromagnetic fields might possibly be employed to achieve radar invisibility.[90] Then, suddenly, in December of 1943, Brown "suffered a nervous collapse that sent him home to rest."[91] Navy doctors soon recommended that he retire from the Navy.[92] Some researchers on the Experiment, Reilly Crabb included, maintained that Brown's nervous collapse was due to his involvement in the Philadelphia Experiment, and his horror at the unexpected results that were achieved and the effects they had on the crew of the test ship.[93] Berlitz and Moore are more cautious, and indicate that they uncovered no evidence to support these speculations.[94]

Brown then joined Lockheed-Vega Aircraft Corporation in California in the early spring of 1944, doing work in radar. He also continued his private work on his "gravitor" devices, though he had now decided to drop speaking of their effects in terms of gravity and "seemed to prefer the more scientifically but decidedly less sensational term 'stress in dielectrics.'"[95] While the shift in

---

[89] Berlitz and Moore, *The Philadelphia Experiment,* p. 143.
[90] Ibid.
[91] Ibid.
[92] Ibid., p. 144.
[93] Ibid.
[94] Ibid.
[95] Ibid.

terminology is less sensational and perhaps a deliberate calculation on Brown's part to sell his ideas under less controversial terms, the terminology still indicates in what direction Brown's thought inclined, for a "stress in dielectrics" could easily translate into a stress – the very type of stress introduced by torsion – in the medium of space-time itself.

After the war, Brown left Lockheed and went to Hawaii to continue his research. While there, an old friend introduced his ideas to Admiral Arthur W. Radford, at that time commander of the U.S. Pacific Fleet and later Chairman of the Joint Chiefs of Staff under President Eisenhower from 1953-1957. Brown's gravitor devices, now capable of much more fantastic losses of weight and increased motion, still failed to impress the Navy. Some authors have attributed this to that "alternative explanation" hinted at earlier, for they described it as simply being due to an "ion wind," that is, to the motion of charged particles in the atmosphere around the devices. Berlitz and Moore point out another possible reason for the Navy's reluctance to back and fund Brown's research, however:

> It is also possible that the Navy had seen more than its share of force-field research during the war and was keeping its distance from any more such projects for obvious reasons. (Carlos Allende's statement that "the Navy fears to use such results" returns to mind at this point.)[96]

This conflicts somewhat with a possibility mentioned in chapter four, namely, that the Navy's interest in the Varo Edition of Dr. Jessup's *The Case for the UFOs* might indicate something other than reluctance to use or pursue the results of the Experiment, as Berlitz, Moore, and Allende suggest. It might rather indicate that the Navy had somehow lost control of the project; it might have gone so black and so deep that a whole new roster of personnel had taken it over, and wrested control of it from the Navy's hands.

The turn of the decade saw the classic early 1950s UFO flaps, and Brown, like Jessup, was interested in the science that the UFOs possibly represented. Brown believed that with proper commitment of scientific resources, the mystery of their propulsion

---

[96] Berlitz and Moore, *The Philadelphia Experiment,* p. 145.

might be solved. And of course, "he remained constantly aware of the possibility that through his own efforts at research into electrograviticis he had hit upon one of the keys to the mystery."[97]

These two interests – his interest in the UFO propulsion mystery and his own "gravitor" work on stresses in dielectrics to produce motion – combined in 1952, after Brown moved back to Ohio, in a project he called "Winterhaven." His research by that time had improved his "gravitors" to such an extent that they were now capable of lifting more than their own weight. The new apparati were much more sophisticated than the originals and their demonstrations "were most impressive," such that they "should have raised the eyebrows of any respectable scientist or Pentagon official."[98] For Project Winterhaven, Brown constructed special disk-shaped dielectrics that involved high potentials and that could be discharged and recharged several thousand times per second. When different amounts of direct current high voltage was applied to these disks, the Biefeld-Brown Effect was observed to a degree never previously seen, for the disc-shaped dielectrics flew under their own power, "emitting a slight hum and bluish electrical glow as they did so."[99] While Brown continued to ascribe this phemomenon as a coupling effect between electricity and magnetism in his Project Winterhaven proposals to the military, the military's own experts had their doubts, and again chose to see in it nothing more than the effect of an ion wind in the atmosphere itself, induced by the strong electromagnetic fields.

It is worth mentioning that Brown was alive to this interpretation of his work. Having failed to sell his ideas to the American military, Brown was contacted by the French firm of La Société Nationale de Construction Aeronautique Sud Ouest to conduct his tests in France, under high vacuum conditions. If the dielectrics continued to fly under these conditions, the likelihood of "ion wind" as an explanation decreased dramatically. According to most of the information available, Brown's disks, when tested in

---

[97] Berlitz and Moore, *The Philadelphia Experiment,* p. 145.
[98] Ibid., p. 146.
[99] Ibid., pp. 146-147.

France under these conditions, were quite successful.[100] Brown was "ecstatic, for not only had he succeeded in proving that his discs flew more efficiently *without* air, but he had also shown that the speed and efficiency of his 'craft' could be increased by providing greater voltage to the dielectric plates."[101] Brown and others had even proposed the idea of using jet engines as electrical generators with the capability of providing potentials of up to 15 million volts as the power plants for such field propulsion aerodynes.[102]

Once again, Brown's research project was dashed by circumstances, for the French corporation was merged with a larger company, whose president was not interested in Brown's fantastic project.[103] Brown returned to the United States in 1956. Was it possible that someone had engineered the corporate takeover to prevent Brown from pursuing his research in France, and thereby handing over whatever technology and results that it achieved to the French? One will never know for sure, but it remains a possibility, and given the pattern of other such alternative energy and propulsion technologies throughout the last century, it remains a relatively *strong* possibility.

Back in the states, Brown eventually ended up at the Bahnson Company in Winston-Salem, North Carolina. The firm's president, Agnew Bahnson, had an interest in UFOs, and accordingly backed Brown's research as best as his small company could. But again, circumstances intervened to sideline Brown's work, for Bahnson

---

[100] And this, of course, raises the question of just what the *French* aerospace and military industrial complexes have been up to since the 1950s!

[101] Berlitz and Moore, *The Philadelphia Experiment,* p. 148.

[102] Ibid. Berlitz and Moore do not mention Brown in this connection, but Brown had in fact conceived of this idea some time before the Winterhaven tests, as he was working out the practical engineering problems of making his dielectric devices practical flying machines. In the Winterhaven tests, the dielectric devices were suspended from the laboratory ceiling, and power fed into them via heavy electrical cabling. Hence the need for on board power plants. Similar proposals had, in fact, already been broached in Nazi Germany as well.

[103] Berlitz and Moore, op. cit., p. 148.

himself, an experienced pilot, crashed when his plane struck power lines at the airport Bahnson had flown in and out of many times.[104]

One of the many results that Brown observed in the many years he tested his "gravitor" devices was that the degree of weight loss that was achieved also varied slightly with the position of the planets and more importantly, the phases of the moon! Toward the end of his life, Brown apparently finally achieved the recognition – quiet though it was – that his work deserved. This project was housed at none other than the Stanford Research Institute – well-known for its connection to the CIA's remote viewing project and a host of other covert military and defense projects – and the Ames Research Center of NASA.[105]

> The object of the research, details of which are still largely under wraps, is to try to determine what connection, if any, there is between the earth's gravitational field and rock electricity (also known as petroelectricity). If Brown can achieve his hoped-for goal of proving that petroelectricity (is) "induced" by the earth's gravitational field, it would go a long way towards strengthening not only Unified Field concepts in general, but Brown's own personal theories on electrogravity as well[106]

While Berlitz and Moore do not state exactly why such research into "rocks" and petroelectricity would constitute generalized confirmation of the Unified Field Theory, it is relatively easy to see why this is so. Rocks, and most especially crystalline rocks such as quartz, carborundum, diamond and so on, are well known to release minute amounts of voltage when subjected to sudden stress. Quartz, for example, when placed in a press, will eventually break. If done in the dark, one can actually see the spark of electricity released by the rock as it shatters. This is because the lattice structure of such crystals functions as a dialectric, storing minute amounts of electricity.

But for our purposes – and Brown's – we note one more important property of crystals. Every crystalline lattice structure

---

[104] Berlitz and Moore, *The Philadelphia Experiment,* p. 149.
[105] Ibid., p.. 150.
[106] Ibid.

contains defects, i.e., *displacements* of some nodes of the lattice. These defects are either *twisted*, in which case they are called "screw" defects, or sometimes they are entirely missing. In any case, *such defects are exactly explainable along the lines of the torsion tensor transform.* As such, these defects can almost be viewed as the physical manifestation of torsion, i.e., as a manifestation of a small twist or fold in space-time that was present locally when the crystal was being grown. Extending this thought somewhat further, *this means that crystals are natural resonators to the geometric, gravitational "shape" of their local space.* [107] No wonder, then, that the results of Brown's final research are "under wraps."

H. Allende's Shenanigans

Since Carlos Miguel Allende and his letters to Morris K. Jessup lie at the heart of the Philadelphia Experiment story, it behooves us to mention the shenanigans that nearly destroyed his credibility as a source. Indeed, Allende himself seems to have set out with the intention of doing precisely that.

The shenanigans began when noted UFOlogist Brad Steiger acquired a copy of the Varo Annotated Edition. Steiger immediately realized the implications of what he was reading, and decided to write an article about it, which ran in the November 1967 issue of the then well-known "paranormal" magazine, *Saga*, now defunct. The article also contained several reproductions of some actual pages of the Varo Edition that Steiger had acquired. [108] As fortune or chance would have it, Allende happened to have read this particular magazine, and was quite exercised about it.

Learning that Steiger was planning to publish a book which would include the article as one of its chapters, and "worried that the book might set the Navy on his trail again, and not wishing publicity in any event"[109] Allende bombarded Steiger's publisher

---

[107]Readers of my *Giza Death Star* trilogy will immediately appreciate the significance of this observation, since the Great Pyramid is exactly analogous to a gigantic crystal, with its own lattice "defects" or displacements.

[108] Berlitz and Moore, *The Phladelphia Experiment,* p. 85.

[109] Ibid., pp. 83-84.

"with several angry letters…asking that the material be suppressed."[110] Needless to say, these salvos were ineffective, and the book not only appeared, but Allende's name actually appeared in the title: *The Allende Letters, New UFO Breakthrough.* [111]

Then Jessup's friend Ivan T. Sanderson published *Uninvited Visitors* in 1967, in which the whole Varo episode and the Allende letters were once again discussed. According to Berlitz and Moore, Allende was not only enraged at the unwanted publicity, but also that others were making money on his story "while he himself was nearly penniless."[112] Allende decided upon a plan of revenge: he would confess that it had all been an elaborate hoax, thereby not only hitting the book sales of the authors that were exposing his story and damaging their credibility, but also diminishing the considerable publicity he was now getting.[113]

Jessup went to the Varo Corporation itself which had first printed the special annotation of Jessup's book, and not only demanded a copy of the book for himself, calling it "my book," but shaking down the company president in order to "get him out of their hair."[114] With this in hand, Allende then journeyed to the home office of the Aerial Phenomena Research Organization (APRO, "the oldest and most influential of the UFO research organizations")[115] in Tucson, Arizona, and declared that the letters to Dr. Jessup were hoaxes "designed specifically to 'scare the hell out of Jessup.'"[116]

To this end, Allende presented to Jim Lorenzen, then highly connected to APRO, the following "confession" which was added to the top of the second page of the Appendix:

> "All words, phrases, and sentences underlined on the following pages in brown ink are false. The below page and the top part of the following were and are the craziest (sic) pack of lies I ever wrote. Object? to

---

[110] Berlitz and Moore, *The Philadelphia Experiment,* p. 86.
[111] Ibid.
[112] Ibid.
[113] Ibid.
[114] Ibid., pp. 86-87.
[115] Ibid., p. 86.
[116] Ibid.

encourage ONR Research and to discourage Professor (sic) Morris K. Jessup going further with investigations possibly leading to actual research. *Then* I feared invisibility and force-field research; I don't now."[117]

And then, "with his plot hatched and the seeds of his revenge sown (or so he thought), Allende again disappeared from public view."[118]

There was, however, a significant problem with Allende's confession, and that was, namely, that in all his underlinings with brown ink to declare the falsity of the statements so underlined, he fell entirely short of stating that the Experiment itself had been a part of the hoax.[119] But in any case, the "confession" appeared to have worked, at least, for the moment, for in 1971 "when Paris Flammonde, producer of the 'Long John Nebel Show' in New York for many years, spoke of the events surrounding Jessup's death, he failed even to so much as mention anything concerning the Allende affair."[120] Things continued in this fashion, in fact, for some years, until, as was seen in the previous chapter, Berlitz's book *The Bermuda Triangle,* appeared and produced the witness to the final days of Jessup's life, Dr. Manson Valentine.[121]

With this cat out of the bag, Allende later on repudiated his confession. And so, it is time at last to turn to the Letters themselves.

---

[117] Berlitz and Moore, *The Philadelphia Experiment,* p. 87.

[118] Ibid., p. 88.

[119] Ibid., p. 87.

[120] Ibid., p. 88. As was mentioned earlier, Paris Flammonde was a well-known author in such subjects as UFOs, and the Kennedy Assassination, in his own right. His book on the JKF assassination conspiracy was, in fact, one of the first to buck the prevailing tide and to review the investigation of New Orleans District Attorney Jim Garrison in a favorable light. Long John Nebel, along with Mae Brussel, was perhaps one of the most popular talk show hosts at that time, specializing in areas of alternative research and conspiracy.

[121] Ibid.

I. What Started It All: The Letters of Carlos Miguel Allende to Dr. Morris K. Jessup

In citing the letters of Allende to Jessup, we once again turn to the Varo Annotated Edition, where they appeared in a more or less public document for the first time. The letters, however, are also reproduced in their entirety in Berlitz and Moore, and as this work is much more readily available, this is the source whose page references will be cited in the footnotes. These letters will be cited in full, preserving the peculiar punctuation, underlinings, highlightings, and misspellings as they are found there. When emphasis has been added to the text by this author, it is so noted in the footnotes. Afterward, Berlitz's and Moore's own summary of the letters will be cited, and then our own commentary will be added. It should be recalled that these two letters are the *second and third* letters that Allende wrote to Jessup, the very first letter having been lost. Additionally, I depart here from the standard block quotation style of indenting the quotation. Full page margins will be retained, and a slightly smaller font used.

1. The Second Allende Letter

Carlos Miguel Allende
R.D. No. 1 Box 223
New Kensington, Penn.

My Dear Dr Jessup,

Your invocation to the Public that they move en Masse upon their Representatives and have thusly enough Pressure placed at the right & sufficient Number of Places where from a Law demanding Research in Dr Albert Einsteins Unified Field Theory May be enacted (1925-27) is Not at all necessary. It May Interest you to know that The Good Doctor Was Not so Much influenced in his retraction of that Work, by Mathematics, as he most assuredly was by Humantics.

His Later computations, done strictly for his own edification & amusement, upon cycles of Human Civilization & Progress compared to the Growth of Mans General overall Character Was enough to Horrify Him. Thus, We are "told" today that that Theory was "Incomplete." [122]

Dr. B. Russell asserts privately that It is complete.[123] He also says that Man is Not Ready for it & Shan't be until after W.W. III. Nevertheless, "Results" of My fiend Dr Franklin Reno, Were used. *These Were a complete Recheck of That Theory, With a View to any & Every Possible quick use of it, if feasable in a Very short time. There Were good Results, as far as a Group Math Recheck AND as far as a good Physical "Result", to Boot.* [124] YET, THE NAVY FEARS TO USE THIS RESULT. The Result was and stands today as Proof that The Unified Field Theory to a certain extent is correct. Beyond that certain extent No Person in his right senses, or having any senses at all, Will evermore dare to go. I am sorry that I Mislead You in MY Previous Missive. True, enough, such a form of Levitation has been accomplished as described. It is also a Very commonly observed reaction of certain Metals to Certain Fields surrounding a current. This field being used for that purpose. Had Farraday concerned himself about the Mag. Field surrounding an Electric Current, We today Would NOT exist or if We did exist, or present Geo-political situations would not have the very time-bombish, ticking off towards Destruction, atmosphere that Now exists. Alright, Alright! *The "result" was complete invisibility of a ship, Destroyer type, and all of its crew. While at Sea. (Oct 1943) The Field Was effective in an oblate spheroidal shape, extending one hundred yards (More or Less, due to Lunar position & Latitude) out from each beam of the ship.* [125]Any Person Within that sphere became vague in form BUT He too observed those Persons aboard that ship as though they too were of the same state, yet were walking upon nothing. *Any person without that sphere could see Nothing save the clearly Defined shape of the Ships Hull in the Water,*[126] PROVIDING of course, that the person was just close enough to see, yet, just barely outside of that field. Why tell you Now? Very Simple; If You choose to go Mad then you would reveal this information. *Half of the officers & the crew of that Ship are at Present, Mad as Hatters.* [127] A few, are even Yet confined to certain areas where they May receive trained Scientific aid when they, either, "Go Blank" or "Go Blank" &

[122] Berlitz and Moore, *The Philadelphia Experiment,* p. 30, italicized emphasis added.
[123] Ibid., italicized emphasis added.
[124] Ibid., italicized emphasis added.
[125] Ibid., italicized emphasis added.
[126] Ibid., italicized emphasis added.
[127] Ibid., p. 31, italicized emphasis added.

Get Stuck." Going-Blank IS Not at all an unpleasant experience to Healthily Curious Sailors. However it is when also, they "Get Stuck" that they call it "HELL" INCORPORATED" The Man thusly stricken can Not Move of his own volition unless two or More of those who are within the field go & touch him, quickly, else he "Freezes".

If a Man Freezes, His position Must be Marked out carefully and then the Field is cut-off. Everyone but that "Frozen" Man is able to Move; to appreciate apparent Solidity again. Then, The Newest Member of the crew Must Approach the Spot, where he will find the "Frozen" Mans face or Bare skin, that is Not covered by usual uniform Clothing. Sometimes, It takes only and hour or so Sometimes all Night & all Day Long & Worse It once took 6 months, to get The Man "Unfrozen." *This "Deep Freeze" was not psychological. It is the Result of a Hyper-Field that is set up, within the field of the Body. While the "Scorch" Field is turned on & this at Length or upon a Old Hand.* [128]

A Highly complicated Piece of Euipment Had to be constructed in order to Unfreeze those who became "True Froze" or "Deep Freeze" subjects. [129] Usually a "Deep Freeze" Man goes Mad, Stark Raving, Gibbering, Running MAD, if His "freeze" is far More than a Day in our time.

I speak of TIME for DEEP "Frozen Men" are Not aware of Time as We know it. They are Like semi-comatose person, who Live, breathe, look & feel but still are unaware of So Utterly Many things as to constitute a "Nether World" to them. A Man in an ordinary common Freeze is aware of Time, Sometimes acutely so. Yet They are Never aware of Time precisely as you or I are aware of it. The First "Deep Freeze" As I said took 6 months to rectify. It also took over 5 Million Dollars worth of Electronic equipment & a Special Ship Berth. *If around or Near the Philadelphia Navy Yard you see a group of Sailors in the act of Putting their Hands upon a fellow or upon "thin air", observe the Digits & appendages of the Stricken Man. If they seem to Waver, as tho within a Heat-Mirage,* [130] go quickly & Put YOUR Hands upon Him, For that Man is They Very Most Desperate of Men in The World. Not one of those Men ever want at all to become again invisible. I do no think that Much More Need be said as to Why Man is Not Ready for Force-Field Work. Eh?

---

[128] Berlitz and Moore, *The Philadelphia Experiment,* p. 31, italicized emphasis added.

[129] Ibid., italicized emphasis added.

[130] Ibid., p. 32, italicized emphasis added.

You Will Hear phrases from these Men such as "Caught in the Flow (or the Push)" or *"Stuck in the Green"* or "Stuck in Molasses" or "I was "going" FAST", These Refer to Some of the Decade-Later after effects of Force-Field Work. "Caught in the Flow" Describes exactly the "Stuck in Molasses" sensation of a Man going into a "Deep Freeze" or Plan Freeze" either of the two. "Caught in the Push" can either refer to That Which a Man feels Briefly WHEN he is either about to inadvertently "Go-Blank" IE Become Invisible" or about to "Get Stuck" in a "Deep Freeze" or "Plain Freeze."

There are only a very few of the original Expieriental D-E's Crew Left by Now, Sir. Most went insane, one just walked "throo" His quarters Wall in sight of His Wife & Child & 2 other crew Members (WAS NEVER SEEN AGAIN), two "Went into "the Flame," *IE They "Froze" & caught fire, while carrying common Small-Boat Compasses, one Man carried the compass & Caught fire,*[131] the other came for the "Laying on of Hands" as he was the nearest but he too, took fire. THEY BURNED FOR 18 DAYS. The faith in "Hand Laying" Died When this Happened & Mens Minds Went by the scores. The expieriment Was a Complete Success. The Men Were Complete Failures.

Check Philadelphia Papers for a tiny one Paragraph (upper Half of sheet, inside the paper Near the rear 3rd of Paper, 1944-46 in Spring or Fall or Winter, NOT Summer.) of an Item describing the Sailors Actions after their initial Voyage. They Raided a Local to the Navy Yard "Gin Mill" or "Beer Joint" & caused such Shock & Paralysis of the Waitresses that Little comprehensible could be gotten from then, save that Paragraph & the Writer of it, Does Not Believe it, & Says "I only wrote what I heard & them Dames is Daffy. So, all I get is a "Hide-it" Bedtime Story."

Check observer ships crew, Matson Lines Liberty ship out of Norfolk, (Company MAY Have Ships Log for that Voyage or Coast Guard have it) The S.S. Andrew Furuseth, Chief Mate Mowsely, (Will secure Captains Name Later) (Ships Log Has Crew List on it.) one crew member Richard Price or "Splicey" Price May Remember other Nmes of Deck Crew Men, (Coast Guard has record of Sailors issued "Papers") Mr Price was 18 or 19 then, Oct. 1943, and Lives or Lived at that time in His old Family Home in Roanoke, VA. A small town with a Small phone book. These Men Were Witnesses, The Men of this crew, "Connally of New England, (Boston?), May have Witnessed but I doubt it. (Spelling May be incorrect) DID witness this. I ask you to Do this bit of Researech

---

[131] Berlitz and Moore, *The Philadelphia Experiment,* p. 32, italicized emphasis added.

simply that you May Choke on your own Tongue when you Remember what you have "appealed be Made Law"

Very Disrespectfully Yours,

Carl M. Allen

P.S. Will Help more if you see Where I can (Z416175)

Days Later

Notes in addition to and pertaining to Missive. (Contact Rear Admiral Rawson Bennett for verification of info Herein. Navy Chief of Research. He may offer you a job, ultimately)

Coldly and analytically speaking, without the Howling that is in the Letter to you accompanying this, I will say the following in all Fairness to you & to Science. (1) *The Navy did Not know that the men could become invisible WHILE NOT UPON THE SHIP & UNDER THE FIELDS INFLUENCE.* (2) *The Navy Did Not Know that there would be Men Die from odd effects of HYPER "field" within or upon "Field".*[132] 3) Further, They even yet do Not know Why this happened & are not even sure that the "F" within "F" is the reason, for sure at all. In Short The Atomic bomb didn't kill the expierimentors thus the expieriments went on – but eventually one or two were accidentally killed But the cause was known as to Why they died. *Myself, I "feel" that something pertaining to that Small-boat compass "triggered" off "The Flames." I have no proof, but Neither Does the Navy.* (4) WORSE & Not Mentioned When one or two of their Men, Visible-within-the-field-to-all-the-others, Just Walked into Nothingness, AND Nothing Could be felt, of them, either when the "field" Was turned on OR off. THEY WERE JUST GONE! Then, More Fears Were Amassed. (5) *Worse, Yet, When an apparently Visible & New-Man Just walks seemingly "throo" the Wall of his House, the surrounding area Searched by all Men & thoroughly scrutinized by & with & under an Installed Portable Field developer AND NOTHING EVER found of him. So Many Many Fears were by then in effect that the Sum total of them all could Not ever again be faced by ANY of those Men or by the Men Working at & upon the Experiments.*[133]

---

[132] Berlitz and Moore, *The Philadelphia Experiment,* p. 33, italicized emphasis added.

[133] Ibid., p. 34, italicized emphasis added.

I wish to Mention that Somehow, also, The Experimental Ship Disappeared from its Philadelphia Dock and only a Very few Minutes Later appeared at its other Dock in the Norfolk, Newport News, Portsmouth area. This was distinctly AND clearly Identified as being that place BUT the ship then, again, Dissapeared And Went Back to its Philadelphia Dock in only a Very few Minutes or Less.[134] This was also noted in the newspapers But I forget what paper I read it in or When It Happened. Probably Late in the experiments, May have been in 1946 after Experiments were discontinued, I can Not Say for sure.

To the Navy this Whole thing was So Impractical due to its Morale Blasting effects Which were so much so that efficient operation of the Ship was Drastically hindered and then after this occurrence It was shown that even the Mere operation of a ship could Not be counted upon at all. In short, Ignorance of this thing bred Such Terrors of it that, on the Level of attempted operations, with what knowledge was then available It was deemed as impossible, Impracticable and Too Horrible.

I believe that Had YOU then been Working upon & With the team that was Working upon this project With yourself knowing what You NOW know, that "The Flames" Would Not have been so unexpected, or Such a Terrifying Mystery. Also, More than Likely, *I must say in All fairness, None of these other occurrences could have happened without some knowledge of their possibility of occurring.*[135] If fact, They May have been prevented by a far More Cautious Program AND by a Much more Cautiously careful Selection of Personnel for Ships officers & Crew. Such was not the case. The Navy used whatever Human Material was at hand, Without Much, if any, thought as to character & Personality of that Material. If care, Great Care is taken in selection of Ship, and officers and crew AND If Careful Indoctrination is taken along with Careful watch over articles of apparel Such as rings & Watches & Identification bracelets & belt buckles, Pus AND ESPECIALLY the effect of Hob-Nailed shoes of Cleated-shoes. U.S. Navy issues hoes, I feel that some progress towards dissipating the fearfilled ignorance surrounding this project Will be Most surely & certainly accomplished. The Record of the U.S. Maritime Service HOUSE Norfolk, Va (for Graduated Seamen of their Schools) Will reveal Who was assigned to S.S. Andrew Furuseth for Month of either Late Sept. or Oct. of 1943. *I remember positively of one other observer who stood beside Me When*

---

[134] Berlitz and Moore, *The Philadelphia Experiment,* p. 34, italicized emphasis added.

[135] Ibid, italicized emphasis added.

tests were going on.[136] He was from New England, Brown Blond Curly Hair, blue eyes. Don't remember Name. I leave it up to you to Decide if further Work shall be put into this or Not, and Write this in Hopes there Will be,
Very sincerely,
Carl M. Allen[137]

§§§

2. A Brief Analysis of the First Letter

Before going directly to the Third Allende Letter, it is necessary to pause and consider some of the implications and allegations that have been highlighted by italics above. The italicized highlights will be cited again, followed by a brief commentary on each point.

1) *His Later computations, done strictly for his own edification & amusement, upon cycles of Human Civilization & Progress compared to the Growth of Mans General overall Character Was enough to Horrify Him. Thus, We are "told" today that that Theory was "Incomplete."*[138]
Dr. B. Russell asserts privately that It is complete.

   Allende alleges that Einstein had apparently used mathematical techniques to model human history and behavior as well. Of course, there is no evidence that this is the case, but it is nonetheless a fascinating idea, and one which would have fascinated someone with Einstein's turn of mind. Additionally, Allende hints here at a "hidden" physics, namely, that the Unified Field Theory was completed – for which there is not a shred of evidence – and that Dr. B. Russell, who can be none other than Bertrand Russell, maintained that it was. Again, Allende offers not a shred of proof of this idea.

---

[136] Berlitz and Moore, *The Philadelphia Experiment*, p. 35, italicized emphasis added.
[137] For the entire letter, Berlitz and Moore, op. cit., pp. 29-35.
[138] Ibid., p. 30.

As noted earlier however, Allende was perhaps merely confusing "completion" with "engineerability", and hence, to him, the fact of the series of experiments themselves indicated to his layman's mind that the theory was "complete."

2) *These Were a complete Recheck of That Theory, With a View to any & Every Possible quick use of it, if feasible in a Very short time. There Were good Results, as far as a Group Math Recheck AND as far as a good Physical "Result", to Boot.* [139]

This comment squares well with the revelations of "Dr. Rinehart" concerning many conferences that were held in preparation for the project. In terms of establishing the benchmarks for the project, one such benchmark would inevitably have been a group vetting of the mathematical foundations of the experiment. The mathematics would first have to have been derived from Einstein's 1928 theory, and then re-checked several times.

This is an important point, for as will be seen later in the letter, Allende also indicates that some of the dire results were foreseen as possibilities by the Navy. Again, vetting the mathematical foundations of the project would likely have revealed some of these consequences to the project's scientists. That the Experiments proceeded is, then, an indicator that these results were considered to be low probability – and therefore unanticipated – possibilities. They were therefore, once again, not part of the original design of the Experiments.

3) *The "result" was complete invisibility of a ship, Destroyer type, and all of its crew. While at Sea. (Oct 1943) The Field Was effective in an oblate spheroid shape, extending one hundred yards (More or Less, due to Lunar position & Latitude) out from each beam of the ship.* [140]

This is the very *first* indication of what the accidental and unexpected results were, and it is also the first ever indication that actual optical invisibility was achieved. Note

---

[139] Berlitz and Moore, *The Philadelphia Experiment*, p. 30.
[140] Ibid.

also the extremely significant point that Allende states that these results were achieved while *at sea*. And he hints at something else, namely, that the results of such experiments seemed to vary due to "Lunar position," i.e., the phases of the Moon, *just as was discovered in the gravitics work of T.T. Brown.* This significant statement reveals one of two things about Allende himself:

a) Either he was involved in observation of the experiments over a prolonged period of time, and had observed variations in its results due to this circumstance; or,

b) Allende had learned of these results from someone within the project's scientific staff who had access to the results of the Experiment.

In any event, this statement affords a clue as to why the unexpected results were achieved: *perhaps some particular condition or arrangement of the celestial space and experimental environment contributed to amplify the results of the Experiment beyond its design parameters.*

4) *Any person without that sphere could see Nothing save the clearly Defined shape of the Ships Hull in the Water,*[141]

Again, Allende provides a detail or clue as to what observers outside the field surrounding the test ship actually saw. The question that consequently occurs is whether or not this alleged observation would be scientifically *feasible.*

5) *Half of the officers & the crew of that Ship are at Present, Mad as Hatters.* [142]

Here is yet another unanticipated result of the Experiment which was performed "at sea," in other words, the presumptive "full scale combat conditions" experiment. One physiological and psychological effect was that exposure to the field made some of the test ship's crew mentally unbalanced and perhaps even insane.

6) *This "Deep Freeze" was not psychological. It is the Result of a Hyper-Field that is set up, within the field of the Body.*

---

[141] Berlitz and Moore, *The Philadelphia Experiment*, p. 30.

[142] Ibid., p. 31, italicized emphasis added.

While the "Scorch" Field is turned on & this at Length or upon a Old Hand. [143]

This is perhaps one of the most crucial allegations that Allende makes. It consists of several components, and it is best to unpack them:

a) Some of the test ship's crew were apparently unable to move at all as a result of exposure to the full-scale test's field; it was not the result of a psychological effect induced by the experiment, and is thus to be considered separately from the psychological effects of unbalancing the minds of the crew referred to above;

b) Allende speaks of a "hyper-field" within another field, the "field of the Body," which apparently Allende takes to mean that some sort of field was imposed within or impressed itself upon the normal electromagnetic field and processes of the human body; this, as will be seen in the next chapter, is yet another very strong indication that the version of the Unified Field Theory that was at the conceptual root of the Philadelphia Experiment is the 1928 version with its torsion tensor;

c) Finally, Allende indicates that this effect resulted primarily in crew members who were exposed to the "hyper-field within the field" for a prolonged period of time in one session, or alternatively, who were "old hands," and apparently subjected to exposure to the field over several distinct tests and experiments. Its effects, in other words, were cumulative and apparently at least quasi-permanent to those exposed to it. This again will be seen to be an important clue, not only in the next chapter, but also in part three, where similarities to effects experienced by those exposed to the field of the Nazi Bell will become quite apparent.

7) *A Highly complicated Piece of Equipment Had to be constructed in order to Unfreeze those who became "True Froze" or "Deep Freeze" subjects.* [144]

---

[143] Berlitz and Moore, *The Philadelphia Experiment*, p. 31, italicized emphasis added.

Allende here notes that because of the unexpected results of the Experiment, new equipment had to be constructed to reverse, or at least neutralize, these cumulative effects outlined above. This is highly significant, because it means the Navy was at least in part learning how to mitigate those effects by means of technology. Again, the parallel with the Bell will become quite evident in part three.

8) *I speak of TIME for DEEP "Frozen Men" are Not aware of Time as We know it.*

This point should be viewed in the context of the two preceding ones. Once the "hyper-field within the field" had been impressed on the human crew of the test ship, one of its effects was apparently that time passed in a fashion quite differently from the way it is normally experienced. As will be seen in the next chapter, this is yet another indicator of the operation of powerful torsion fields. And once again, there is a direct conceptual connection with the Nazi Bell.

9) *If around or Near the Philadelphia Navy Yard you see a group of Sailors in the act of Putting their Hands upon a fellow or upon "thin air", observe the Digits & appendages of the Stricken Man. If they seem to Waver, as tho within a Heat-Mirage...*[145]

Again, Allende and "Rinehart's" testimony corroborate each other, since one of the effects that the early project conferences decided would result from a field strong enough to affect optical light was precisely a "heat mirage" effect, with test ship appearing to outside observers to shimmer and bounce back and forth. Viewed against the backdrop of Allende's other allegations, however, the effect seems to be due not so much to the field refracting optical electromagnetic waves, but rather due to the effect that the test ship itself was undergoing a phase shift of

---

[144] Berlitz and Moore, *The Philadelphia Experiment,* p. 31, italicized emphasis added.

[145] Ibid., p. 32, italicized emphasis added.

154

some sort into a different phase state from the rest of matter.

10) *IE They "Froze" & caught fire, while carrying common Small-Boat Compasses, one Man carried the compass & Caught fire,*[146]

Another significant allegation from Allende: once the "hyper-field within the field" had impressed itself into the bodies of the test ship's crew, some of them, when re-exposed to relatively weak and normal magnetic fields either became immobile once again, or, apparently, spontaneously combusted.

11) *"Stuck in the Green..."*

This short phrase is a significant though often overlooked detail. Under the conditions of a full scale test, the electromagnetic fields surrounding the test ship would presumably have been quite strong, if not extremely so. In this case, then, the atmosphere exposed to the field would have been ionized, producing the familiar pale green "ozone" glow that people in the Midwest are used to seeing just prior to tornados. Being "stuck in the green" thus seems to indicate the "freezing" or immobility experienced by some of the test crew.

12) *IE They "Froze" & caught fire, while carrying common Small-Boat Compasses, one Man carried the compass & Caught fire,*[147]

Again, exposure to ordinary and quite weak magnetic fields, after exposure to the Experiment's "fields within fields," could induce the disastrous physiological effects

13) *The Navy did Not know that the men could become invisible WHILE NOT UPON THE SHIP & UNDER THE FIELDS INFLUENCE.*

Allende here draws out the implications of his previous points concerning the results that the Experiment had for the test ship crew: exposure to the "field within the field" impressed itself on their bodies such that, under certain

---

[146] Berlitz and Moore, *The Philadelphia Experiment,* p. 32, italicized emphasis added.

[147] Ibid, p. 32.

conditions such as reexposure to a weak magnetic field, it could reintroduce the effects of the actual experiment itself. Thus, once again, *is there a way of explaining this theoretically or scientifically?* If there is, then Allende's allegations gain in credibility. As will be seen in the next chapter, there is indeed an explanation, one fraught with dire implications.

14) *The Navy Did Not Know that there would be Men Die from odd effects of HYPER "field" within or upon "Field".*

Allende again repeats his "hyper-field within or upon the Field" formula, and now adds the information that this actually caused the death of some crewmen, though he does not state or offer a guess as to how or why.

15) *Myself, I "feel" that something pertaining to that Small-boat compass "triggered" off "The Flames." I have no proof, but Neither Does the Navy.*

Again, Allende comes to the logical conclusion his previous examples imply: namely that the "field within the field" could apparently permanently impress itself on the test ship's crew; the longer the exposure, the most powerful the impression. Reexposure to a magnetic field, even a weak one such as a ship's compass, could reinduce the effect of the actual experiment itself.

16) *Worse, Yet, When an apparently Visible & New-Man Just walks seemingly "throo" the Wall of his House, the surrounding area Searched by all Men & thoroughly scrutinized by & with & under an Installed Portable Field developer AND NOTHING EVER found of him. So Many Many Fears were by then in effect that the Sum total of them all could Not ever again be faced by ANY of those Men or by the Men Working at & upon the Experiments.*

Once again, Allende provides another clue into the nature of the Experiment and its effects on the crew: they not only could become invisible once again, but they could also, apparently, move through solid objects. This, if true, is yet another indicator into the nature of the Experiment's "unanticipated" results: ***the structure of matter itself was***

profoundly altered, much as Jessup had speculated with his "invisible solidities." It was thus perhaps this speculation that in part formed part of the reasoning process of Allende when he finally decided to write the scientist. The only question is, is it scientifically possible?

17) *I wish to Mention that Somehow, also, The Experimental Ship Disappeared from its Philadelphia Dock and only a Very few Minutes Later appeared at its other Dock in the Norfolk, Newport News, Portsmouth area. This was distinctly AND clearly Identified as being that place BUT the ship then, again, Dissapeared And Went Back to its Philadelphia Dock in only a Very few Minutes or Less.*

Allende finally states the other result of the Experiment, the one for which, along with "invisibility", it is most famous, the "teleportation" aspect of the story. Notably, Allende does not really indicate whether or not this was an expected or unanticipated result. So the question is not only is it scientifically possible, but was it a design concept of the Experiment, or another unexpected result?

18) *I remember positively of one other observer who stood beside Me When tests were going on.*

Finally, Allende clearly indicates that his role in the Experiment was that he *witnessed it*. He does not indicate whether or not this was of one test, or several, nor does he indicate whether or not he had a role in the project. Allende's frequent comments that in order to save those who looked as if they were going to be "frozen" one would have to "lay hands on them" has the sound of someone who actually observed such events. And this point also implies that, somehow, a "grounding" effect was taking place, that someone, not exposed to the field, could keep someone who was exposed to it anchored in this reality.

With this, we may now examine Allende's Third Letter to Dr. Jessup.

§§§

3. The Third Allende Letter

Carlos M. Allende

RF Box 223
New Kensington, Pa.

Dear Mr Jessup:

Having recently gotten home from my long travels around the country I find that you had dropped me a card. You ask that I write you "at once" and So after taking everything into consideration, I have decided to do so. You ask me for what is tantamount to positive proof of something that only the duplication of those devices that produced "This phenomenon" could ever give you, at least, were I of scientific bent, I presume that, were I of Such a Curiosity about something, the which has been produced from a theory that was discarded (1927) as incomplete, I am sure that I would be of such a curious interaction of Forces & Fields, in operations & their product Mr Jessup, I could NEVER possibly satisfy such an attitude. The reason being that I could not, Nor ever would the Navy Research Dept (Then under the present boss of the Navy, Burke) ever let it be known that any such thing was ever allowed to be done. For you see, it was because of Burke's Curiosity & Willingess & prompting that this experiment was enabled to be carried out. It proved a White-elephant but His attitude towards advanced & ultra-advanced types of research is just "THE" THING that put him where he is today. (Or at least, to be sure, It carries a great weight). Were the stench of such an Experiments results EVER to come out, He too would be crucified.

However, I have noticed, that throo the ages, those who have had this happen to them, once the vulgar passions that caused the reaction have colled-off AND further research OPENLY carried on, that crucified ones achieve something akin to Saint hood. You say that this, "is of the greatest importance." I disagree with you Mr Jessup, not just whole Heartedly, but vehemently. However at the same time, your ideas & your own sort of curiousity is that of mine own sort and besides my disagreement is based upon philosophical Morality and not upon that curiosity which Drives Science so rapidly. I can be of some positive help to you in myself but to do so would require a Hypnotist, Sodium Pentathol, a tape recorded & an excellent typist-secretary in order to produce material of Real value to you.

As you know one who is hypnotized cannot Lie and one who is hypnotized AND given "truth serum" as it is colloqually known,

158

COULD NOT POSSIBLY LIE, AT ALL. To boot, My Memory would be THUS enabled to remember things in such great detail, things that my present consciousness cannot recall at all, or only barely and uncertainly that it would be of far greater benefit to use hypnosis. I could thus be enabled to not only Recall COMPLETE Names, but also addresses & telephone numbers AND perhaps the very important Z numbers of those sailors whom I sailed with them of even came into contact with. I could too, being something of a Dialectician, be able to thusly talk exactly as these witnesses talked and imitate or illustrate the Mannerisms & Habits of thought, thus your psychologists can figure IN ADVANCE the Surefire method of dealing Most Successfully with these. I could NOT do this with someone with whom I had not observed at length & these men, I lived with for about 6 months, so you are bound to get good to excellent results. The mind does NOT ever forget, Not really, As you know. Upon this I suggest this way of doing this with Myself but further, the Latter usage of Myself in Mannerism & Thought pattern illustration is suggested in order that the Goal of inducing these Men to place themselves at & under your disposal (HYPNOTICALLY OR UNDER TRUTH SERUM) is a Goal, the Which could Have Far greater impact, due to co-relation of Expieriences remembered Hypnotically by men who have NOT seen or even written to each other, at all, for Nearly or over Ten years. IN this, With such Men as Witnesses, giving irrefutable testimony It is my belief that were, Not the Navy, but the Airforce, confronted with such evidence, (IE Chief of Research) there would be either an uproaro or a quiet and determined effort to achieve SAFELY "that which" the Navy failed at. *They did NOT fail to, I hope you realize, achieve Metalic & organic invisibility nor did they fail, unbesoughtedly, achieve transportation of thousands of tons of Metal & Humans at an eyes blink speed. Even though this latter effect of prolonged experimentation was (to them) The thing that caused them to consider the experiment as a failure,*[148] I BELIEVE THAT FURTHER EXPERIMENTS WOULD NATURALLY HAVE PRODUCED CONTROLLED TRANSPORT OF GREAT TONNAGES AT ULTRA-FAST SPEEDS TO A DESIRED POINT THE INSTANT IT IS DESIRED throo usage of an area covered by: (1) those cargoes and (2) *that "Field" that could transport those goods, Ships or Ship parts* (MEN WERE TRANSPORTED AS WELL) *to go to another point.*[149]

---

[148] Berlitz and Moore, *The Philadelphia Experiment,* p. 38, italicized emphasis added.

[149] Berlitz and Moore, *The Philadelphia Experiment,* pp. 38-39, italicized emphasis added.

Accidentally & to the embarrassed perplexity of the Navy, THIS HAS ALREADY HAPPENED TO A WHOLE SHIP, CREW & ALL. I read of this AND of THE OFF-BASE AWOL ACTIVITIES OF THE crew-Men who were at the time invisible in a Philadelphia NEWSPAPER. UNDER NARCO-HYPNOSIS I CAN BE ENABLED TO DIVULGE THE NAME, DATE & SECTION & PAGE NUMBER of that Paper & the other one. Thus this papers "Morgue" will divulge EVEN MORE POSITIVE PROOF ALREADY PUBLISHED of this experiment. The name of the REPORTER who skeptically covered & wrote of these incidents (OF THE RESTAURANT-BARROOM RAID MWHILE INVISIBLE & OF THE SHIPS SUDDEN AWOL) AND WHO INTERVIEWED the Waitresses CAN THUS BE FOUND, thus HIS and the Waitresses testimony can be added to the Records. Once on this track, I believe That you can uncover CONSIDERABLY MORE evidence to systain this, ---- (what would you call it ---- SCANDAL or DISCOVERY?) You would Need a Dale Carnegie to maneuver these folks into doing just what you wish. It would be cheaper than paying everyone of all these witnesses & Much more Ethical. The Idea Is, to the Layman type of person, utterly ridiculous. However, can you remember, all by yourself, the Date of a Newspaper in which you saw an interesting tiem more than 5 years ago? Or recall names of Men, their phone #s that you saw in 1943-44.

I do hope you will consider this plan. You will Progress as Not possible in any other way. Of course, I realize that you would need a Man Who can cause people to want to have fun, to play with Hypnotism, one that can thusly those he- you need to: #1 come to His Demonstration & thus call on them to be either or both "Honored" as Helping with the show" & for doing Him a Great favor, & /or being part of the act for the mite of a small fee He would HAVE to be a Man of such an adroit ingenuity at Manufacturing a plausible story on the-instant-he-sizes-up-his-" personality-to be dealt with THAT had cost PLENTY. The ability to convince people of an outright Lie as being the absolute truth would be one of his prime prerequisites. (Ahem.) Yes, some such skullduggery would have to be thought well out & done. THE ULTIMATE END WILL BE A TRUTH TOO HUGE, TOO FANTASTIC, TO NOT BE TOLD. A WELL FOUNDED TRUTH, BY UNOBFUSCATIVE PROOF POSITIVE. I would like to find where it is that these Sailors live NOW. It is known that some few people can msomehow tell you a mans name & His Home address UNDER HYPNOSIS EVEN THOUGH NEVER HAVING EVER MET OR SEEN THE PERSON. These folks have a very high or just high PSI factor in their make-up that can be

160

intensified by Hypnosis, thus is like reading from the Encycloppedia Brittanica. Even through that Barroom-Restaurant Raid was staged by invisible or partly invisible men, those men <u>CAN SEE EACH OTHER</u> THSU NAMES, In the excitement, were sure to have been Mentioned, whether last or first Names or Nicknames. A check of the Naval Yards Dispensories or Hospital of aid stations or prison RECORDS of that particularl day that the Barroom-Restaurant occurred May reveal the EXACT NAMES OF PRECISELY WHO WERE THE MEN, THEIR SERVIVE SERIAL NUMBERS & THUS THE INFORMATION ON WHERE THEY ARE FROM BE SECURED & by adroit "Maneuverings" of those stuill at Home, THE NAME OF THE PLACE where they are at present can be secured.

HOW WOULD YOU LIKE ATO ACTUALLY SPEAK TO (or some of THE MEN) A MAN WHO WAS ONCE AN INVISIBLE HUMAN BEING? (MAY BECOME SO IN FRONT OF YOUR VERY EYES IF HE TURNS-OFF HIS HIP SET) Well, all this fantastically Preposterous sort of rubbish will be necessary, Just do that, the Hynotist-psychologist & all that. Maybe I suggest something too thorough & too Methodical for your taste but then, I, as first subject, Don't care to be Hypnotized at all, But too, feel that certain pull of curiosity about this thing that, to me, is irresistible. I want to crack this thing wide open. My reasons are simply to enable more work to be done upon this "Field Theory."

I am a star-gazer Mr Jessup. I make no bones about this and the fact that I feel that IF HANDLED PROPERLY, I.E. PRESENTED TO PEOPLE AND SCIENCE IN THE PROPER PSYCHOLOGICALLY EFFECTIVE MANNER, *I feel sure that Man will go where He now dreams of being - to the stars via the form of transport that the Navy accidentally stumbled upon (to their embarrassment) when their EXP SHIP took off & popped-up a minute or so later on several Hundred sea travel-trip miles away at another of its Berths in the Chesapeake Bay area*[150]. I read of this in another newspaper & only by Hypnosis could any man remember all the details of which paper, date of occurance & etc., you see? Eh. Perhaps already, the Navy has used this accident of transport to build your UFO's It is a logical advance from any standpoint. What do you think???

VERY RESPECTFULLY
Cal Allen[151]

---

[150] Berlitz and Moore, *THe Philadelphia Experiment,* p. 41, italicized emphasis added.

[151] Berlitz and Moore, *The Philadelphia Experiment,* pp. 36-41.

§§§

4. A Brief Analysis of the Third Allende Letter

While in many respects Allende's Third Letter to Dr. Jessup is at once less sensational in its contents and more jumbled in its diction, there *are* some points that should be noted.

1) *They did NOT fail to, I hope you realize, achieve Metalic & organic invisibility nor did they fail, unbesoughtedly, achieve transportation of thousands of tons of Metal & Humans at an eyes blink speed. Even though this latter effect of prolonged experimentation was (to them) The thing that caused them to consider the experiment as a failure...*[152]

Once again, Allende insists that some sort of teleportation effect was an accidental result of the Experiment. But here he seems just ever so slightly to imply that optical invisibility may have been part of the conceptual design of the project, since his remark stands in a context where he emphasizes the accidental nature of the teleportation effect achieved. Again, the proper question is whether or not there was a scientific basis for this result in the theory that Allende emphasized in his Second Letter was the basis for the Experiment: the 1928 Unified Field Theory of Albert Einstein.

2) *That "Field" that could transport those goods, Ships or Ship parts... to go to another point.*[153]

In light of the previous point this is significant, for Allende now attributes the accidental teleportation effect to the "field" that was used. So again, we have Allende insisting upon

---

[152] Ibid., p. 38, italicized emphasis added.
[153] Berlitz and Moore, *The Philadelphia Experiment,* pp. 38-39, italicized emphasis added.

a) optical invisibility
b) "frozen" men
c) teleportation

as all being results of the Experiment. Again, are these effects explainable on the basis of the theory he cites as the foundation for the Experiment?

3) *I feel sure that Man will go where He now dreams of being - to the stars via the form of transport that the Navy accidentally stumbled upon (to their embarrassment) when their EXP SHIP took off & popped-up a minute or so later on several Hundred sea travel-trip miles away at another of its Berths in the Chesapeake Bay area[154].*

Allende emphasizes again the accidental nature of the teleportation results, and couples the effect to Jessup's interest in UFO propulsion, doubtless in a play to get Jessup interested in supporting his idea for hypnotic regression.[155]

5. Final Thoughts

What emerges from all these points, however, is that Allende, if he indeed concocted an elaborate hoax, had concocted one so outlandish that an ordinary person would scarcely give it the time of day: invisible ships? Disappearing men who could walk through walls or who spontaneously combusted if exposed to a compass magnet? Men frozen in time and unable to move? And all of this with the technology of World War Two?!?

Preposterous!

---

[154] Ibid., p. 41, italicized emphasis added.
[155] Berlitz and Moore's summary of the letters may be found on pp. 61-64.

Why then, did the Navy take notice and go to the effort of printing the Varo Edition? And why would a scientist, for that matter, give it serious consideration? To answer these questions requires a look at the science itself.

7.

THE CORUM PROOF OF CONCEPT
EXPERIMENT:
THE IMPORTANCE OF UNANTICIPATED NON-LINEAR
EFFECTS

*"Did the U.S. Navy, as Allende allges, and as the evidence we have examined
thus far seems to indicate, actually use the DE 173 to conduct such an
experiment in electronic camouflage? And were the results as horrifying as he
says they were?.... Can such proof be found? Probably not unless the
government files on the project can be discovered and made public."*
Charles Berlitz and William Moore[1]

The epigraph of Berlitz and Moore cited above indicates just
what the problem with the Philadelphia Experiment is: it lies in the
same category – or at least *appears* to – as the UFO phenomenon
itself, and like many UFOlogists, Berlitz and Moore strongly imply
throughout their now classic book on the story that the government
is deliberately covering up vital information concerning the
project. *If* the Experiment indeed took place more or less as
Allende alleged it did in his letters to Dr. Jessup, then such a
cover-up and conspiracy makes eminent rational sense. But is it
entirely true that the Philadelphia Experiment inhabits the same
realm of suppressed documents and non-provable data as UFOs?

No it is not.

As the previous chapters have demonstrated time and again, the
Philadelphia Experiment story contains a number of details that are
on the surface verifiable, the first and most important of which is
that the Experiment's conceptual foundations were based upon
engineerable considerations of the 1928 Einstein Unified Field
Theory, based upon a Kron-like application of its principles to
rotating electrical machinery and/or fields. Thus, while
documentary proof may not be forthcoming from the Pentagon or
the American national archives, strong corroboration is a
possibility *if a "proof of concept experiment" can be designed and
tested to verify certain aspects of that theory.*

---

[1] Berlitz and Moore, *The Philadelphia Experiment,* pp. 153-154.

Fortunately, we are in the position of not even having to perform such an experiment, for it has already not only been done, but done by some eminent engineers and scientists, K.L. Corum, J.F. Corum, Ph.D., and J.F.X. Daum, PhD. Moreover, we do not even have to apply interpretation to their experiment, for it was conceived and designed precisely with the idea of testing the conceptual foundations of the Philadelphia Experiment. As will be seen in this chapter, the results are startling.

A. The Conceptual History of the Philadelphia Experiment According to the Corums and Daum

The Corums and Daum present their scientific examination of the Philadelphia Experiment in an important, and unfortunately little-known paper,[2] "Tesla's Egg of Columbus, Radar Stealth, The Torsion Tensor, and the 'Philadelphia Experiment,'" presented in 1994 to the Tesla Symposium at Colorado Springs. In doing so, they also offer a well-considered conceptual history and evolution of the Experiment.

This history, and their scientific approach, may be appreciated by a careful consideration of their abstract at the beginning of the paper:

> In this paper we follow the thread leading from Tesla's spinning "Egg of Columbus" demonstration, through his proposal of a large rectangular helix disposed about the hull of a ship for U-boat detection, to Arnold Sommerfeld's discussion of magnetically biased ferrites creating electromagnetic stealth for WW-II submarines. *By calculation, the required magnetic field to reduce ship's radar reflection to less than 1%, at L-Band (1.5) GHz, is in excess of 15,000 A/m. Fields this order of magnitude would appear to fulfill the requirements of a "Philadelphia Experiment". Such intense fields would create green mist and cavities in salt water, and magnetophosphenes and Purkinji patterns in humans, particularly if driven at frequencies in the range of 10-125 Hz, as was available from the synchronous generators on WW-II electric drive ships. We conclude that with the knowledge available, the DSRB (under Vannevar Bush) would have been derelict not to have conducted such an experiment.*

---

[2] Unknown except in certain circles of the American defense and engineering community that is!

166

Finally, we present speculation on temporal bifurcations. Assuming Hehl's hypothesis that localized Cartan Torsion tensors are generated by ferromagnetic spin, we propose two physical experiments which distinguish temporal anisotropy arising from anholonomy (the Sagnac effect) from that arising in the torsion of the 1929 version of the unified field (Eddington's "crinkled manifold").[3]

Note what is being said here:

1) The original design concept of the Experiment was to achieve radar reflection reduction;
2) The field strength required to reduce radar reflection to less than 1% is precisely calculable;
3) Fields of that strength not only fulfill the requirements for a "Philadelphia Experiment"- style project, but moreover would generate not only an ionized atmosphere and a "green mist" around the ship, but also cavities in the salt water around it, and deleterious physiological effects in humans within the field; in other words, *some of Allende's wild allegations have a basis in scientifically verifiable fact;*
4) This strength of field is within the capabilities of ship-borne electric drive generators available on American ships during World War Two;
5) Faced with these possibilities, the authors argue that the Navy would have been far more likely to pursue them as not, since not to do so would have been a dereliction of duty; and finally,
6) Based on the experimental and theoretical considerations that they will survey in the main body of their work, they will present speculations on "temporal bifurcations," in other words, on the possible bases for Allende's more sensational allegations that the Experiment actually, and quite unexpectedly, achieved optical invisibility, and even a "teleportation" or "spatio-temporal" displacement.

---

[3] K.L. Corum, J. F. Corum, Ph.D., and J.F.X. Daum, Ph.D., "Tesla's Egg of Columbus, Radar Stealth, the Torsion Tensor, and the 'Philadelphia Experiment,'" p. 1, emphasis added.

Like everyone else, the Corums and Daum began to muse on the scientific possibility and plausibility of the Experiment when they acquired and read Berlitz's and Moore's now classical book on the story.[4]

They began – as we have attempted to do throughout this book thus far – by trying to reconstruct *"the sort of physical arguments, both classical and relativistic, that would have been available by scientists of the decade preceding the* Philadelphia Experiment."[5] As indicated by their abstract, they quickly settled upon the Torsion Tensor transform in the 1928 version of the Unified Field Theory as a possible conceptual basis for the Experiment.

One interesting revelation that the Corum and Daum paper makes – though without substantiation – is the list of names that they maintain were associated with the Experiment, some of whom we have encountered in the Varo Edition, Berlitz's *Bermuda Triangle,* and of course in Berlitz's and Moore's *The Philadelphia Experiment*: Albert Einstein, Rudolph Ladenburg, John Von Neumann, David Hilbert, Nikola Tesla, Oswald Veblin, Bertrand Russell, *Gabriel Kron,* and *Vannevar Bush.*[6]

The inclusion of Kron in this list is explainable for all the reasons outlined in previous chapters, and the inclusion of Vannevar Bush is understandable for the simple reason that, as FDR's scientific research Tsar, he would have had his hands in every secret research project in the country. Both men are almost inevitable logical necessities to such a project. The list also reveals something else that the Corums and Daum are quick to point out: if the Philadelphia Experiment story *is* a myth or hoax, then it could not have originated with Allende, for its details are too precisely aligned with the scientific implications of the torsion tensor for it to be the creation of laymen.[7]

---

[4] Corum, Corum, and Daum, "Tesla's Egg of Columbus…", p. 2.
[5] Ibid.
[6] Ibid., emphasis added.
[7] Ibid., p. 3.

1. Tesla's Meeting with FDR

In the reconstruction of the conceptual history of the Experiment, the Corums and Daum begin with a meeting that took place during World War One between the famous physicist and inventor Nikola Tesla and then Assistant Secretary of the Navy, Franklin Delano Roosevelt.[8] Roosevelt, and his immediate superior and mentor, Secretary of the Navy Josephus Daniels, were both intensely interested that the Navy have absolute legal control of the entire electromagnetic spectrum.[9] During this time Dr. Vannevar Bush was also occupied in the problem of submarine detection for the Navy. And in a final, and interesting "coincidence," it is known that during the 1920s Tesla was in some sort of contractual or consultative position with the E.G. Budd Mfg. Co. in Philadelphia. The Corums and Daum also put a new spin to the story that the government secretly examined and removed Tesla's papers upon his death in early 1943. In the normal version of this story, it is the FBI that raids Tesla's hotel room and removes his papers. But in the Corums' and Daum's version, MIT Professor John G. Trump, an associate of Dr. Vannevar Bush no less, was accompanied by "Naval Intelligence officers" to examine the coveted papers.[10]

Thus, there is a strong association of the famous inventor with the Navy, dating from World War One. But the Corums and Daum argue for a much stronger relationship than a series of mere coincidences:

> We think that not only can the Philadelphia Experiment be tracked to statements which Tesla published during World War I, and were grasped by men like Bush, but that the physics of the experiment can

---

[8] Corum, Corum, and Daum, "Tesla's Egg of Columbus...", p. 3.

[9] Ibid.

[10] Ibid. On p. 8 in a footnote, the Corums and Daum add the following information about Trump: "Recall that John G. Trump, accompanied by three Naval personnel, examined Tesla's personal papers when he died in January of 1943. Trump was Secretary of the Microwave Committee of the National Defense Research Committee from 1942 until 1944 when, as a member of General C.A. Spaatz's Advisory Special Group on Radar, he went to Europe as the Director of the British Branch of the (MIT) Radiation Laboratory. ...General Spaatz, by the way, was Air Force Chief of Staff and headed the 'very secret' committee on UFOs."

actually be traced back to Tesla's invention of the rotating magnetic field. Furthermore, to us there appears to be a legitimate link between Tesla's rotating fields and the Torsion tensor which appears in Einstein's 1927-29 Unified Field Theory publications. This connection was first identified and published by Gabriel Kron at GE (Schenectady) during the 930's.[11]

And there it is, the link between the technology of Tesla, the torsion tensor of Einstein, and its application by Gabriel Kron. The conceptual outlines of the Experiment, in other words, were between the technology of Tesla and the theory of Einstein, with Kron's engineering supplying the link between the two. Needless to say, a similar if not identical, set of connections might be drawn for the Nazi Bell, as will be seen in the next section of this book.

But what, exactly, in Tesla's work might have formed the conceptual core of the Experiment?

> Listen as, filtered by the pen of a journalist, Tesla narrates the electrical preparation of a ship:
> "Now, suppose that we erect on a vessel, a large rectangular helix or an inductance coil of insulated wire. Actual experiments in my laboratory at Houston Street (New York City), have proven that the presence of a local iron mass, such as the ship's hull, would not interfere with the actions of this device. To this coil of wire, measuring perhaps 400 feet in length by 70 feet in width (the length and breadth of the ship) we connect a source of extremely high frequency and very powerful oscillating current."[12]

As the Corums and Daum go on to conclude, "we think that Vannevar Bush was aware of this suggestion, and it is our thesis that these words are the seed that later blossomed as the 'Philadelphia Experiment.'"[13] Further on in this article, Tesla spells out more fully what he had in mind: "The average ship has available from 10,000 to 15,000 HP.... The electric energy would be taken from the ship's plant for a fraction of a minute only, being absorbed at a tremendous rate *by suitable condensers* and other

---

[11] Ibid.

[12] Corum, Corum, and Daum, "Tesla's Egg of Columbus...", p. 6, citing Secor, H.W., "Tesla's Views on Electricity and the War," *The Electrical Experimenter,* Vol. V, No. 52, August, 1917, pp. 229-230, 370.

[13] Ibid.

apparatus, from which it could be liberated at any rate desired."[14] While Tesla was writing all this for *The Electric Experimenter* magazine, Vannevar Bush was similarly engaged in discovering means of submarine detection.[15] And there is, of course, another obvious Tesla connection to the Philadelphia Experiment, for it was Tesla who had first proposed the idea of radar in the first place.[16]

Having thus dug into the conceptual history of the Experiment as far as radar and the salient theoretical and technological foundations in the work of Tesla, Einstein, and Kron are concerned, they pass immediately to a consideration of the conceptual foundations of radar *stealth* involved.

2. Arnold Sommerfeldt and Electromagnetic Radar Stealth

It was Einstein's colleague Arnold Sommerfeld, an expert on radar, electromagnetism, and radar stealth, that provided the next conceptual layer in their building case, and what a layer it is, with implications that spin out in some very breathtaking directions. They begin by making an extremely important observation about Sommerfeld's famous *Lectures on Theoretical Physics* and its section concerning electromagnetic radar stealth, which "presents a surprising discussion of *German* war research on stealth and radar absorbing materials."[17] In other words, all the theoretical considerations that now follow are based on *Nazi* concepts and experimentation.

a. Magnetic Permeabilities of Two Media

Sommerfeld begins his discussion by noting the case when two media - the air and the target – are of unequal magnetic permeabilies, μ_1 and μ_2, where μ stands for the magnetic permeability of the medium, and the subscripts denote the air and target respectively. Thus $\mu_1 \neq \mu_2$.

---

[14] Ibid., p. 7.
[15] Ibid., p. 8
[16] Ibid., p. 9.
[17] Ibid., p. 10.

> During the war the problem arose to find, as a counter measure to
> allied (sic) radar, a largely nonreflecting ("black") surface layer of
> small thickness. This layer was to be particularly non-reflecting for
> perpendicular or almost perpendicular incidence of the radar wave. In
> this case the angle of incidence and the angle of transmission are both
> almost equal zero. The problem is solved by making *the ratio of the
> two wave impedances* equal to unity...[18]

For the Germans, in Sommerfeld's own words, "the criterion is,
thus, not the index of refraction but the ratio of wave
impedances."[19]

The Corums and Daum are quick to see the enormous
implications: "*Sommerfeld's suggestion is similar to the idea of
making the radar target surface a 'conjugate match' to eliminate
radar reflections. If one could make the impedance of the second
medium be the same as free-space, the target would become radar
invisible.*"[20] I now beg the indulgence of those readers who have
been following my presentation of phase conjugation throughout
my previous books, in order to present it to those who have not.

*b. Electromagnetic Phase Conjugation, Phase Conjugate Mirrors,
and Templates*

In my previous book *The Cosmic War: Interplanetary Warfare,
Modern Physics, and Ancient Texts,* I presented the following
summary of physicist Paul LaViolette on electromagnetic phase
conjugation:

> The term "phase conjugation" refers to a special kind of "mirror" that is
> able to reverse the trajectories of the incident light waves and cause
> them to *precisely retrace the path they followed to the phase
> conjugating mirror. The outcome is as if the photons had been made to
> travel **backward** in time.* If you shine a flashlight beam at an angle
> toward a regular silvered mirror, the beam will reflect off at an equal
> angle in the opposite direction. But if you angle a flashlight beam at a

---

[18] Corum, Corum, and Daum, "Tesla's Egg of Columbus...", p. 10,
emphasis added, citing Sommerfeld.

[19] Ibid., citing Sommerfeld again.

[20] Ibid., emphasis added.

phase conjugate mirror, the returned beam will instead shine directly back at your flashlight!

Optical phase conjugation is most commonly known for its use *in military laser weapons systems for destroying enemy missiles.* In this application, a laser beam *is directed at a distant moving missile target and light rays scattered back from the target are allowed to enter the phase conjugator, a chamber containing a medium having nonlinear optical properties. In this nonlinear medium, the scattered rays interact with two opposed laser beams of similar wavelength to form a hologram-like electrostatic light refracting pattern called a "grating." Once this grating pattern is formed, the system has essentially locked onto its target. A powerful laser weapon is then discharged into this holographic grating pattern, whereupon the coherent laser light reflects (from the grating) in such a way as to produce an intense outgoing laser beam that retraces the paths that had been followed by the incoming rays that had originally been scattered from the missile. Consequently, the outgoing laser pulse converges precisely back onto its missile target.*[21]

In other words, phase conjugation is a means of compensating for the distortion that the atmosphere (or for that matter, any intervening medium) causes in electromagnetic waves being reflected from a target. Thus, a laser beam aimed through such a "grating" that is formed from phase conjugation arrives at its target fully cohered *and at full strength.* It is easy to see how Sommerfled's electromagnetic version of radar stealth is related to this concept, for a kind of "reverse" phase conjugation is being implied, where the target is being made to resemble the medium around it.[22] Thus, not only was Nazi Germany taking enormous strides toward the acquisition of phase conjugate weaponry during World War Two, but the United States as well, in its Philadelphia Experiment, was also – though unlike its Nazi enemy,

---

[21] Paul LaViolette, *The Talk of the Galaxy,* p. 132, emphasis added. Cited in my *The Cosmic War: Interplanetary Warfare, Modern Physics, and Ancient Texts,* p. 125.

[22] For more on the relationship of Nazi Radar stealth and RAM (radar absorbing materials) experiments and the relationship to the discovery of phase conjugation, see the entire fifth chapter of my book *The SS Brotherhood of the Bell.* For a fuller discussion of the weaponization of this principle, see my *The Cosmic War: Interplanetary Warfare, Modern Physics, and Ancient Texts,* 124-130.

inadvertently – taking the same enormous strides to the same weaponry.

c. Back to Sommerfeld: Permeability and Dielectric Constant

Sommerfeld reveals a great deal more about Nazi radar stealth materials, their theoretical foundations, and Nazi electromagnetic stealth research:

> In order to *"camouflage" an object against radar waves,* one must cover it with a layer for which this ratio of wave resistances has the value 1 *in the region of centimeter waves.* According to (the law of refraction and the boundary conditions) this means that if we call the constants of the desired material ε and μ and those of air ε_o and μ_o, then
>
> $$\varepsilon/\varepsilon_o = \mu/\mu_o$$
>
> Hence, the problem concerns not only the dielectric constant (ε) but also the relationship between the dielectric constant and the permeability. A substance must be formed whose relative permeability...is of the same magnitude as its relative dielectric constant....[23]

But as Sommerfld goes on to observe, this does not yet solve the problem, for behind this layer of radar absorbing material the target metal still forms a reflective surface. And thus, the radar absorbing material had to absorb sufficiently strongly. This in turn imposed the conditions that the magnetic permeability and dielectric constants of the material were given by complex, rather than real, numbers.[24] The material, in other words, had to be "ferromagnetic" and of such a nature that its structure could "relax" sufficiently to absorb the incident radar waves.

This was a difficult technological problem, and one that was not likely solvable in the course of the war. Accordingly, the Nazi scientists resorted to the expedient of layering materials over the target surface whose thickness was ¼ of the incident wavelength of Allied radars, and, as I detailed in my book *The SS Brotherhood of*

---

[23] Corum, Corum, and Daum, "Tesla's Egg of Columbus...", p. 10, emphasis added by those authors.
[24] Ibid.

the Bell, impregnated with small metal balls of various metals and alloys, of varying diameters resonant to different frequencies of radar waves. The material into which these balls were impressed was rubber. Thus, incident radar waves would stimulate a small current in the balls via resonance, and this current, in turn, would be dissipated in the rubber. By the time the incident radar wave struggled through all the layers of this material to the metal surface of the target, its signal was considerably weakened, though never entirely absorbed. The reason was that complete absorption required a layer of RAM materials about 2.5 thick, far too thick and too much weight to incorporate completely on German U-boats, which had to settle for a partial layer of the material.[25]

Nonetheless, German radar absorbing materials exhibited precisely the type of nonlinear properties that are used in phase conjugation, and indeed, as I disclosed in my book *The SS Brotherhood of the Bell,* the Germans actually discovered radar phase conjugation during their late war experiments.[26]

The Corums and Daum, however, raise one final question, a disturbing one: "Is there any connection between the remarks of Soomerfeld and the supposed German version of the 'Philadelphia Experiment' which has been rumored to have occurred at the Kiel Shipyards in Germany during World War II?"[27] This rumor has circulated for years in the community following the Philadelphia Experiment story, yet no evidence has ever been forthcoming to corroborate the story to any degree. All that can be said is that Nazi Germany, like the United States, was vigorously pursuing a program of radar stealth, both through development of RAM materials and through electromagnetic camouflage, in concert with each other, as Sommerfeld's remarks indicate. And like the United States, it would have been dereliction of duty had not the German *Kriegsmarine* attempted some sort of full scale eperiment.

B. The Corum-Daum Experiment and its Results

---

[25] Corum, Corum, and Daum, "Telsa's Egg of Columbus...", p, 11.
[26] See again chapter five of my *The SS Brotherhood of the Bell.*
[27] Corum, Corum, and Daum, op. cit., p. 11.

1. Initial Surface Impedance Measurements and Its Results

Going back to Sommerfeld's statement that the solution to the problem of radar stealth by electromagnetic means was to make the ratio of wave impedances in air and in the target equal to unity, thus rendering the target "invisible" to radar, the Corums and Daum "ask if there exists any phenomenon by which power line currents in a large coil around a steel (or ferromagnetic) body could somehow bring about a reduction in the reflection of microwave energy from the steel body."[28] They begin by determining the surface impedance of a "ferromagnetic slab that is immersed in a constant magnetic field oriented" parallel to its surface. This would, they maintain, "simulate the situation of a destroyer escort, with coils wrapped around it, illuminated broadside by microwave radar pulses."[29]

Taking measurements over a variety of bandwidths,[30] they cautiously concluded that "the evidence, meager though it is, appears to indicate that the radar reflection can be minimized and the use of electronic camouflage would probably have been studied experimentatlly." However, they also point out that "we do not claim that any material is capable of such deep nulls in the radar reflection, or is tunable over such broad bandwidths."[31] In other words, complete radar invisibility was an impossibility for any material, much less over various frequencies in the microwave range.

2. A Second Experiment

These measurements taken and conclusions drawn, they decided to modify the experiment somewhat, and to conduct a more elaborate test. Removing a toroidal steel core from a Tesla "Egg of Columbus" device, with a power source that would yield much larger currents through the coil windings, they illuminated

---

[28] Corum, Corum, and Daum, "Tesla's Egg of Columbus...", p. 13.

[29] Ibid.

[30] These results are found and charted on pp. 14-22.

[31] Ibid., p. 22.

the toroid or coil broadside with a klystron (at 100-250mW and 9.98-11.98 GHz), measuring the radar backscatter with a crystal detector.[32]

Then, they did more in order to simulate the Philadelphia Experiment's conditions.

Immersing the coil in a tub of water with rocksalt in solution, they energized the coil with their modest power supply. The resulting high current in the coil, however, brought a rather astonishing result: "The water 'flew out of the tub' (literally)!"[33] They then draw their first speculative conclusion, though one not at all beyond the bounds of the experimental evidence that they reproduce in their paper: "Clearly, with up to 4.5 MW available, eddy currents in salt water *would not only burrow out a hull-shaped hole in the water, but would probably levitate the ship somewhat."*[34] Carlos Miguel Allende consequently stands at least partially vindicated, for this is precisely what he reported, not only a "boiling" of the water but a hull-shaped cavity in it! And with the admission that a partial levitational effect may have resulted, one is a little bit along the way to Allende's fanstastic claims for teleportation.

But we are not quite there yet.

Before we get there, we must note the conclusions that the Corums and Daum draw from these initial series of "proof of concept" experiments:

> The analysis would appear to lend credence to the hypothesis that something more than mythology is involved, and it renders plausible the conclusion that sufficient motivation existed to actually conduct a "Philadelphia Experiment" to examine radar stealth on ships with electric drives. Independent of whether our assumed values are practical or not, the analysis which uses no phenomenology that wasn't known subseuqnet to 1938, would probably have brought WWII Naval investigators to the point of radar stealth experimentation. In fact, it would have been derelict behavior for the Defense Science Research Board *not* to have conducted such experiments if it were aware of this phenomenology(as it must have been) in 1943.[35]

---

[32] Corum, Corum, and Daum, "Tesla's Egg of Columbus...", pp. 22-23.
[33] Ibid., p. 23.
[34] Ibid., emphasis added.
[35] Corum,, Corum, and Daum, "Tesla's Egg of Columbus...", p. 23.

In other words, radar stealth was the most likely conceptual foundation for the experiment, and even when a "proof of concept" experiment such as the Corums and Daum designed was tested, some of the more extraordinary claims and observations of Allende were experimentally observed.

But what of Allende's *other claims?* What about the total optical invisibility of the ship? What of his extraordinary and incredible claim of actual teleportation?

This, as they say, is where it gets *really* interesting…

C. The Corum-Daum Analysis of the Moore-"Rinehart" Interview

…it gets really interesting because the Corums and Daum subject the statements of "Dr. Rinehart" as outlined in Berlitz's and Moore's book to a rather thorough scientific analysis, which opens the door for them to consider the other sensational aspects of the Philadelphia Experiment story.

They preface this analysis by a review of a typical magnetic degaussing installation on a ship. There were, as they note, "basically five different types of coil systems used on a ship."[36] Two of them are commented upon more fully. These are:

1) The "L-coil", which was a helical solenoid type arrangement, having its axis paralleling the length axis of the ship, with the loops of the coil running in vertical planes around the hull of the ship, perpendicular to its centerline, from its keel to the weatherdeck;[37] and,

2) The "M-coil", which encircled the ship inside the hull in a horizontal plane at the approximate level of the waterline.[38]

The cable of these coils could be almost five inches in diameter, and oftentimes three or four of these cables were racked together.[39] As the Corums and Daum go on to observe, even when one

---

[36] Ibid., p. 26.
[37] Ibid.
[38] Ibid., pp. 26-27.
[39] Corum, Corum, and Daum, "Tesla's Egg of Columbus…", p. 27.

discounts the heat sink effect of the ship's hull and its surrounding seawater, "it appears that the standard bundles could probably handle quite some current if pressed to the limit."[40] The coils in a ship, in other words, were quite beyond the power output needs of whatever equipment was used in the "proof of concept" experiments that led to full-scale shipborn testing of the Experiment.

With these thoughts in hand, the Corums and Daum begin their own examination of the detailed claims in Berlitz's and Moore's book. They begin by citing the work of a critic of the story, J. Pothier:

> The book by Moore and Berlitz is a source of surprising descriptive information. Recently, one critic examined the book and concluded, "Not only does the information presented by Moore and Berlitz in *The Philadelphia Experiment* fail the most fundamental test of verification, but he massive amount of the evidence available has demonstrated the thesis patently invalid." *We think the contrary to be true. Not only is the phenomenology supplied, but the independent statements of various witnesses corroborate the basic **technical** issues.* [41]

They begin by asking how, within the limitations of the ship's coils, the current could be stepped up, and the voltage decreased.[42]

The two answers were, obviously, (1) to use transformers, or (2) via "the resonant rise in circulating currents which occurs in a parallel resonant tank circuit."[43] At this point, they cite two statements of "Dr. Rinehart", and one statement of Jessup's friend, Dr. Manson Valentine:

---

[40] Ibid.

[41] Ibid., p. 28, emphasis added, citing J. Pothier, "The Philadelphia Experiment Revisited – Part II," *Electrical Spacecraft Journal,* Issue 8, October-December, 1992, pp. 14-21.

[42] Corum, Corum, and Daum, op. cit., p. 28.

[43] Ibid., p. 29.

Dr. R.F. Rinehart

"I think that the conversation had turned at this point to the principles of resonance and how the intense fields which would be required, for such an experiment, might be achieved using this principle."[44]

"I feel confident that the idea of producing the necessary electro-magnetic field for experimental purposes by means of the principle of resonance was also initially suggested by Kent- possibly as a result of these discussions with Professor Allen."[45]

Dr. (Manson) Valentine

"The experiment (Dr. Jessup) said had been accomplished by using naval type magnetic generators, known as degaussers, which were 'pulsed' at resonant frequencies so as to create a tremendous magnetic field on and around a docked vessel."[46]

The Corums and Daum then observe that

if they had placed a capacitor in parallel with the ship's coils (as Tesla suggested in the 1917 interview...) and brought the system to parallel resonance at the ship's generator frequency, then the circulating current in the coils would be stepped up by the Q of the parallel resonant system. That is, the AC current circulating *in the tank circuit coil* is larger than the imput current by the amount

$$I_{coil} = I_T \sqrt{1+Q_T^2} \ ...^{47}$$

In other words, the use of resonance was the most logical way to step up the current to obtain the desired field strengths for the full scale test. So this aspect of the details that Berlitz and Moore recorded in their book makes a great deal of sense.

---

[44] Corum, Corum, and Daum, "Tesla's Egg of Columbus...", p. 29, citing Berlitz and Moore, *The Philadelphia Experiment* (Ballantine Books, 1979), p. 191 (please note these page numbers of the Ballantine paperback edition that the Corums and Daum cite are different from the hardback version cited elsewhere in this book).

[45] Ibid., citing Berlitz and Moore, *The Philadelphia Experiment* (Ballantine), p. 187.

[46] Ibid., citing Berlitz and Moore, *THe Philadelphia Experiment* (Ballantine), p. 130.

[47] Corum, Corum, and Daum, "Tesla's Egg of Columbus...", p. 29.

Rather than review their comparison of the actual science with the detailed statements of Allende and others in Berlitz's and Moore's book, I present the following table of the Corum's and Daum's scientific analysis of those details, for ease of compairion.

The Corum's and Daum's Statement of Scientific Basis of Observed Effects	Detailed Statements of Allende and Others in Berlitz's and Moore's Book
Low Frequency Magnetohydrodynamics in Salt Water: **1. Green Fog and Mist[48]** "Ionization in the air could result as follows. Large magnetic fields rapidly changing in time can cause an ionizing breakdown of air."[49]	"After a time the central ship, a destroyer, disappeared slowly into a transparent fog until all that could be seen was an imprint of that ship in the water. Then, when the field, or whatever it was, was turned off, the ship reappeared slowly out of thin fog."[50] "I saw, after a few minutes, a foggy green mist arise like a thin cloud."[51] "...suddenly, the green fog returned..."[52]
Low Frequency Magnetohydrodynamics in Salt Water: **2. A cavity in the water:[48]** "The circulating AC eddy currents would agitate the sea water, at acoustical frequencies, (pumping the salt water, making steam, mist, and fog) and, in all probability, hollow out a cavity under the magnet. (Consider what happens with a high current AC electromagnet in a plastic tub of salt water. (It's even more exciting with	"The men on the ship were apparently able to see one another vaguely, but all that could be seen by anyone outside of the filed was 'the clearly defined shape of the ship's hull in the water.'"[54] "I watched as the DE 173 became rapidly invisible to human eyes. And yet, the precise shape of the keel and underhull of the ship remained impressed into the ocean water as it

---

[48] Corum, Corum, and Daum, "Tesla's Egg of Columbus...", p. 30.

[49] Ibid., p. 32.

[50] Ibid., p. 30 citing Berlitz and Moore, *The Philadelphia Experiment* (Ballantine), p. 240.

[51] Ibid., citing Berlitz and Moore(Ballantine), p. 110.

[52] Ibid., citing Berlitz and Moore(Ballantine), p. 249.

[53] Ibid., p. 31.

[54] Ibid., p. 30, citing Berlitz and Moore(Ballantine), p. 88.

[55] Ibid., citing Berlitz and Moore(Ballantine), pp. 110-111.

[56] Ibid., citing Berlitz and Moore(Ballantine), p. 41.

polyphase AC and a rotating magnetic field!)"[53]	and my own ship sped along somewhat side by side and close to inboards."[55]
	"The field was effective in an oblate spheroidal shaped, extending one hundred yards out from each beam of the ship… Any person outside that could see nothing save the clearly defined shape of the ship's hull in the water."[56]
Unsettled Conditions[57]	"…a boiling of the water, ionization of the surrounding air, and even a 'Zeemanizing' of the atoms…"[58]
Acoustic Whine and Hum[59] "It would seem reasonable to assume that the media immersed in the bias coil's low frequency magnetic fields (the ship and the sea water) would respond with mechanical vibrations, much like the acoustical hum of conventional power transformers for example. (The ship and sea water have become the output of an *acoustical transducer*, driven by the bias coils.) More than likely, the power content of harmonic spectra would be substantially well into the ultrasonic region, (think of all the electrical, mechanical, and physiological nonlinearities present), accounting for the perception of 'unbearable whine.'"[60]	"I felt the push of that force field against the solidness of my arm and hand outstretched into its humming, pushing, propelling flow."[61] "In trying to describe the sounds that the force field made as it circled around the DE 173…it began as a humming, pushing, propelling flow."[62] "A special series of electrical power cables had been laid from a nearby power house to the ship. When the order was given and the switches were thrown, 'the resulting whine was almost unbearable.'"[63]
Biological (Physiological) Effects[64] "Let us zero in on perceptual	"We couldn't stand the effects of the energy field they were using…It affected us in different ways. Some

[57] Corum, Corum, and Daum, "Tesla's Egg of Columbus…," p. 31.
[58] Ibid., citing Berlitz and Moore (Ballantine), p. 198.
[59] Ibid., p. 32.
[60] Ibid., pp. 32-33.
[61] Ibid., p. 32, citing Berlitz and Moore (Ballantine), p. 110.
[62] Ibid., citing Berlitz and Moore (Ballantine), p. 111.
[63] Ibid., citing Berlitz and Moore (Ballantine), p. 248.
[64] Corum, Corum, and Daum, "Tesla's Egg of Columbus…", p. 33.

effects which we would expect under such circumstances: Magneto-phosphenes and Purkinji figures. A phosphene is a sensation of light produced by physical stimuli other than light. A magnetophosphene is one stimulated by time-varying magnetic fields. What about Purkinji patterns?

"Johannes Purkinji, the renowned Czech physiologist of the 19th century.... Was famous for studying a number of variously shaped, subjective optical patterns that can be excited by electrical stimulation."[65]

"We think that visual distortion, magneto-phosphenes and Purkinji patterns (whether they were the alien humanoids reported as being seen by some sailors, or not) would certainly have accompanied the experiment. Such cerebral cortex stimulation...would probably also play a role in the 'blanking-out' experienced by some participants, even after the fields had been turned off...."[66]

only saw double, others began to laugh and stagger like they were drunk, and a few passed out. Some even claimed that they had passed into another world and had seen and talked to alien beings."[67]

"Any person within that sphere became vague in form but he too observed those persons aboard the ship as though they were of the same state, yet were walking upon nothing."[68]

"As he stood there trying to comprehend what had happened, and looking for his ship, he watched indistinct figures in motion whom he could not identify as sailors and some other shapes 'that did not seem to belong on the dock, if that is where I was.'"[69]

This table serves to demonstrate that, as far as the Corums and Dr. Daum are concerned, there are plausible scientific explanations for some of the more extreme effects reported by Carlos Allende in his letters. Moreover, these effects clearly emerge from the design parameters of the Experiment.

With these observations in hand, they then go on to pose the most significant question of them all:

[65] Corum, Corum, and Daum, "Tesla's Egg of Columbus...", p. 33.
[66] Ibid., p. 35.
[67] Ibid., p. 33, citing Berlitz and Moore (Ballantine), p. 19.
[68] Ibid., citing Berlitz and Moore (Ballantine), p. 41.
[69] Ibid., citing Berlitz and Moore (Ballantine), p. 248.

All this leads to a relatively unpretentious question. If the physics of the experiment is so easy to explain, and the physiological symptoms so easy to rationalize, then why would there be such a shroud of mystery in the Navy, and such unwillingness to acknowledge it? (Surely, with the National debt the size it is, they must have figured this all out years ago.) The military have conducted many experiments that went awry and where people were seriously injured. Why cover up this one?

The reluctance implies deeper issues. It would seem to suggest that something of an unusual nature occurred during the experiment. What was it?[70]

The careful reader will have noted that, in the Corums's and Daum's reading of the Experiment, radar stealth was the avowed goal. Yet, in the table outlined above, passages from Allende's letter are cited which in context are drawn from his first letter, which states that one unanticipated outcome was the optical invisibility of the ship. In one of the quotations the Corums and Daum cited above, this is clearly referred to, yet it has called forth no comment on their part.

The other sensational allegation that Allende clearly made on more than one occasion was that the DE 173 was "teleported" or "instantaneously transported" hundreds of sea travel miles from Philadelphia to its alternative berth in Norfolk, Virginia.

D. The Corum-Daum Analysis of the Torsion Tensor:
A Speculative Basis for Allende's Invisibility and Teleportation Claims, and
The Importance of Unanticipated Non-Linear Effects

At this juncture, it is necessary to pause and consider what the Corums' and Daum's paper indicates is verifiably established by experimental "proof of concept" testing, and what is realiably established on the basis of reasoned conjecture from that experiment to scaled up versions:

---

[70] Corum, Corum, and Daum, "Tesla's Egg of Columbus...," p. 35, emphasis added.

Verifiably Established By Proof of Concept Experiment	*Reliably Established by Reasoned Conjecture from the Proof of Concept Experiment to Fuller Scale Versions*
1. Radar refraction incident upon strong magnetic fields over a variety of bandwidths.	1. Ionization of the Air and Atmosphere around the test coils producing the "green mist" effect;
2. Boiling of Brine solution (created to simulate the effect of sea water).	2. Boiling of sea water, creation of a "cavity" in the sea water in the shape of the ship's hull; Zeemanizing of atoms; this boiling would likely have created fog, contributing to the "green mist effect" of atmospheric ionization noted above.
	3. Stepped up current in the field-inducing coils via the principles of resonance and the incorporation of capacitors in parallel, as per the suggestion of Tesla;
	4. Extreme physiological effects explainable as Purkinji patterns induced by the strong fields produced in a fuller-scale experiment.

With this in hand, they now begin to answer their own question of why the Navy would cover up such an experiment when the physics and *some* of the results of the experiment were so easy to explain or rationalize. As their own beginning glimmer of an answer indicates, it can only be because the military's "reluctance implies deeper issues," that is, that some of the extreme claims made for the experiment by Allende and others – optical invisibility and teleportation – might have, in fact, actually occurred. If so, then how would one rationalize them? How would one find a plausible scientific basis of speculation for them?

"At this point," in answer to these questions, they respond that they are not only "going to go out on a limb, but, metaphorically speaking, we also will saw the tree off."[71] Then they present some of the "bizarre testimony" that has been outlined in the previous chapters:

> "The experimental ship also somehow mysteriously disappeared from its Philadelphia dock and showed up early only minutes later in the Norfolk area. It then subsequently vanished again only to reappear at its Philadelphia dock. Total elapsed time – a matter of minutes."[72]

> "Suddenly, the deep fog 'flashed off,' leaving Silverman in a very confused state and wondering, 'what in the world I was doing in Norfolk.' He said he had recognized the place as Norfolk 'because I had been there before to the ship's other dock there.' Then, just as suddenly, the green fog returned; it lifted again and Silverman found himself back at dockside in the Philadelphia Navy Yard."[73]

> "One day, looking at the harbor from the dock (five British merchant seamen in Norfolk, Virginia) were understandably amazed to see a sea-level cloud suddenly form in the harbor, and almost immediately dissipate, leaving a destroyer escort in full view, which stayed by a few moments before it was covered by a cloud and vanished again."[74]

Their commentary is illuminating, because it records the natural response of any scientist when confronted by such claims, namely, that on any *standard* theoretical examination of such allegations based in quantum mechanics or the geometry of General Relativity, such things are practically impossible:

> These (quotations) sound like the unmitigated blabberings of some science fiction writer. Look, you can't do a macroscopic job like this with quantum mechanics, *or even general relativity.* Nine megawatts is one bodacious rate of energy delivery, but (worm holes, black holes and *Zitterbewegung* notwithstanding) *it's not enough to distort Schwarzschild's metric, Kerr's metric, or anybody else's solution to the extent that something like this could happen, even in a small locality.* The obvious rational explanation would be that some people that saw it were confused or intoxicated. Certainly one might expect the former to

---

[71] Corum, Corum, and Daum, "Tesla's Egg of Columbus…," p. 35.

[72] Corum, Corum, and Daum, "Tesla's Egg of Columbus…," p. 36, citing Berlitz and Moore (Ballantine), p. 89.

[73] Ibid., citing Berlitz and Moore (Ballantine), p. 249.

[74] Ibid, citing Berlitz and Moore (Ballantine), p. 250.

be the case for those sailors immersed in the intense fields of the experiment.[75]

But, here, for once, their analytical skills break down somewhat, for having previously vindicated the allegations of Allende on a number of points – the boiling of the seawater, the green mist and ionization of the air, even the harmful physiological effects – they fail to note that Allende himself, by his own admission, was *not* so immersed in the field, and therefore, this "intoxication" explanation fails in his case. He was, by his own insistence, a witness to the optical invisibility of the ship, and relates the stories of its teleportation.

They do, however, indicate where the flaw in the scientific reasoning of *standard* physics explanations of the experiment break down, for any approach from the standpoint of quantum mechanics or General Relativity are bound to break down, for the simple reason that these theories, and in particular, the *geometry of the latter,* are simply inadequate to explain these types of allegations.

And this is precisely the point, for Allende *nowhere* maintained that the conceptual basis of the series of experiments was to be found in General Relativity; it was to be found in the 1928 Unified Field Theory, with its torsion tensor and resulting "spiraling crinkled aluminum can" geometry. So, they ask, what about all those allegations of teleportation? "How could these topics become part of the associated lore" of the Philadelphia Experiment?[76] Their answer attempts to examine this speculative history in the light of the torsion tensor, which is the basis of maintaining "mathematical sensibility."[77]

They begin by citing a very important little quotation from the physicist Friedrich Hehl:

> One find that distant observers, who measure only the metric field, cannot distinguish between a (ferromagnetically) *polarized source of spinning matter* (**which causes torsion locally**) *and a rotating*

---

[75] Corum, Corum, and Daum, "Tesla's Egg of Columbus…," p. 36.
[76] Ibid.
[77] Ibid.

distribution of matter with the same total angular momentum (which nowhere causes torsion).[78]

Those who have read my *SS Brotherhood of the Bell* will immediately sense the relevance of this quotation to the conceptual foundations and actual configuration of the Bell.

Here we must remain focused on the Philadelphia Experiment, and the relevance of the torsion tensor to it, for they then continue with a breathtaking paragraph that unfolds the implications of this tensor transform for the wilder allegations of Allende and others that constitute the "unanticipated results" of the full-scale tests:

> Could it be possible that, as a result of magnetically biasing the ship to radar stealth, torsion deformations were excited in the fabric of space-time itself? (We told you that we were going out on a limb, in this section.) Were that possible, *then there might be teleportation and time-travel **without** the crushing effects of gravitational curvature, or squeezing through the Schwarzschild radius down the throat of a black-hole, or thoughts of bubbling out through a white-hole at some unknown place in the universe, or 10^{44} joules required to make the machine run. The torsion technique might even be within reach of pre-WWII electrical engineering.* If the spin were right, one might leap ahead along his world line (or perhaps even backwards) without traveling all the distance in between.[79]

Torsion, in other words, can accomplish what black holes or worm holes can accomplish- practical teleportation and forward time-travel – and do so without crushing the object to the incredibly tiny dimensions needed to squeeze through such a hole! Torsion, as was seen in the very first chapter, is this a change "in the properties of the underlying manifold" of space-time itself, and thus cannot be "transformed away" by any mathematical technique.[80]

When a field involving strong torsion is suddenly "turned on" the result, in other words, is that a "fold" or "pleat" is made along

---

[78] Corum, Corum, and Daum, "Tesla's Egg of Columbus...," p. 37, citing Hehl, F.W., P. von der Heyde, and G. D. Kerlich, "General Relativity with Spin and Torsion: Foundations and Prospects," *Reviews of Modern Physics,* Vol. 48, No. 3, July 1976, pp. 393-416, italicized and bold face emphasis by the Corums and Daum, italicized emphasis added.

[79] Ibid., p. 37, italicized emphasis added.

[80] Corum, Corum, and Daum, "Tesla's Egg of Columbus...," p. 41.

the time axis of space time, and similarly, such "folds or pleats" may also occur spatially.[81] Thus, we obtain a theoretical explanation for some of the wilder allegations of Allende concerning the Philadelphia Experiment, namely:

1) that the ship was suddenly teleported to and back from Norfolk, a distance of several hundred sea miles, in a matter of mere minutes, without the ship or the crew experiencing any gravitational crushing; and,

2) that – in some versions of the Philadelphia Experiment story – some crew members were tragically embedded in the bulkheads of the ship in a kind of grizzly metallo-organic chimera; if such spatial distortions resulted from strong torsion fields, then the sudden "turning off" of the field would have "unfolded" the pleats, with the sad results suggested.

But how explain the fact that Allende maintained that such results were entirely accidental?

Recall the earlier observations about resonance, and the Corums' and Daum's own hinted at suggestion of unanticipated non-linear effects. Non-linearity, as understood in this context, simply means that the normal mathematically predicted effects are magnified several orders of magnitude by the presence of unaccounted for parameters in the Experiment. Perhaps, then, the use of resonance was one such effect. Perhaps the coils were so in resonance that they kept stepping up the field until a non-linear threshold was unexpectedly crossed, and extreme torsion effects resulted. Similarly, external factors – planetary positions and so on, as indicated in the experiments of T.T. Brown on his gravitors – may have even played a factor.

In this case, then, there may be laws of torsion effects and non-linearity that can only be teased out of nature by further experimentation. If so, then it is small wonder the Navy was reluctant, given the effects of the Experiment on the ship's crew, to do so. But if this was the case, we may be certain that it did

---

[81] Ibid., p. 59.

undertake a very highly classified study of what "went wrong" and "why", and learned the basic outlines of what factors and parameters might have induced the unanticipated results.

Whatever one makes of these speculations, one thing emerges from the Corums' and Daum's breathtaking paper, and that is, that even in its most sensational elements, a scientific basis of speculation and reasoned mathematical argument may be presented to account for the Philadelphia Experiment in almost *all* of its details.[82]

---

[82] Even Allende's description of a "hyper-field within the field" can be construed along this line of interpretation, as implying a torsion field within the normal electromagnetic field induced by the Experiment. A further speculation is necessary, for the Corums and Daum do not, to my mind, adequately address Allende's allegations of some of the test crew becoming invisible, walking through walls, or spontaneously combusting in the presence of weak magnetic fields subsequent to the Experiment. It is a highly speculative suggestion, nevertheless I make it: perhaps one of the unknown "laws" referred to above would include the fact that organic materials somehow preserve or manage to have such torsion fields impressed upon them, so that they remain present after the inducing electromagnetic field is no longer present. In this respect, such results would square well with the research result of Russian torsion physicist Kozyrev, and would further resemble Bearden's ideas of "impressed dynamics" in living systems via electromagnetic fields. The obvious implications both for a new kind of medicine and a new kind of weapon are immediately apparent.

8.

THE HISTORY OF THE *U.S.S. ELDRIDGE*, DE 173, AND CARLOS ALLENDE, RECONSIDERED:
OR, THE STRANGE CASE OF THE RESEARCHERS WHO WERE NEVER HEARD FROM AGAIN

"Most importantly, however, Allende actually pointed to the specific time in which it occurred, though missed by all. Researchers and investigators of this incident, over the past four and a half decades, failed to connect this one very significant passage written by Allende. Why? Most of them, if any at all, placed very little stock into his writings, and seem to know very little, if anything, about naval procedure and regulations imposed during World War II."
Dru (a.k.a Howard A. Strom), and Debra Cunningham[1]

One of the strangest episodes concerning the Philadelphia Experiment occurred when two researchers, Howard A. Strom, a.k.a. "Dru", and Debra J. Cunningham appeared one night on the famous overnight radio talk show, Coast to Coast AM, with talk show host George Noory, who had only a few years earlier taken over the show from its creator and founder, well-known radio celebrity Art Bell. In some small way, this author became involved in this strange episode, because he happened to be listening to the show that night.

The guests proceeded to hold me, and I presume many others in the audience, spellbound with their account of their own research into the Philadelphia Experiment, which had turned up a wealth of new details from the ships' logs that Berlitz and Moore either could not find, or did not know how to find. I sat and listened with rapt attention, and when I learned that the contents of the show were available in a small booklet, I of course rushed off the following morning, mailed my payment, and a few days later received the booklet. There is nothing strange in *this*.

What was strange was that the two guests, Mr. Strom and Ms. Cunningham, provided *such* a wealth of new details that when they indicated that they were planning the first real comprehensive book

---

[1] Dru (a.k.a. Howard A. Strom), and Debra J. Cunnningham, *Special Investigative Report #1: Case Solved! Carlos Miguel Allende's Witness Account of "The Philadelphia Experiment"* (Oceanside, California: 2003), p. 7.

on the history and science of the Experiment since Berlitz's and Moore's now classic work, a book which they were titling *Phase,* I paid close attention. I visited their website, and sure enough, there was a picture of the tentative book cover with projected price, and a little notice indicating that it was still in press.

Contenting myself for the moment with the booklet, I simply placed an advance order for their book... and waited...

....and waited...

...and waited.

Finally, after about a year, I popped into their website again, or at least, *tried* to. The website was gone. Completely gone. This just did not "feel right," since the authors of the little booklet I now possessed had given solid indications during their appearance on Coast to Coast AM that much more would be coming out in the full sized book. So, I decided to write them once again.

My letter was returned, with the usual post office rubber stamp indicating that the letter could not be delivered. My attempts since then to track these authors down have proven totally unsuccessful, and it is a shame, for the quality of work exhibited in the little booklet is first class research. The authors, whose voices and personalities I had heard on the Coast to Coast AM show, had simply vanished as thoroughly as had some of the crew members of the *U.S.S. Eldridge!* Their one and only appearance on that show was never to be repeated, presumably because the Coast to Coast AM producers were having as much difficulty as I in locating them. All that remains to testify to the show's occurrence and to their research is the little booklet that I, and presumably a few others, had ordered using the information given out during the show!

The little booklet, somewhat clumsily but accurately entitled *Special Investigative Report #1: Case Solved! Carlos Miguel Allende's Witness Account of "the Philadelphia Experiment",* for its relatively few 71 pages, proved to be a goldmine of new information about the actual history of the *performance* of the full-scale Experiment. Accordingly, it is reviewed here, to present its information to those who have an interest in this story, and who may not have had the opportunity to hear that program or buy the booklet.[2]

The booklet, plus an entry on the Coast to Coast AM website for Debra J. Cunningham, is all that remains to attest their appearance on the radio show on Monday, Sept. 15th, 2003. Their website, and postal mailing address simply no longer function.

A. The Missing Logbooks and the Broad Outline of Their Reconsruction of the "At Sea" Test

The basic premise of Strom's and Cunningham's research is that normal naval procedure required that merchant ships keep two sets of logs, an "official" one and a "secret" one. With the declassification in 1981 of the S.S. *Andrew Furuseth's* secret logbooks – the ship on which Allende served according to the research of Berlitz and Moore – the critical tools were finally available "to advance Allende's claims beyond its current known version," that version outlined in Berlitz's and Moore's book.[3] These are, to say the least, a *"major, major revelation!"*[4]

Armed with these records and Allende's letters, Strom and Cunningham painstakingly reconstructed a very different history of the Philadelphia Experiment. One of their most significant points of departure in this new analysis is that "Allende actually pointed to the specific time in which it occurred, though *missed by all."*[5] They begin with a careful analysis of Allende's letters, and in particular, his Second Letter to Jessup:

> ...Allende describes the shape and size of the energy field encasing the ship. To use a simple analogy, it took the form similar to that of a football, and since the typical length of a destroyer escort was 306 feet, the entire force field was approximately, if not larger than three football fields in length and size. *This is massive! For him to define its exact form and size from one beam of the ship to the other, the* Andrew

[2] It is also presented in the hopes that, if there are any readers who do know more about these authors or any further publications they may have made concerning the Experiment, that they will contact me via my publisher.
[3] Strom and Cunningham, *Special Investigative Report #1,* p. 15.
[4] Ibid., emphasis in the original.
[5] Ibid., p. 7, emphasis added.

193

Furuseth *had to have been positioned either on the port or starboard side of the experimental ship. ...*

...For Allende to speak about what a person inside this field would experience or see, requires the personal knowledge of one who was, in fact, within such a field at one time and survived. Therefore, *we believe that Allende had unprecedented access to some of the men on board this experimental ship. The questions that immediately come to mind are: How, When, and Where?*

....To spot the defined shape of the ship's hull in the water after the vessel disappeared indicates that the ship was still physical enough to displace water, though you couldn't see it. At the same time, the ship could evade radar detection, because the signals, once absorbed by the surrounding magnetic field, *were entrapped within and couldn't return back to its sender. For Allende to observe this would mean, that the incident had to have taken place sometime during daylight hours.*

...Allende discusses the physical conditions of both men and ship. The actual operation was hindered, because the men could no longer tolerate the awesome forces besieging them; thus, to the men on board, the operation of the ship became secondary. The ship was also found to be beyond the point of seaworthiness. This would mean that the tremendous electro/magnetic forces formed around the vessal had caused untold destruction. Substantial damages occurred, no doubt caused by obvious electrical surges, which in turn would cause fires throughout the ship. To speak of the conditions of both men and ship, reveals that the experiment was still ongoing. What Allende had actually witnessed, was **not** the beginning stages of the experiment, but only one aspect of it. Remember, he only stated that he saw the ship disappear. *Therefore, we can conclude that the* Andrew Furuseth *had accidentally come upon the experimental ship while she was in distress. It too is highly probable, that the* Andrew Furuseth *was part and parcel to a hastily put together rescue mission. All of this would also help explain how Allende had come into contact with some of the men who were on board the experimental vessel.*[6]

This, then, is the basic outline and thesis of Strom and Cunningham's *Special Investigative Report #1:*

1) That the test had occurred *at sea*, ostensibly under normal combat and seafaring conditions;
2) That Allende's merchant ship, the S.S. *Andrew Furuseth* came upon the test ship while the test was underway;

---

[6] Strom and Cunningham, *Special Investigative Report #1,* pp. 8-9, italicized emphasis added, bold face emphasis original.

3) That he saw it disappear;
4) That the test therefore occurred in daylight hours;
5) That the S.S. *Andrew Furuseth* may have formed part of a rescue mission; and
6) That this is how Allende learned the details of what it was like to have been a crewman on the test ship and inside the field.

B. The Puzzle of the Furuseth's Missing Logbooks

As was seen in chapter six, Berlitz and Moore encountered the curious fact that the logbooks of the S.S. *Andrew Furuseth* were missing "on executive orders." I speculated there that perhaps a cover-up had been initiated at the highest levels of the government: FDR's Oval Office itself. But Strom and Cunningham have a very different, and much more plausible explanation, one that nevertheless ends with a cover-up!

As they note, after the war all *original* official logs of merchant ships were confiscated, and in the early 1970s, "believing that these *original* logs no longer held any significance or historical value, authority was granted to destroy them."[7] However, this did not mean that the official log books no longer existed, for it was standard practice to keep *carbon copies* that were then turned over to the ships' home Port Directors upon conclusion of a voyage.[8] Knowing this bit of naval and merchant marine procedure, Strom and Cunningham contacted the National Archives and Records Administration to obtain copies of the *carbon copies* of the Furuseth's Official Logbook.

But like Berlitz and Moore before them, they ran into a puzzling circumstance:

> All "**Official**" Log Books for the *Andrew Furuseth* were found to be on file, except those for the very period in question, August 16, 1943 to January 17, 1944. We had requested and received all of the logs on file, and what came with them, caught our attention. *The National Archives inadvertently sent us a file copy of a "Charge-Out" sheet in place of*

---

[7] Strom and Cunningham, *Special Investigative Report #1,* p. 12, emphasis in the original.
[8] Ibid.

those that were missing. Somebody, who went by the last name of Hollman, checked out these logs on August 31, 1978 and never returned them. Hollman filled-out (a Request for Records form), representing the U.S. Coast Guard! It this discovery just a coincidence? We believe not! Is this a cover-up? It's suspiciously beginning to look like it.[9]

"Hollman's" charge-out sheet is reproduced on the next page. It should be noted that all records facsimiles that appear in this chapter are from Strom and Cunningham's book, and are the fruit of their meticulous research. Unfortunately, as already detailed, all attempts by this author to contact them to request use of their material ended in failure. Thus, even while these records are public domain, I wish to acknowledge – gratefully - that the documents appearing in this chapter are *solely* the fruits of *their* research, not mine.[10]

In any case, the "charge-out" sheet is quite revealing for what it implies. As a close examination will demonstrate, Strom and Cunningham are correct: "Hollman" did indeed request the logs for the approximate period in question. But notice one thing that Strom and Cunningham do not mention: "Hollman" requested records from *October of 1943,* the *very month* that Allende so often mentioned in his Second Letter to Dr. Jessup as having been the time of the Experiment.

And finally there is the Coast Guard itself, America's "forgotten" military service branch (except for those who serve or served in it, of course!). It is perhaps worth speculating a bit...if one were going to "hide" a very covert black project, where better to hide it than in the most "forgotten" military service branch? It does give one pause, for why would "Hollman", if indeed he was from the Coast Guard, have zeroed in so precisely to this time period *unless someone in that service was very well-informed and knew exactly where to look?*

---

[9] Strom and Cunningham, *Special Investigative Report #1,* p. 12, italicized emphasis added, boldface emphasis in the original.

[10] Similarly, I am trying to be as comprehensive and thorough in reviewing the salient points of their research as possible, to make their work available to a wider audience that may not even know that they did this excellent work, and in hopes that someone will come forward and indicate what may have happened to their planned large-scale book on the Experiment.

"Hollman's" Request for SS Andrew Furuseth Logs Oct 1943-Jan. 20, 1944.

C. The Convoy GUS-15's "After Action" Report and the Furuseth's Secret Logs

As we saw in chapter six, Berlitz and Moore indicated that the *Furuseth* and the *Eldridge* were both connected with convoy duty.[11] The reason why GUS-15 is significant is that Allende's ship, the S.S. *Andrew Furuseth* was a member of this convoy. When the course of the convoy - as revealed in the newly acquired logs reveals – is plotted on a map, on the date of September 18, its course takes it within 120 miles northward of Bermuda.[12] During the same time period, the U.S.S. *Eldridge's* Deck Log reveals that is within 120 miles of GUS-15.[13]

But as noted in chapter six, Allende repeatedly and insistently points to October of 1943 as being the time he observed the Experiment. Strom and Cunningham ask the obvious question: "Will these two vessels be found coming together in the same location at the same time during the month of October?"[14]

The only way of answering this question is by recourse to the *Furuseth's* Secret Logbooks. It is here that Strom and Cunningham's research shows its remarkable quality, and where it most distinguishes itself from that of Berlitz and Moore, who simply did not even know of the *existence* of such logbooks. These secret logs were "required by the Department of the Navy". They could only be handled by a ship's master and were to be stored in the "overboard bag" along with all other confidential records. When a merchant vessel returned from a voyage, they were to be immediately turned over to the local U.S. Navy Routing Officer in the first U.S. seaport which they entered.[15] "Mandatory entries included: latitude and longitude; courses steered; bearing or

---

[11] Berlitz and Moore maintain that is was GUS 22, whereas Strom and Cunningham, on the basis of their newly uncovered documentary evidence, maintain that it was GUS 15.

[12] Strom and Cunningham, *Special Investigative Report #1,* p. 14.

[13] Ibid.

[14] Ibid., p. 15.

[15] Ibid.

Top Secret: Torsion

PART III
CONFIDENTIAL

Page 55

UNITED STATES SHIP Eldridge (DE-173) Saturday 18 September, 1943

Zone description +4

Position	0800	1200	2000
Lat.	33°-13' N	32°-37' N	32° 17' N
Long.	65°-13' W	65°-06' W	64° 21' W

OPERATIONAL REMARKS
(WAR DIARY)

12-16

Steaming as before. 1355 c/c to 350°(T), 350°(pgc), 353°(psc). 1442 c/s to 15 Knots (442 r.p.m.), c/c to 000°(T), 000°(pgc), 003°(psc). 1444 c/s to 19.5 Knots (600 r.p.m.). 1445 c/s to 350°(T), 330°(pgc), 335°(psc), c/s to 295 rpm, 10 Knots. 1446 c/c to 325°(T), 325 (pgc), 328°(psc). 1447 c/c to 5 Knots (140 r.p.m.). 1451 c/s to 15 Knots (442 r.p.m.). 1453 c/s to (215 r.p.m.) 10 Knots. 1453 c/c to 270°(T), 270°(pgc). 1454 c/s to 15 Knots (442 r.p.m.) 1458 c/c to 206°(T), 200°(pgc), 274°(psc). 1500 c/c to 201°(T), 267°(pgc), 276°(psc) 1501 c/s to 265°(T), 265°(pgc), 275°(psc). 1509 stood into a marked channel, steaming at various courses and speeds conforming to the channel. 1541 G.E. Welch, pilot, came aboard from motor launch. 1545, stood into the Narrows, Captain, Executive Officer, and navigator on bridge, pilot at the conn. 1636 stood into Dundonald channel.

Charles E. Hart 3d
Lieut. (jg) USNR, O.O.D.

16-20 Steaming as before. 1705-Wheel boat water borne. 1715- Steering gear casualty, switched to after steering. 1716- Steering gear repaired, switched to bridge control. Made fast to buoy E-1, Great Sound. 1746- Cast off on orders from U.S.S. Hamul. Steered course and speed to conform with Harbor Regulations 1802- Rudder jammed, steering control switched to after steering Casualty repaired, control switched to bridge. 1808- Moored starboard side to D.E. 245 lying in nest on port side of U.S.S. Hamul. Secured special sea detail. R. ? USNR, OOD

Approved: C.K. Hamilton
Commanding Officer.

Examined: H. K. Van Allen
Lt. USNR Navigator.

To be forwarded direct to the Commander in Chief, U.S. Fleet, either at end of an operation or at the end of the calendar month.

Log Entry of the U.S.S. Eldridge, DE 173, for September 18, 1943

199

distances of land, lights and other markers; names and positions of any ships sighted; and movements made in the convoy."[16] Thus, with these entries, the exact course of the *Furuseth's* movements could be precisely charted. Recalling for the moment that the *Edlridge* "remained in the Bermuda area until October 15, when she returned to New York after having completed her training operations," we may now examine whether or not the *Furuseth's* course would have taken her within close range of the *Eldridge* in October of 1943.

> According to Navy Lietenant William S. Dodge (Master of the *Andrew Furuseth*), he reports, after having boarded 427 German POWs and one passenger, they got underway departing Cadablanca the afternoon on September 18.

On the following day the *Furuseth* then joined up with the Mediterranean section of the convoy, under the command of Commodore Atkins. When the convoy was fully formed, orders were given to steam west on a course of 270^0 true at a speed of 9 knots.[17]

The following seven days were rather uneventful and, according to the secret logs, passed without incident. Then, on September 26th, the escort aircraft carrier *U.S.S. Santee* and her screen left the convoy. Some 16 hours later at 0240 hours September 27th, general quarters were sounded, and the log records that the convoy's remaining screens were seen dropping depth charges off the convoy's port side.[18] Obviously, if a German U-boat had been tracking the convoy for any time, it had wisely waited until the departure of the aircraft carrier and her escort group before attacking the convoy.

On the following day, Dodge requested medical supplies and assistance from the convoy's commander, Commodore Atkins, as the German military doctor accompanying the POWs detected cases of diphtheria and malaria among the prisoners. Having taken on these supplies which were passed along a line from the U.S.S. *Walter Brown*, DE 258, things returned to normal. Later that

---

[16] Strom and Cunningham, *Special Investigative Report #1,* p. 15.
[17] Ibid.
[18] Ibid., p. 17.

afternoon general quarters were again sounded and the convoy was ordered to turn sharply to port to avoid mines that had been laid in the path of the convoy. The rest of the voyage was uneventful, with the *Furuseth* steaming into Chesapeake Bay on the morning of October 3rd.[19]

Thus, the Secret Logbooks gave no indication whatsoever of anything remotely approaching the sensational events alleged to have occurred by Allende in his Second Letter to Jessup. Strom and Cunningham state that they "began to feel that maybe Allende's claims might, in fact, not be true. It's very hard to dispute the information contained in…Lt. Dodge's logs, when all you have is a lone allegation made by a simple deckhand over 40 years ago."[20]

But there was a problem…

D. More on The Convoy's "After Action" Reports

As noted above, at one point the convoy appeared to have been attacked by a German U-boat after the aircraft carrier U.S.S. *Santee* and her escorts steamed away from the group. Dodge, it will be recalled, recorded that general quarters were sounded, and the convoy's escorts were observed dropping depth charges. However, *Commodore Atkins did not even mention this anti-submarine activity and operations in his convoy's "After Action" Report*. This was and is a significant and highly unusual discrepancy between the documentation, and Strom and Cunningham had to investigate it further. What they found only conpounded the discrepancy, which was fast becoming a significant mystery:

> There are a number of different methods that can be used to determine valid WWII enemy submarine activity:
>
> First, we called for an additional record – the *U.S.S. Tarazed's* Deck Logs. Remember, this was Commodore Atkins' convoy Flagship, of which should have some mentioning of the sighting, noted counter-measures taken, and possible zigzagging or laying of smoke by the Navy escorts. If anything, at the very least, we should see the *Tarazed's*

---

[19] Strom and Cunningham, *Special Investigative Report #1*, p. 17.
[20] Ibid.

crew called to *"General Quarters"*. ***Upon review of the*** Tarazed's ***deck logs…we found that Watch Officers made no mention, whatsoever, of any submarine or subsequent actions taken to the likes described by Lt. Dodge.*** <u>*Very strange!*</u>[21]

But Strom and Cunningham had another ace up their sleeves:

> Second, we also knew that this region of the Atlantic Ocean came under the direct responsibility of Bermuda's Naval Operating Base(NOB). And, since this was the Navy's convoy base course used regularly by hundreds of vessels, at the very least, (the base commander) would have sent planes out to hunt this predator down. Therefore, we ordered Bermuda's War Diaries to see what action, if any, were taken by the naval forces staged there. ***These declassified pages…show that the Commandant was not even aware of, nor did he report to higher headquarters, that an enemy submarine was east of Bermuda on either September 27 or 28.*** <u>*This is very unusual!*</u>[22]

Finally, knowing that the convoy's escorting destroyers would also each have had to file a separate mandatory "Anti-Submarine Action Report" to the Tenth Fleet's Anti-Submarine Warfare Assessment Committee, Strom and Cunningham consulted the post-war compilation of all such reports, and found that *no such reports were filed by any of the convoy's escort screens.*[23]

Needless to say, all this is "highly suspicious."[24] Who was one to believe? Lt. Dodge, master of Allende's ship, the S.S. *Andrew Furuseth*, whose secret logs recorded a flurry of anti-submarine operations and depth-charging, or everyone else?[25] Strom and Cunningham decided to follow a hypothesis: Lt. Dodge's secret log entry was a "red herring, leading us to believe that something else had occurred."[26] It was when viewed in this light that the Navy's carefully contrived log books, action reports, and so on began to unravel.

---

[21] Strom and Cunningham, *Special Investigative Report #1,* p. 18, bold and italicized emphasis added. Underlined emphasis in the original.

[22] Ibid, with emphases as before.

[23] Ibid., p. 19.

[24] Ibid.

[25] Ibid.

[26] Ibid.

1. And the "Green Very Star"

The tapestry of documentary inconsistencies began to unravel when Strom and Cunningham re-examined the U.S.S. *Tarazed's* Deck Logs:

> Watch Officers of the *Tarazed* briefly reported the sighting of a green flare at 2212 hours at 130° True on September 27. The reason why it's peculiar to us is because Commodore Atkins, in his *"After Action"* report, also remarks about a green flare. It was his unambiguous language that captured our attention:
>
> "While passing through the Straits of Gibraltar, convoy was fully illuminated by searchlights from Gibraltar. On night of __ September, *a green very star was fired from point about 3000 yards from port side of convoy. No escort or ship in that position. Radar showed no vessel. Escort informed. I suspected this to be survivor, not found.*"
>
> We're confused! Why would Atkins suspect that the source of this green flare would be a *"survivor, not found"*? *A green flare is typically used to identify one's position to other known friendly military forces in the area, and simply means "all is clear."* But, all clear of what? It was also noted, thinking it too was unusual, that he had left blank the actual day this event occurred.[27]

But, it will be recalled that according to the *Furuseth's* master, he had set out from Casablanca on September 18 and formed up with the Mediterranean section of the convoy the following day. Atkin's flagship was therefore running the Straits of Gibraltar around September 17th, not September 27th. Why then this new discrepancy?[28] As Strom and Cunningham quip, "With all these inconsistencies popping up among these related official documents, it was almost like the *Andrew Furuseth* was part of another convoy, not GUS-15. Though, all of the official records reviewed say otherwise.... It appears that Commodore Atkins,

---

[27] Strom and Cunningham, *Special Investigative Report #1*, pp. 19, 23. Strom and Cunningham's narrative is interrupted by their placement of three pages of the Bermuda War Diary, which are found here at the end of the chapter.
[28] Ibid., p. 23.

Commander Hoffman and Lieutenant Dodge are all very busy covering something up."[29]

2. *"Romping Ahead"*

All of these inconsistencies merely made Strom and Cunningham "scrutinize this period like never before, beginning with September 26. In other words, everything is suspect now."[30] When they reexamined the positions of the S.S. *Andrew Furuseth* relative to the convoy flagship, the S.S. *Tarazed,* a new revelation popped out: the *Furuseth* was a "romper." A "romper" is simply a ship in a convoy that is 10 or more nautical miles out of formation with the rest of the convoy, running *ahead* of the main body of ships. Conversely, a "straggler" is a ship running 10 or more nautical miles behind the main body of a convoy.[31]

Their careful reexamination of the logs of the two ships revealed something more. The *Furuseth* was not only a "romper," but apparently the romper to end all rompers, for at one point she was some 31 nautical miles ahead of the advance units of the main body of the convoy![32]

Careful comparison of the logs revealed even more. Around noon of September 26th, the *Furuseth* was abeam of the convoy flagship *Tarazed* on her port side, though two columns away. But by 3:50 that afternoon, the *Furuseth* had traveled some 67 nautical miles, an impossibility at the convoy's speed of 9 knots. "For the *Andrew Furuseth* to travel a distance of 67 miles in four hours, she had to be traveling greater than 16.75 knots."[33] This was pushing the ship, rated for a top speed of only 11-12 knots, rather hard. By noon of the 27th, she is ahead of the convoy only 16 miles, and by noon of the 28th she was once again in formation with the convoy. Thus, she was a "romper" for almost 48 hours![34]

[29] Strom and Cunningham, *Special Investigative Report #1,* p. 23.
[30] Ibid.
[31] Ibid., p. 24.
[32] Ibid.
[33] Ibid., p. 25.
[34] Ibid.

It is now worth citing in full Strom's and Cunningham's commentary on this peculiar behavior:

> This would explain and satisfy the reasons why there were noted inconsistencies between all of the related official documents up to this point.... And, for the first time, we have identified a period in which Allende had a prime opportunity to see something along the line of that alleged, without being in full view of all the other GUS-15 merchant vessels.
>
> *By all accounts, neither Commodore Atkins nor Commander Hoffman is seen reporting this unusual ship movement of the* Andrew Furuseth, *which indicates that Dodge was not acting independently. But, was under orders sanctioned by these two senior Naval Officers in charge of the convoy. Thus, all three are deeply involved in covering up something really big! What was so paramount that it was necessary to order Dodge and the crew of the* Andrew Furuseth *beyond the protective shield of the Navy escorts?*[35]

But Strom and Cunningham should also have asked another question: *Why order the Furuseth to "romp" ahead of the convoy so dramatically, and not some other ship?*

While no evidence exists as to the exact reasons the *Furuseth* was tasked with this unusual duty, we are permitted to speculate on what Strom and Cunningham uncovered. Recall that the *Furuseth* had taken on over four hundred German POWs in Casablanca. From a certain standpoint, then, she might have been viewed as more expendable than the other ships in the convoy.[36] Another alternative is possible, namely, that Commodore Atkins was gambling that German military intelligence might have seen the *Furuseth* taking on German POWs at Casablanca, and accordingly alerted U-Boats not to attack the ship. Whatever the reasons actually were, something *like* these speculations may have run through Commodore Atkin's mind as he made the selection of which ship was to undertake the dangerous "romp." And there is a

---

[35] Strom and Cunningham, *Special Investigative Report #1*, p. 26, emphasis added.

[36] It should be noted, however, that with the final failure of the German *Afrika Korps* in Tunisia during this same period, thousands of German POWs were probably being transferred to the United States on returning convoy vessels, so it is likely that other ships in GUS-15 carried German prisoners as well.

final consideration. Perhaps Lieutenant Dodge was known to be a competent officer who could perhaps squeeze every last bit of speed out of the lumbering merchant vessel.

Which leaves Strom's and Cunningham's question to be answered: Why have *any* ship "romp" so dangerously far ahead of the convoy, and make it an easy target for a U-boat's torpedoes?

3. And **Erasing** Log Entries

Further reexamination of the *Furuseth's* Secret Logs revealed to Strom and Cunningham an even *more* revealing bit of information. Lieutenant Dodge had crossed out one set of coordinates written in the log for September 26th and recorded the correction on the line below. All of this is in accordance with normal Navy procedure. But Strom and Cunningham looked a little closer.

> (Now) in total disbelief, we noticed that Dodge had actually expunged both latitude and longitude coordinates once written in the logs. He then printed new coordinates on top of those erased.
>
> Realize that this disturbing fact of erasing entries in a logbook is in direct conflict with Navy regulations and was not to occur under any circumstances. Those of us, who have served in our great military institutions, know well the regulations that govern official unit logs → *you don't do this, period! Standing alone, this is more than sufficient evidence, which proves that events surrounding this period in question were being concealed.*[37]

And to make matters worse, Strom and Cunningham discovered a letter that the Naval Historical Center maintained on file

> a letter from Lieutenant Junior Grade William S. Dodge, USNR, (Ret.) the master of *Andrew Furuseth* in 1943, categorically denying that he or his crew observed any unusual event while in Norfolk.[38]

---

[37] Strom and Cunningham, *Special Investigative Report #1,* p. 26, emphasis added.

[38] Ibid.

But this is, by now, an obvious and pure obfuscation, the *Furuseth* was nowhere near Norfolk when "something" happened that required all the juggling of the official records thus far surveyed.

4. Romping Ahead, Unescorted?

As outlined above, the movements of the *Furuseth* between September 26 and September 28, as it romped ahead of the convoy, have all the hallmarks of having been ordered to do so by Commodore Atkins. But does it stand to reason or operational logic that he would have done so without providing an escort for it, as we speculated above?

Not really.

Moreover, in his logs Lt. (J.G.) Dodge actually does mention that he *is* traveling in a convoy. "So, with what convoy of Navy escorts were he and the *Andrew Furuseth* traveling."[39] Recall that Lt. Dodge indicated the departure from the convoy GUS-15 of the escort aircraft carrier U.S.S. *Santee* and her escort group. This was on the morning of September 26th. The *Furuseth* departed the main convoy group some two hours later, the decision apparently having been made to have her join up with the *Santee* group.

> There had to have been a very good reason as to why both Atkins and Hoffman would release the *Andrew Furuseth* on this highly unusual mission, no doubt designated as a *"Special Operation"*. At this moment, we can only guess that the *Santee's* Commanding Officer, sometime between departing GUS-15 and 12 noon of September 26, had called back requesting for additional ship support. If this were true, what was the rationale behind needing a merchant vessel? This was not a training exercise they were on. Therefore, we believe that the *Santee* group was responding to an urgent SOS call from a ship in distress, otherwise this group would have immediately complied with the orders received from CINCLANT[40] headquarters to return to the Azores. To discover the real reason, we need to pull another "Ace" from our sleeve.[41]

---

[39] Strom and Cunningham, *Special Investigative Report #1,* p. 27.

[40] CINCLANT: Commander in Chief's headquarters, Atlantic Fleet. These documents are reproduced at the end of this chapter.

[41] Ibid., p. 29.

Strom and Cunningham's argument now becomes very subtle. Noting again that the *Furuseth* had taken on German POWs at Casablanca, they draw the logical and inevitable conclusion that the *Furuseth* was one of those Liberty ships designed to carry troops. Given the fact that she could carry from 9,000 to 10,000 tons, and was now carrying only 427 German POWs, meant that she was much lighter, and thus could steam faster. Moreover, her complement of prisoners meant that she could probably carry some 100 more people.[42]

Strom and Cunningham now played their "ace." Knowing that the *Furuseth* was carrying German prisoners, this meant that she would also have carried a complement of 12-24 armed guards. "Therefore, we ordered and received the voyage reports that were submitted to the Armed Guard Center, Brooklyn, New York."[43] Lt. (J.G.) Edward J. Russell, the *Furuseth's* armed guard commander, records the same things Dodge recorded in his Secret Log: the departure of the CVE *Santee* and her group of escorts, the alleged contact with the German U-Boat and the depth-charging by the Navy escorts.[44]

But then, on September 27th, Russell records that both he and Lt. Dodge are listening to the *Furuseth's* radio, where the escorts of their group are reporting another U-boat contact. *But in this case absolutely no submarine counter-measures are taken.*[45] After this point, Dodge's Secret Log records no more...but Russell's does.

> No more than 35 minutes later, Russell mentions sighting, three or four columns over on the *Andrew Furuseth's* starboard side, an unidentified vessel with a fire on its stern. This too is strange, because the only vessels with which the *Andrew Furuseth* was traveling were the "*Hunter/Killer*" group that consisted of one carrier[46] and three destroyers, not a convoy or merchant vessels. *Hence, this (new) ship was not part of the convoy, but the very ship they had been searching for since the morning of September 26.*
>
> At 2030 hours, no less than 45 minutes after sighting the unidentified ship, Russell reports sighting a "*Blue Rocket*" bearing 130°

---

[42] Strom and Cunningham, *Special Investigative Report #1,* p. 29.
[43] Ibid.
[44] Ibid., p. 31.
[45] Ibid.
[46] The *U.S.S. Santee*

True. For those who may not know, a blue rocket is a bluish/white pyrotechnic flare with an attached parachute used tor the purposes of illumination.[47]

Then, abruptly, Lt. Russell also ceases recording in his log.

E. Pulling it All Together

Strom and Cunningham then begin to pull together their evidence in order to construct a new scenario. Obviously, they believe that the stricken ship that the *Santee* group and the *Furuseth* had raced westward to rescue was the DE 173, stricken by the disastrous results to the crew – and evidently the ship – of a full scale test of the Experiment. The reports of enemy submarine activity was a diversion, but a diversion not intended for the public, but rather, for the many hundreds of Navy sailors involved in the rescue operation, as well as in the convoy itself.[48] How then account for the sudden silence of Lts. Dodge and Russell in their logbooks? The fact that they both ceased recording entries within an hour of each other is "a good indication that an order was sent out to all ships to stop the recording of operational data in the deck logs until further notified," a procedure in fact authorized un Naval regulations when conducting special operations.[49]

And what of the flares? Recall that both the *Tarazed* and Lt. Russell both recorded seeing flares, bearing 130° True. Russell, however, had seen a bluish flare, and the *Tarazed* a green one. But Commodore Atkins, it will be remembered, *did not record the date* when he reported the sighting of the green flare. The green flare was sent up, in Strom's and Cunningham's reasoning, as a kind of coded signal between the *Santee* group and Commodore Atkins, as his convoy finally caught up with the carrier group, that "all was clear," meaning most likely that is was "safe to approach," that all incriminating evidence had been removed from the stricken and rescued ship.[50]

---

[47] Strom and Cunningham, *Special Investigative Report #1*, pp. 31, 33, italiczed and boldface emphasis added.

[48] Ibid., p. 33.

[49] Ibid.

[50] Ibid., p. 34.

Some sixteen hours after sending up the green flare, GUS-15's Commander Hoffman then dispatched priority traffic to the base in Bermuda, a message meant "to inform and update all of the ship units and commands that were involved with this incident."[51] But Hoffman's actual message is a heartstopper:

> *At 280014Z in 35-50 47-16 sighted green very star, investigating vessel unable to locate source. Prospects good something was or is there.*[52]

Strom and Cunningham spell out the implications of this deliberately selected language in no uncertain terms:

> How, after sending an investigating vessel in the area where the flare was visually sighted, could Hoffman *still believe something was or is still there? Could it be that the experimental ship was still displacing water, and couldn't be seen? Better yet, how could a ship, whether friend or foe, get well within the boundary of the protected umbrella of Navy escorts as Commodore Atkins described, and at the same time evade radar detection?*[53]

This reconstruction, obviously, has a great deal to commend it, and it casts a whole new light on the story of the Philadelphia Experiment.

Clearly, Strom and Cunningham's research indicates a great deal of effort was expended by the U.S. Navy to cover-up something that had happened near Bermuda from September 26-28, a time frame close enough, perhaps, to Allende's insistence on October as the time he observed the Experiment and its results. The Navy, as was seen, went to great effort to camouflage the movements not only of the S.S. *Andrew Furuseth,* but also of convoy GUS-15's carrier escort group.

But it raises as many questions as it answers, and perhaps Strom and Cunningham intended to address these questions in their full-length book. Whether or not they shall ever do so, remains to be seen. However, in view of the fact that they seem to have

---

[51] Strom and Cunningham, *Special Investigative Report #1,* p. 35.

[52] Ibid., emphasis added.

[53] Ibid., bold and italicized emphasis added, italicized emphasis in the original.

disappeared, or at least, no longer want to be contacted, we must raise these questions and attempt to speculate on the answers for ourselves.

From all that has been surveyed in the previous and present chapters, it is apparent that the incident (that Strom and Cunningham finally placed where Allende said it occurred – *at sea)* was the full-scale test that ran into those "unanticipated non-linear results." In this light, it is perhaps significant that the Experiment took place close to Bermuda, the region that first set Charles Berlitz on the trail of the Philadelphia Experiment story. It is perhaps even worth mentioning that the Sci-Fi channel's miniseries, *The Triangle* made a deliberate connection between the Triangle and the Experiment. Again, *perhaps* the famous "Triangle" played a role in the resulting unanticipated non-linear effects.

Its accidental character is confirmed by their new interpretation of the final phase of the Experiment's history, for it is apparent that the field, once engaged, not only rendered the ship radar invisible, but optically invisible as well. In fact, the Navy seems to have *lost* the ship altogether, and sent other ships looking for it. Whether or not this may have something to do with the "teleportation" result that Allende also mentions cannot be known. At best it remains, thanks to the speculations of the Corums and Daum, a mathematical "maybe."

But, in the final analysis, whatever one makes of these questions and speculations, the fact remains that by uncovering the documentation that they did, they have given the *historical* aspects of the Experiment and of Allende's allegations fresh validation and a new history.

Green Very Star Message of Convoy GUS-15 to CINCLANT

DECLASSIFIED
SECRET

ORIGINAL

ACTION REPORT

COMMANDER TASK GROUP 21.11
(COMMANDING OFFICER, (USS SANTEE))

SERIAL 0027   12 OCTOBER 1943

HUNTER/KILLER GROUP OPERATIONS, REPORT OF.

REPORT OF OPERATIONS IN NORTH ATLANTIC.
AIR COVERAGE WAS PROVIDED FOR CONVOYS
UGS-16 AND GUS-15 AND ASW OPERATIONS
WERE CONDUCTED ON DETACHED DUTY DURING
26 AUGUST - 12 OCTOBER 1943.

NAVAL HISTORY DIVISION

Anti-Submarine Action Report of USS Santee Carrier Group

DECLASSIFIED
NND 908/33
by OI

NAVY DEPARTMENT

DRAFTER	EXTENSION NUMBER	ADDRESSEES	PRECEDENCE	1
		ASTERISK (*) MAILGRAM ADDRESSEES		2

FROM CINCLANT (INDEF CALL)

RELEASED BY

DATE 26 SEPT 1943

TOR CODEROOM 0129

DECODED BY SAPP

PARAPHRASED BY SCHNEIDER

ROUTED MILL

FOR ACTION	CTG 21.11	ROUTINE
	CTG 21.4	
	COM 10TH FLT	DEFERRED
	COMINCH	
INFORMATION	CTF 64	
	COMMORSEAFRON	PRIORITY
	CTF 61	
	CTF 62	ROUTINE
	CTG 21.12	
	COMAIRLANT	DEFERRED

PRIORITY ... 4
ROUTINE ... 5
DEFERRED ... 7, 8
... 9, 10
PRIORITY ... 11, 12
ROUTINE ... 13, 14
DEFERRED ... 15, 16

UNLESS OTHERWISE INDICATED THIS DISPATCH WILL BE TRANSMITTED WITH DEFERRED PRECEDENCE

252307   NCR 1355

ORIGINATOR FILL IN DATE AND TIME   DATE   TIME   OCT

ON OUTGOING DISPATCHES PLEASE LEAVE ABOUT ONE INCH CLEAR SPACE BEFORE BEGINNING TEXT

CINCLANT ORIGINATOR.

RELIEVED OF TASK OF SUPPORTING TF 61. REMAIN IN
AZORES AREA GIVING SUPPORT TO OTHER GUS-UGS
CONVOYS AND TO IO CONVOYS UNTIL SUCH TIME AS
NECESSARY TO ARRIVE NORFOLK 12 OCTOBER UNLESS
EARLIER ARRIVAL REQUIRED BY LOGISTIC NEEDS.

FX37...19...19C...FILE....

GUS-15

TOR NCR 260445

S E C R E T

Make original only. Deliver to Code Room Watch Officer in person. (See Art. 76 (4) NAVREGS.)
OPNAV-NCR-15   U. S. GOVERNMENT PRINTING OFFICE 16—28312 a—6

October 3, 1943

From: Lt.(jg) Edward J. Russell, USNR., Armed Guard Commander
          Aboard SS Andrew Furuseth

To: Vice Chief of Naval Operations, Washington, D. C.

Via: *PO S N O*

Subject: Return Voyage Report

1. Ship data:

   a. Name of Vessel: SS Andrew Furuseth.
   b. Type of Vessel: Steam Cargo.
   c. Gross Tonnage: 7182 Gross Tons.
   d. Owner of Vessel: War Shipping Administration.
   e. Chartered by: War Shipping Administration.
   f. Agent: Matson Navigation Company.
   g. Sub Agent: Isthmian Steamship Company, New York,
                         N. Y.

2. Departures and Arrivals:

   a. Departed Casablanca, Morocco, September 13, 1943 at 1615.
   b. *arrived Norfolk, Va. October 3, 1943.*

3. Unusual Incidents:

   a. September 18, 1943:
      2105 -- Sighted white flash on horizon off starboard--
             nothing on TBY.

      2113 -- Sighted another white flash at approximately
             the same position. No developments.

      DECLASSIFIED
      NND 750065
      By NHL   NARS, Date 4/2/91

S.S. Andrew Furuseth's Armed Guard Reports (Lt. J.G. Russell)

3. Unusual Incidents: (Continued)

    b. September 20, 1943:

        1625 -- Aft lookout sighted what seemed to be one
            man on a life raft passing off our starboard
            quarter between our column and the next. Es-
            cort Commander was notified by TBY. Apparent-
            ly escort astern of us given instructions, for
            it immediately investigated the raft. No move-
            ment of man noted on raft and no further devel-
            opments.

    c. September 22, 1943:

        0705 -- Carrier based plane sighted off port bow.

        1010 -- Carrier sighted off Starboard bow of Convoy.

    d. September 24, 1943:

        1339 -- Captain reported having felt depth charges --
            TBY manned and nothing reported. It was the
            Captain's opinion that it must have been a noise
            from the ship. Gun crew lookouts had nothing to
            report. No developments.

    e. September 26, 1943:

        1010 -- Carrier departed from Convoy.

    f. September 27, 1943:

        0240 -- Lookouts reported three depth charges.
            General Alarm immediately sounded and TBY
            manned.

        0255 -- Conversation between Escort Commander and
            attacking vessel was overheard on TBY to the
            effect that contact was lost.

        0327 -- Secured General Quarters and resumed normal
            sea watch.

        1905 -- Dusk General Quarters.

        1008 -- Overheard over TBY that destroyer abaft our
            port beam had a contact and that she was pre-
            paring to lay a pattern of depth charges. At-
            tacking vessel was told to proceed with plan;

S.S. Andrew Furuseth's Armed Guard Report 2

CONFIDENTIAL

3. Unusual Incidents: (Continued)
    f. September 27, 1943: (Continued)
        1008 --
            however, contact was lost before depth charges
            could apparently be dropped. Attacking vessel
            was ordered to return to her convoy position.

        1945 -- Sighted fire on stern of ship three or four
            columns over off our Starboard beam.

        1950 -- Fire on ship apparently distinguished.

        2010 -- Secured General Quarters after having re-
            ceived no further developments on contact. Re-
            sumed normal sea watch.

        2030 -- Sighted blue rocket bearing 130 degrees true.
            No developments.

    g. September 28, 1943:
        1435 -- Emergency turn to port. General Alarm immedi-
            iately sounded and TBY manned. Received inform-
            ation to the effect that objects were seen float-
            ing ahead of convoy and that it was possible to
            clear them.

        1445--- Emergency turn to Starboard was made.

        1450 -- Secured General Quarters and resumed normal
            sea watch.

    h. September 29, 1943:
        1703 -- Overheard conversation between Escort Comman-
            der and destroyer on our port bow to the effect
            that objects, similar to mines, were floating
            ahead of the Convoy, and that an emergency turn
            would be made. Gun crew put on the alert -- used
            binoculars on bow and bridge and 20 mm's #1 and
            #2 were loaded.

        1705 -- Emergency turn made to Starboard.

        1708 -- Overheard conversation between escorts on TBY
            to the effect that they should return to their
            stations.

S.S. Andrew Furuseth Armed Guard Report 3

CONFIDENTIAL

3. Unusual Incidents: (Continued)
   h. September 29, 1943: (Continued)
      1710 -- Emergency turn to port was made.

      1715 -- Secured the alert and instructed bow watch
      to use binocular in covering their assigned
      arcs.

   i. September 30, 1943:
      1010 -- Sighted friendly plane -- believed to be
      from Bermuda.

      2055 -- Light sighted off port bow. One ship fully
      lit -- TBY manned and from coded conversation,
      assumed it to be a neutral ship.

      2105 -- Sighted another ship fully lit approximately
      five miles astern of the above ship off our
      port bow. TBY manned and from conversation
      learned that ship's course would be altered to
      miss Convoy.

   j. October 3, 1943:
      2140 -- Sighted first lighted buoy outside Norfolk,
      Va.

S.S. Andrew Furuseth Armed Guard Report 4

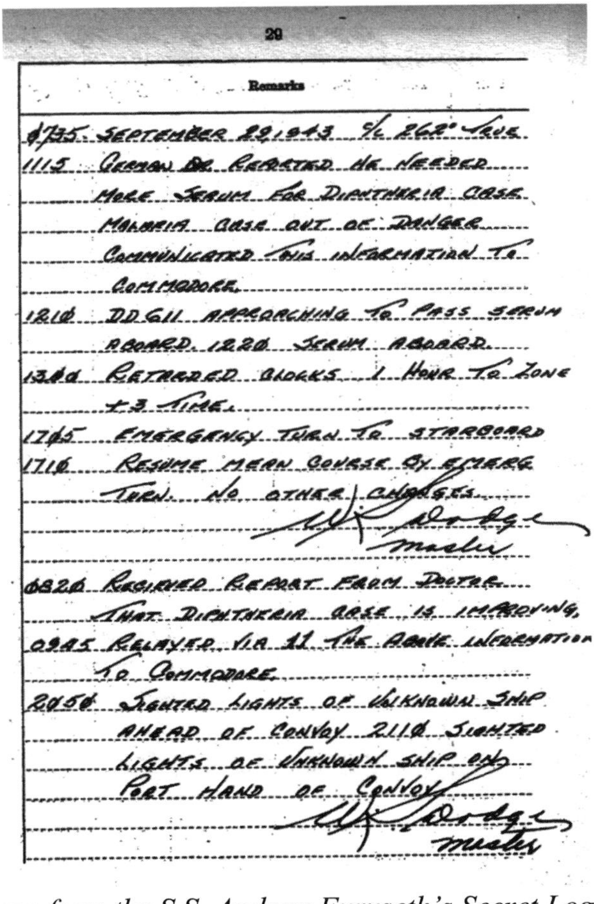

29

Remarks

0735 SEPTEMBER 29 1943 C/C 262° TRUE
1115 GERMAN DR. REPORTED HE NEEDED
MORE SERUM FOR DIPHTHERIA CASE.
MALARIA CASE OUT OF DANGER.
COMMUNICATED THIS INFORMATION TO
COMMODORE.
1210 DD 611 APPROACHING TO PASS SERUM
ABOARD. 1220 SERUM ABOARD.
1300 RETARDED CLOCKS 1 HOUR TO ZONE
+3 TIME.
1705 EMERGENCY TURN TO STARBOARD
1710 RESUME MEAN COURSE BY EMERG
TURN. NO OTHER CHANGES.
Master
0820 RECEIVED REPORT FROM DOCTOR
THAT DIPHTHERIA CASE IS IMPROVING.
0945 RELAYED VIA 11 THE ABOVE INFORMATION
TO COMMODORE.
2050 SIGHTED LIGHTS OF UNKNOWN SHIP
AHEAD OF CONVOY 2110 SIGHTED
LIGHTS OF UNKNOWN SHIP ON
PORT HAND OF CONVOY
Master

A Page from the S.S. Andrew Furuseth's Secret Logbook

Reg. No. 4 37 5 99

R.S. No.

WAR DIARY

U. S. NAVAL OPERATING BASE

BERMUDA

SEPTEMBER 1943

E44

From: The Commandant.

To: The Commander in Chief, U. S. Fleet

RECEIVED S-C FILES
Room 2055
8 NOV 1943
ROUTE TO:- 30
Op File No. A12-1/NB28
Doc. No. 98999
Copy No. ...

Return to comirich

)9462 **FILMED**

SECRET

Bermuda Naval Operations Base War Diary Cover

S.S. Andrew Furuseth Secret Logbook Cover

LOG BOOK

OF THE

U. S. S. _____ TARAZED _____

_____ AF13 _____ Rate,

COMMANDED BY

_____ RAYMOND W. CHAMBERS, _____ COMMANDER, _____ , U. S. Navy, R.

Attached to {
_____ Division,
_____ Squadron,
_____ ATLANTIC _____ Fleet,

Commencing _____ 0000 1 September, _____ , 19 43 ,

at _____ AT SEA _____ ,

and ending _____ 2400 30 September _____ , 19 43 ,

at _____ AT SEA.

U.S.S. Tarazed Deck Log Cover

9.
CONCLUSIONS, COVER-UPS, CABALS, AND CONNECTIONS

"The mystery of the Philadelphia Experiment has not yet been clarified, and its eventual answer may lie deep within the files of the Department of the Navy."
Charles Berlitz and William Moore[1]

If anything reveals the fact that the Philadelphia Experiment is a story that will not go away, it is the fact that almost two decades had passed between the work of Berlitz and Moore, and the Corum-Daum scientific proof of concept experiments and mathematical analysis of torsion; and that nearly *three* decades had passed between the work of Berlitz and Moore and the historical reconstructions of Strom and Cunningham.

These two very different approaches – the Corum's and Daum's scientific one and the historical one of Strom and Cunningham – are the surest signs that a cover-up *is* in place regarding this story, that the Navy *is* dissembling when it says no such experiments ever took place nor any such technology developed during World War Two. They are the surest sign as well, that there is more work to be done, that there is more research to do, and more documents to pry loose from government vaults and archives.

What *has* emerged from our two track investigation, however, is, astonishingly, that *most* of Carlos Miguel Allende's sensational allegations concerning the experiment have either some basis in solid science, or at least in solid scientific speculation, and moreover, that most of his detailed clues and hints about the timing and location of the Experiment are themselves within the bounds of historical plausibility.

Even Allende's bizarre assertions that the whole Experiment was hatched from hard-boiled scientific considerations of the engineering possibilities of Einstein's 1928 Unified Field Theory and its torsion tensor has been shown to be the *most likely conceptual candidate* for the Experiment, a theory that, moreover,

---

[1] Berlitz and Moore, *The Philadelphia Experiment,* p. 181.

is capable of sustaining even the wildest of Allende's allegations: optical invisibility and teleportation.

Obviously, there had been a cover-up regarding the events, the location, the results, and the technologies and actual details of the physics used in the Experiment. And this implies someone to do the covering-up. It implies that somewhere in the government there is a group of people whose responsibility it is to ensure that no significant and conclusive data about the Experiment ever sees the light of day.

It implies, too, that perhaps one reason that Einstein's 1928 Unified Field Theory was sidelined was not that it was theoretically incomplete, as the standard and public version of science history would have it, but rather, because it was eminently engineerable *even though* incomplete. And if the results of the Philadelphia Experiment were in fact achieved, as the evidence presented here indicates, then there was every reason to sideline the theory as much as possible.

The U.S. Navy would have realized – again, if the results that Allende alleges were achieved – that it had stumbled on something truly significant, whose weaponization potential, whose propulsion and travel and energy production potentials, were all implications of the conceptual foundations and achieved results of the Experiment. Thus if, as the Corums and Daum argued, it would have been a dereliction of duty for the Navy *not* to have investigated the means of electromagnetic radar stealth, then by the same token it would have been dereliction of duty for it not to investigate these potentials after the results – unanticipated though they were – of the full scale Experiment were achieved.

Rotation, torsion and non-linear effects, were the core of that Experiment, and these in turn, depended upon that small mathematical tensor transform that Einstein had included in his 1928 Unified Field Paper.

And the Germans, on the other side of the war, could do the mathematics, too...

PART THREE:
THE NAZI BELL AND THE
INTENTIONAL WEAPON

"According to the SS man, Hitler had a hidden facility in the mountains of the Harz region. There, deep under a mountain Hitler had constructed a time machine."
Henry Stevens,
Hitler's Suppressed and Still-Secret Weapons, Science, and Technology, p. 249.

"In connection with this high-energy research, various mysterious 'transmitters' were erected at several 'key points' in the Reich. In 1938 the Brocken, a celebrated peak in the Harz Mountains, was the site of feverish construction work."
Nigel Pennick, cited in Henry Stevens,
Hitler's Suppressed and Still-Secret Weapons, Science, and Technology, p. 172.

10.
THE ALLIES MISS THE CLUES

"Missing technology is a clue that something is wrong. Missing technology is missing because it has been suppressed. If technology is suppressed, then there is a suppressor."
Henry Stevens[1]

As many historians and researchers of Nazi secret weapons have repeatedly pointed out, when the advancing Allied armies rolled into the collapsing Third Reich, teams of special intelligence officers were in the vanguard, entering Germany's many secret research facilities, and literally suctioning every conceivable technological advance, patent, and document out of the Reich in what would go down as the largest technology transfer in history. As they did so, they were confronted with a vast and bewildering array of secret weapons projects encompassing everything from exotic conventional technologies such as prototype digital computers, semi-conductors, miniaturized klystron tubes, phased radar arrays, heat- and infrared-seeking missiles, television-guided missles, wire-guided missiles and torpedoes, acoustic homing torpedoes, U-boats that could cruise to sustainable underwater speeds of 21 knots, and radar stealth materials, to technologies that were not only exotic but downright bizarre and seemingly only the stuff of science fiction: acoustic and electromagnetic "death rays", foo fighters, allegations of flying saucers, super-dense metal alloys, sonic oil distillation and refinement, electrical rail guns, wind and vortex cannon... and on and on the list could go.

For many in the British and American teams assigned the monumental task of securing, cataloguing, and analyzing this vast arsenal, it was nothing more than an indicator not only of how desperate the Nazi regime had become, but also how woefully inefficient it had been in squandering its precious human and material resources on what – for all intents and purposes – appeared to be nothing more than an irrational and ultimately

---

[1] Henry Stevens, *Hitler's Suppressed and Still-Secret Weapons, Science, and Technology* (Kempton, Illinois: Adventures Unlimited Press, 2007), p. ii.

unsuccessful hodgepodge of "get victory quick super-weapons" schemes. And to some extent this was true.

Moreover, this apparently irrational hodgepodge and squandering of scarce resources led many post-war Allied apologists to speculate that it was also one of the main causes, if not the *main* cause, for Germany's failure to obtain the atom bomb prior to the end of the war. This version of the Allied Legend of Nuclear Superiority maintained that Germany had frittered away the scientific and technological advantages that she had begun the war with, on projects many of which could only be characterized as charlatanry. For other versions of the Allied Legend the hodgepodge was the ultimate symbol of an insane and irrational regime, and of its utter and abject scientific and technological failure.

But as I outlined in my earlier book *Reich of the Black Sun: Nazi Secret Weapons and the Cold War Allied Legend*, a strong circumstantial case can be made that the Nazi atom bomb project was much more successful – horrendously so – than the post-war Allied Legend would have us believe. It was so successful, in fact, that it has every appearance of having been deliberately obfuscated and buried by the victorious Allies because it was achieved in complete secrecy under the auspices of the very branch that the Allied Legend wished the public to associate with the Nazi regime's irrationality, inefficiency, corruption, and brutality: the Waffen SS. That it was achieved by that Nazi agency was a part of the story that made it convenient for the Allies to concoct their Legend, for the Nazi atom bomb was achieved at the cost of the incalculable human suffering and misery of the concentration camp slave labor that made it possible.[2] Moreover, there are even two specific indications that Nazi atomic success very likely contributed to subsequent American atomic success in the Manhattan Project.[3] If the Allies did indeed use Nazi technology to

---

[2] See my *Reich of the Black Sun,* Part One, for this story.
[3] The two specific instances are (1) the probable use by the Manhattan Project of enriched Nazi U235 to supply the missing amount of uranium needed for a critical mass for a bomb, an amount that, as late as March of 1945, according to the Manhattan District's own records, it was short of and would only obtain – by using solely American sources – in November of 1945, well

complete their own atom bomb project, a technology bought at the cost of enormous human suffering, then there was more than political motivation for the creation of the Allied Legend.

But there is more.

Among the hodgepodge of bizarre research projects there were scattered clues that the Nazis were indeed deliberately researching the possibilities of weapons based on electromagnetic energy. And scattered among *these,* there were further clues that the Nazi regime was researching the possibilities of a weapon based on torsion physics and the tearing of the space-time continuum, the same kind of physics that led to the astonishing and unanticipated results of the Philadelphia Experiment. The Nazis were in effect after a kind of "torsion bomb." The clues, however, were not only scattered throughout the hodgepodge of projects the Allied intelligence teams encountered as they entered the Reich, but the projects themselves were similarly spread across the landscape of Nazi Germany. The Allied intelligence teams can therefore hardly be blamed for having missed the clues, for who would have reasonably thought that the Nazis were after a weapon that was potentially far more destructive than mere atom bombs? But there was a final reason the clues were missed besides their dispersion across the catalogue of projects and the landscape of Germany.

They were missed because, like so many other cases of classified research in Nazi Germany, they were most likely being coordinated by the super-secret think tank of SS *Obergruppen-führer* Dr. Ing. Hans Kammler, the *Kammlerstab.* The hodgepodge of secret weapons, at least in some cases, was no hodgepodge at all; it was all being secretly coordinated, but unless one knew of this controlling and coordinating agency, one would miss the clues. And it is true that most members of the Allied intelligence teams vacuuming the Reich of her technology and patents had never even

---

after Little Boy was dropped on Hiroshima. Where did the extra enriched uranium come from? There is only one other option: Nazi Germany. (2) The Manhattan District also most likely was forced, due to the difficulties inherent in using plutoniam for a bomb, to employ German infrared proximity fuses in the implosion detonator that assembled the plutonium in a super-critical mass, and tested for the first time at the Trinity site in New Mexico in July of 1945. Again, for these aspects of the story, see my *Reich of the Black Sun,* part one, and Carter P. Hyrick's superb study, *Critical Mass.*

heard of Kammler, much less that he headed the world's largest secret weapons think tank.

A. The Kammlerstab and Its Survival:
Missing the Clues of the Shape of the Post-War Nazi International

As recounted in my previous books on wartime Nazi secret weapons research, *Reich of the Black Sun: Nazi Secret Weapons and the Cold War Allied Legend,* and *The SS Brotherhood of the Bell: NASA's Nazis, JFK, and Majic-12,* much of the most highly classified Nazi secret weapons research, including their most highly classified weapon, the Bell,[4] was coordinated by a super-secret think tank housed within the engineering division of the Skoda Munitions Works in Pilsen, Czechoslovakia.

SS *Obergruppenführer* Dr. Ing Hans Kammler headed the think tank. Born on August 26, 1901 in the German Baltic port city of Stettin, Kammler held a doctorate in engineering, and, by dint of his command of all German secret weapons research *and* of the SS' Building and Works Department, could tap into a slave labor pool of perhaps as many as 14 *million* people.[5]

Within the Skoda Works, Kammler had established a think tank whose mission brief was to map out technology trees for first, second, third, and even fourth generations of weapons of every conceivable variety, including nuclear weapons *and weapons far more destructive.*[6] Since Kammler also spoke Czech, his choice of Skoda inside of Bohemian Czechoslovakia to headquarter his think tank was entirely logical, for Bohemia had been made a Reich Protectorate, and fell under the immediate jurisdiction of the SS. The SS had, in effect, turned all of Bohemia into a military reservation which to enter or leave required proper SS authorization and clearances. The SS had in effect turned a whole country into the Nazi equivalent of the Nevada test ranges. And

---

[4] Q.v. Igor Witkowski, *The Truth About the Wunderwaffe,* pp. 255-256, and my *SS Brotherhood of the Bell,* pp. 157-159.

[5] Henry Stevens, *Hitler's Suppressed and Still-Secret Weapons,* p. 1.

[6] For an outline of the first, second, and third generation nuclear weapons and its relevance to the Nazi atom bomb and Bell projects, see my *SS Brotherhood of the Bell,* pp. 283-287.

within this already cloistered country, Kammler had turned the engineering division of the Skoda Works into the nerve center of a vast secret weapons empire, a veritable rats' run of underground laboratories and production facilities, many of which were never even known to Allied intelligence until after the war.

This think tank existed behind a triple belt of security. Indeed, the *Kammlerstab's* security is itself "the last piece of the puzzle," for as researcher Henry Stevens puts the case, it was a puzzle

> because Kammler's security was never breached. It was not breached by the U.S., British Intelligence or even Soviet Intelligence which thought they knew everything. Kammler was able to pull Alberich's Cloak of Obscurity over himself and his staff using a triple-wall of counter-intelligence units, the political counter-intelligence unit, and the industrial counter-intelligence unit.
>
> This security arrangement was so successful that when the Allies began advancing into Germany in the early spring of 1945, nobody asked the local population anything about Kammler or the Kammler Group. Neither side knew anything at all about it. By the time the "boots on the ground" realized who Dr. Kammler and his organization really were, his very name became a forbidden subject. This was probably so lest the other Allied Powers, especially the Soviets, learn of any potential treasure trove of scientific secrets.[7]

Moreover, this triple belt of security not only answered to Kammler, but to another notorious figure in the Third Reich, Heinrich Müller, head of the Gestapo, and whose very nickname "Gestapo Müller," says it all. In any case, Stevens is correct; Kammler's think tank was never penetrated.

This, from the historical standpoint, is an interesting association of names, for Müller in turn owed his promotion to the upper echelons of Nazi power to none other than Martin Bormann. Müller had, with Bormann's connivance, turned a blind eye when as a local Munich police investigator he was called in to handle the suspicious suicide of Hitler's niece and then mistress, Geli Raubal, prior to the Nazi assumption of power. There was strong evidence that Hitler had either deliberately murdered her, or in a fit of rage, had killed her. Hitler had called Bormann, so the story goes, in a panic. Bormann calmly told him he would fix it. Bormann then

---

[7] Henry Stevens, *Hitler's Suppressed and Still-Secret Weapons,* pp. 4-5.

called Müller. And Müller suppressed the evidence, and for his efforts, became the chief of the notorious *Geheime Staatpolizei*. Small wonder then that, toward the end of the war, we find Bormann giving direct command of all of Germany's heavy lift aircraft, the Luftwaffe unit *Kampfgeschwader 200,* to Kammler, which he then used to smuggle himself and Nazi Germany's most sensitive secrets, including the Bell, out of Europe. Small wonder, then, that suspicions always abounded after the war that Bormann and Müller had also escaped after carefully contriving their "deaths."[8]

Bormann, Müller, and Kammler.

It is an interesting and unholy trinity to contemplate, for in it, one discerns the outlines of a very sinister shadow, the shadow of a post-war "Nazi International", beginning to emerge. Consider: if there was to be a post-war Nazi International continuing to develop its own secret projects, it would need lots of money and someone who knew how to handle it: Bormann; it would need lots of security and someone who knew how to run it: Müller; and lots of engineering expertise and management experience in coordinating large projects and keeping them secret: Kammler. And they would need a suitably advanced project to work on within the limits imposed by post-war circumstances. Large uranium enrichment plants for a-bombs were out, as were large, and very visible rocket gantries. Something truly sensational, which would not require large physical plants (other than large power supplies), and which could pay much larger dividends than any other of the above alternatives, was needed: the Bell.

But there are other discernible clues to the lineaments of this post-war Nazi International as well, and in my two previous books on this topic – *Reich of the Black Sun* and *The SS Brotherhood of the Bell* – I hinted at these, and it is now time to tie them all together into a more comprehensive package. In *The SS Brotherhood of the Bell* I observed the curious fact – often commented upon by other authors as well – that the early "Space

---

[8] For the story of Bormann placing Kammler in charge of the special "evacuation command" and placing him in charge of *Kampfgeschwader* 200, and the disappearance of the Bell, see Nick Cook's *The Hunt for Zero Point*, pp. 182 ff.

Race" between the Soviet Union and the United States gives every appearance of having been *contrived.* First one side would launch a series of probes, and then the other, and then back to the first. The launch schedules of the two superpowers has every appearance of having been coordinated.[9]But coordinated by whom? The only entity that has the requisite presence of personnel and hence penetration into both programs, the only entity for which there is actual *evidence*, is the Nazi penetration into both programs.

But this would require a further component, a means of *coordinating* the "marching orders" of its personnel in both programs, and it would also require that it have some historical connection with the Nazi war machine. Is there such an entity?

Yes.

Recall that it was General Reinhard Gehlen, head of the German Army's military intelligence branch, *Fremde Heere Ost* (Foreign Armies East) who approached Allen Dulles, America's OSS station chief in Zurich, in 1944 with a deal. The deal was that Gehlen would turn over to the nominal control of the American OSS his entire *Fremde Heere Ost*, Nazi Germany's entire intelligence apparatus in Eastern Europe and the Soviet Union, an organization that included thousands of agents, and scores of "émigré exile" societies from countries that fell under the Soviet yoke. This means that when Present Harry S. Truman signed the National Security Act of 1947 into law, creating the National Security Agency and the Central Intelligence Agency,[10] its civilian charter had already been compromised by the deal worked out between Dulles and Gehlen, for effectively that deal meant that the entire operational Soviet desk of the CIA was but a front office for a network of Nazis! Thus, once again, while one may speculate that other entities may have been involved in secret coordination of the Soviet and American space programs, *the only entities* **historically** *in evidence, and known to be in a position to do so are*

---

[9] Q.v. my *SS Brotherhood of the Bell,* pp. 121-123.

[10] Two agencies with their own "Nazi" resonances, for Nazi Germany had a similar such agency, the *Reichssicherheithauptamt,* or RSHA, the umbrella organization that covered the SS, the Gestapo, the SD and so on. Its basic meaning, when translated into English, is precisely Reich Security Department, or "national security agency," a kind of central intelligence clearing house.

the Nazi personnel present after the war in both programs, and the descendent organization of General Gehlen's Fremde Heere Ost. Indeed, that last organization was, per the agreement reached between Dulles and Gehlen, to be turned back over to German control once a sovereign post-war German government was constituted. Thus, the Gehlen Organization or "Gehlenorg" as it was known, actually became the foundation for the modern German equivalent of the CIA, the *Bundesnachrichtendienst* (BND). If there *was* a coordinating entity in the two superpowers' space programs, then this organization, the Gehlenorg, was most likely the actual on-the-ground pipeline between the two.

And this puts an entirely new spin on the Kennedy assassination as well. This author remembers in the early 1970s a series of articles that appeared in the French and British press, attributing the ultimate orders for the assassination as having originated with none other than Martin Bormann, now very elderly, but, according to the articles, very much alive and well in South America, and still very much "in control." The articles would have been dismissible as sheerest fantasia if they had not appeared in such prestigious papers as the British *Guardian.*

Is it, however, so far fetched? It was, after all, Allen Dulles whom Kennedy had fired for the Bay of Pigs invasion fiasco, the same Allen Dulles who brokered the deal with General Gehlen. And it was the same Allen Dulles who, in the ultimate irony, was chosen by Lyndon Johnson as one of the members of the Warren Commission investigating the assassination. But the most important clue to a possible Nazi involvement was Kennedy's threat "to smash the CIA into a thousands pieces" and turn all covert operations over to the direct control of the military. Viewed against the backdrop of the Dulles-Gehlen deal, Kennedy's threat is revealed as nothing less than a threat to smash the very cover umbrella for a network of Nazis inside of American intelligence. This *would* constitute sufficient motivation for a Nazi involvement in the assassination.

And finally, there was Oswald's notebook itself. As I pointed out in *The SS Brotherhood of the Bell*, Oswald's notebook contained the addresses and phone numbers of some very unusual contacts: that of Dallas FBI agent James Hosty is well-known;

right-wing American General Walker – whom Oswald wa.
accused of trying to assassinate – less so. But what n.
Americans never hear about is that Oswald's address book also
contained the name and phone number of one last, and most
interesting, person: George Lincoln Rockwell, president of the
American Nazi Party.[11]

Of course, if conspiracy researchers are correct and Oswald
was being "sheepdipped", i.e., deliberately told to cultivate certain
types of extremist contacts for what he thought was a "mission,"
when in fact it was nothing but an attempt to make him look like a
"lone nut," then the presence of these names is explicable, if not
unusual.

However, there is a problem with this explanation as well.
During the time that Oswald was in Atsugi, Japan supposedly
receiving training in Russian, one of Oswald's marine buddies –
according to the Warren Report itself – supposedly overheard
Oswald speaking a language he believed was German. Russian *and*
German linguistic training? Oswald, in other words, gives every
appearance of being handled by the CIA, as many JFK
assassination researchers have concluded. *But what they have
missed is that Oswald also gives every appearance of being
handled by the Gehlenorg, acting as the mediator between him and
his CIA handlers.*

What has all this to do with the outlines of a Nazi
International? Consider what has been outlined. We have:

1) Penetration into sensitive military and space projects by
   German personnel after the end of the war, both in the
   United States and in the Soviet Union;
2) Penetration into American intelligence via the Gehlenorg by
   German intelligence agents and networks, agents and
   networks, moreover, with a large on-the-ground presence in
   Eastern Europe and the Soviet Union;
3) And, as I outlined in *SS Brotherhood of the Bell*, a highly
   suspicious German financial connection to the assassination
   of JFK with the German-Argentine firm of Bunge and

---

[11] *The SS Brotherhood of the Bell*, p. 400.

Born, which profited immensely by carefully placed short-sell orders on Wall Street on the day of the assassination.[12]

Finance. Intelligence. Science. The outlines are writ large in the events of the decades following World War Two. But they were already visible with the less-than-convincing "deaths" of the unholy trinity who were the ikons of that post-war outline:
Bormann. Müller. And Kammler:
Finance. Intelligence. And Science.

But back to Kammler and the *Kammlerstab* itself.
The fact that it had not been penetrated during the war by any Allied or Soviet intelligence operation led both Igor Witkowski, in his book *The Truth About the Wunderwaffe,* and I in my books *Reich of the Black Sun* and *The SS Brotherhood of the Bell,* to speculate that U.S. General Patton's Third Army thrusts into Bohemia, Austria, and south central Germany and the Harz Mountain region were too precisely coordinated with some of Kammler's most secret facilities to be coincidental. Rather, they seem to have been steered to their objectives by someone highly placed in U.S. Intelligence.

However, given the *Kammlerstab's* extreme secrecy and security countermeasures – all coordinated by Gestapo Müller - then this makes it very likely that the source of these intelligence objectives came from within the Kammler Group itself, from someone equally highly placed, perhaps even Kammler himself, who turned traitor as the was drew near its end. Another possibility is Bormann, for as researcher Carter Hydrick has pointed out, the German U-Boat, U-234 - which was carrying canisters of highly enriched uranium 235, infrared proximity fuses, their inventor, and two Japanese officers, to Japan – made every effort to surrender itself to American, and *only* American authorities after the German capitulation. Carter speculates, offering a great deal of evidence, that it was Bormann himself who brokered this deal. And given Bormann's placement and association with Müller and Kammler, he alone, along with the other two men, would have been in a

---

[12] *The SS Brotherhood of the Bell,* pp. 403-411.

position to know the entire catalogue of weaponry being developed by Kammler's think tank, and where the facilities doing the research were located. So the conclusion is inevitable: the ultimate source guiding General Patton's Third Army movements at the end of the war is likely to be one of three men: Bormann, Müller, or Kammler. And the go-between for these sensitive and delicate transfers of information and objectives would likely have been either SS General Wolff, already negotiating with Allen Dulles for the surrender of German forces in northern Italy, or General Reinhard Gehlen, already angling to preserve German military intelligence in Eastern Europe after the war.

*Two Views of SS Obergruppenführer Dr. Ing. Hans Kammler:
On the Left, Kammler's Nazi Party Identification Photo, on the
Right Kammler in Full SS Dress Uniform*

A More Familiar Picture of SS General Kammler, as his Many Thousands of Victims Would Have Seen Him

B. The Scattered Clues to the Science

There are, however, other types of clues that the Allies missed, besides the ones pointing to a highly organized effort to constitute a post-war Nazi International.[13] These were the clues that should have alerted the Allied intelligence teams entering Nazi Germany that the Germans were investigating a form of physics potentially far more destructive than mere atom or, worse, mere hydrogen bombs. Not surprisingly, these clues hid themselves among secret projects that, by contrast, looked comparatively benign, from weapons referred to as "methods to stop motors," to some mysterious – and to date ill-understood – secret installations along the Rhine valley, to a little town east of Berlin called Gut Alt Golssen, and even to rumors of a super-secret "time machine" buried in the Harz Mountains of Thuringia in south central Germany! We shall consider each of these scattered clues in turn.

---

[13] Of course, Allied intelligence was well aware of Bormann's plans for a strategic evacuation of Nazi economic and technical resources out of Germany after the war, and, as far as it could, rolled up many of these operations. But the fact of the matter remains, that many of them completely escaped, like General Kammler on his Junkers 390 six-engine long range airplane, the Bell, and all its project documentation.

1. The "Motorstoppmittel," or "Method to Stop Motors"

While the rest of the UFOlogy world was happily writing off stories of Nazi flying saucers as an unsubstantiated myth promulgated by disillusioned German veterans or post-war pro-Nazi sympathizers, researcher Henry Stevens quietly continued to research the story, undeterred by the fashions and fads of UFOlogy, eager as it was to crown and anoint ET as its favored hypothesis to explain all sightings not otherwise accounted for. During the process, he also unearthed and documented a wealth of hitherto unknown details about Nazi secret weapons, research that rivals in the scope of its detail and significance the work of Polish researcher Igor Witkowski.

One of these forgotten Nazi technologies was the *Motorstopp-mittel* or "means" or "method to stop motors." There is an unusual set of circumstances surrounding this curious technology, circumstances that relate directly to the type of physics suggested by the Nazis' "war decisive" (*Kriegsentscheidend*) weapon, the Bell. Accordingly, Stevens' research concerning this device will be surveyed in detail:

> One of the first accounts of a test involving this device comes from Germany's Axis ally, Italy, in 1936. It involves no less than the electric genius Dr. Guglielmo Marconi, Italian leader Benito Mussolini, and Mussolini's wife.
>
> It seems that in 1936 Mrs. Mussolini informed her husband of her intention to travel on the Rome-Ostia highway in the afternoon. Mussolini told his wife she would experience something special if she made the trip between 3:00 and 3:30 P.M. As a matter of fact he said that she would be struck with wonder at seeing something. Mrs. Mussolini was at the prescribed place and time along with dozens of other cars both in front of her and behind her. What happened which was of such wonder was that their cars stopped running. Her Chauffer as well as other stranded motorists attempted to restart their vehicles but to no avail. At exactly 3:35 P.M. all the cars mysteriously restarted and proceeded normally.

> That evening Mussolini gave his wife the story behind her trouble. Marconi had invented something that halted engines. Pope Pius XI got wind of the experiment and called it the work of the devil.[14]

From there the device or its blueprints either made its way to Nazi Germany, or something similar was invented there.

When requesting information on the *Motorstoppmittel* through FOIA requests submitted to the American federal government, Stevens at first received nothing but "no record" responses of such a device ever having been learned about by the Allies.[15] However, Stevens was not unaware of the work of German researcher Friedrich Georg, who discovered what Stevens calls the "mini-Rosetta stone" of documentation concerning German wartime secret research, an official U.S. government document entitled "An Evaluation of German Capabilities in 1945," that ereferred to the device as a *Magnetic Wave!*[16] The implications and obvious conceptual connections to the Philadelphia Experiment of this terminology are immediately and obviously self evident. The terminology is eerily reminiscent of similar expressions from the Varo Annotated Edition, and similar to Jessup's own terminology surrounding his ideas concerning "invisible solidities".

Notes Stevens, "The American reports are based on many sources. There are reports from German scientists, from prisoners of war, and from the American military, all speaking of the same thing. They all describe an alleged German weapon able to made motor vehicles, including airplanes, stop running."[17] Needless to say, the reports caused some concern to American military leaders, and as a consequence, flights of aircraft were "even sent into areas suspected of being defended by this weapon in order to evaluate it."[18] Stevens mentions a report from January 24, 1945, of a flight of two P-38 fighters sent to reconnoiter one such area of suspect activity near Frankfurt-am-Main. British author Nigel Penneck summarized the operation:

---

[14] Stevens, *Hitler's Suppressed and Still-Secret Weapons,* p. 171.
[15] Ibid.
[16] Ibid., emphasis added.
[17] Ibid., p. 172.
[18] Ibid.

> In connection with this high-energy research, various mysterious "transmitters: were erected at several "key points" in the Reich. *In 1938 the Brocken, a celebrated peak in the Harz Mountains, was the site of feverish construction work....*
>
> *This "transmitter" was a strange contraption, a tower surrounded by an array of posts with pear-shaped knobs on top. At the same time a similar system was erected on the peak of the Feldberg near Frankfurt. When it began operation, there were soon reports of strange phenomena in the vicinity of the Brocken tower. Cars traveling along the mountain roads would suddenly have engine failure.* A Luftwaffe sentry would soon spot the stranded car, and tell the puzzled morotist that it was no use trying to get the car started at present. After a while, the sentry would tell the driver that the engine would work again now, and the car would then start up and drive away.[19]

Note now what we have: two antenna arrays atop mountain peaks in Germany, some distance from each other, and the same effects as were reported with Mussolini's device: stopped motor engines that would then be capable of restarting, presumably after the transmissions were stopped.[20]

But there's more.

One American P-38 pilot, Lt. Hitt, suddenly experienced the malfunction of his electrical instruments as he was flying on this mission near Frankfurt at approximately 17,000 feet altitude. "His fuel pressure indicator, rpm gauge, gyro gauge, artificial horizon gauge all started to malfunction.... *The gyro compass started spinning through 360 degrees revolutions.*"[21] Shades of the Bermuda Triangle! In addition, both engines on his twin-engine fighter started running very rough. As we shall see, this is another significant "missed clue," into the nature of the device the Americans called the "magnetic wave."

The other pilot, who was at least a mile away, experienced no such difficulties. When the pilots landed after their mission, the

---

[19] Stevens, *Hitler's Suppressed and Still-Secret Weapons,* p. 172, citing Nigel Penneck, *Hitler's Secret Sciences,* (Neville Spearman Limited, 1981), p. 189, emphasis added.

[20] There is also a slight physical resemblance between the description of the antenna array atop the Brocken and Nikola Tesla's Wardenclyffe Tower project, and a superficial resemblance to the HAARP phased antenna array.

[21] Stevens, op. cit., p. 175, emphasis added,

usual investigations were conducted on the mechanical and electrical systems of Lt. Hitt's P-38.

> The title of the final report reflects the verdict of the inquiry: "Preliminary Report on Suspected Magnetic Ray." This report was given "Secret" status and was produced by headquarters, United States Strategic Air Forces Europe (rear), Office of the Director of Intelligence, dated January 24, 1945.
> Even prior to this, a report had been generated by the Director of Intelligence, U.S. St. A.F., dated 12/6/44 and titled: "Engine Interference By Electro-Magnetic Disturbances." This was sub-titled on the second page: Project 1217, "Investigation Into German Possible Use of Rays to Neutralize Allied Aircraft Motors."[22]

Calculations were done by a British engineer to ascertain how large a facility would be needed for such a device, and it was concluded that it would have been a very large facility "using ground-based coils" that were "enormous in size and therefore impractical."[23] But then Stevens notes that "Obviously, the actual German device was a little more intelligent, adaptable, flexible and target specific than a simple, huge, ground-based, gigantic coil pumping out a single, steady pulse as envisioned by Hollywood."[24] This implies that the German device operated on different principles than what the Allies expected, given that the description of these antenna do not resemble that of a huge set of coils. What is of highest interest here are Lt. Hitt's spinning compass. A small clue, to be sure, but perhaps a significant one.

2. The Gut Alt Golssen Facility

An even more peculiar "missed clue" was an alleged facility at the town of Gut Alt Golssen, some thirty miles east of Berlin. British UFOlogist Nicholas Redfern recounts the story in his book *The F.B.I. Files: The FBI's UFO Top Secrets Exposed.* According to Redfern, the FBI's records reveal that this report was received by the agency on Nov. 7, 1957 after "news reports of a mysterious

---

[22] Stevens, *Hitler's Suppressed and Still-Secret Weapons,* p. 175. The Photostat of the report is reproduced by Stevens on p. 174.
[23] Ibid., p. 176.
[24] Ibid.,

vehicle in Texas *causing engines to stall*" prompted a witness to "communicate with the United States Government concerning a similar phenomenon observed by him in 1944 in the area of Gut Alt Golssen."[25] The witness, whose name has been deleted in the declassified version of the document, came to the Detroit office of the Bureau to file his report, which then passed it along to its headquarters in Washington, D.C.

It is worth citing this report extensively:

> (Witness was) born February 19, 1926 in the State of Warsaw, Poland (and) was brought from Poland as a Prisoner of War to Gut Alt Golssen approximately 30 miles east of Berlin, Germany, in May 1942, where he remained until a few weeks after the end of World War II. He spent the following years at Displaced Persons camps at Kork, Strasburg, Offenburg, Milheim and Freiburg, Germany. He attended a radio technician school at Freiburg and for about a year was employed in a textile mill at Laurachbaden, Germany. He arrived in the United States at New York, May 2, 1951, via the "SS General Stewart" as a Displaced Person...
>
> According to (witness), during 1944, month not recalled, while enroute to work in a field a short distance north of Gut Alt Golssen, their tractor engine stalled on a road through a swamp area. No machinery or other vehicle was then visible although a noise was heard *described as a high-pitched whine similar to that produced by a large electric generator.*

The "electric generator sound" is similar to the sound many of the Philadelphia Experiment witnesses heard.

> *An "SS" guard appeared and talked briefly with the German driver of the tractor,* who waited five to ten minutes, after which the noise stopped and the tractor engine was started normally. Approximately 3 hours later in the same swamp area, but away from the road where the work crew was cutting "hay," he surreptitiously, because of the German in charge of the crew and "SS" guards in the otherwise deserted area, observed *a circular enclosure approximately 100 to 150 yards in diameter* protected from viewers by a tarpaulin-type wall *approximately 50 feet high, from which a vehicle was observed to slowly rise vertically to a height sufficient to clear the wall and then to*

---

[25] FBI Report of Nov 7, 1957, cited in Nicholas Redfern, *The F.B.I. Files: The FBI's UFO Top Secrets Exposed,* (London: Simon and Schuster, 1998), p. 202, emphasis added.

move slowly horizontally a short distance out of his view, which was obstructed by nearby trees.

This vehicle, observed from approximately 500 feet, was described as circular in shape, 75 to 100 yards in diameter, and about 14 feet high. The approximate three foot middle section appeared to be a rapidly moving component producing a continuous blur similar to an aeroplane propeller, but extending the circumference of the vehicle so far as could be observed. The noise emanating from the vehicle was similar but of somewhat lower pitch than the noise previously heard. The engine of the tractor again stalled on this occasion and no effort was made by the German driver to start the engine until the noise stopped, after which the engine started normally.

Uninsulated metal, possibly copper, *cables one and one-half to two inches in diameter, on and under the surface of the ground, in some places covered by water,* were observed on this and previous occasions, *apparently running between the enclosure and a small concrete column-like structure between the road and enclosure.*

This area was not visited by (witness) again until shortly after the end of World War II, *when it was observed the cables had been removed and the previous locations of the concrete structure and the enclosure were covered by water.* (Witness) stated he has not been in communication since 1945 with any of the work crew of 16 or 18 men, consisting of Russian, French and Polish POWs, who had discussed this incident among themselves many times. However, of these, (Witness) was able to recall by name only (one), no address known, described as then about 50 years of age and presumed to have returned to Poland after 1945.[26]

There are a number of connections between this Polish POW's account of what he saw at Gut Alt Golssen, and the sound made by the Bell and the peculiar installations at its test site further south in Silesia at the Wenceslas Mine in Ludwigsdorf, northwest of Breslau.

One can only guess at the consternation that this report might have elicited at the highest levels of the American government, for not only does it clearly allude to the existence of some advanced form of "flying saucer" field propulsion test site near Berlin, a fact that would place very *advanced* technologies in the hands of the Nazis during the war, a technology that they can also clearly *handle,* but the location of Gut Alt Golssen itself would have given

---

[26] FBI Report of November 7, 1951, cited in Nicholas Redfern, *The FBI Files,* pp. 202-205, emphasis added.

rise to concern since it lay so deep inside the Soviet zone of post-war occupied Germany!

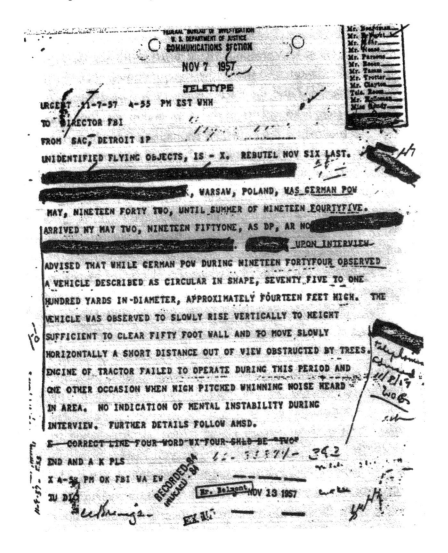

Portion of the FBI's "Gut Alt Golssen" Flying Saucer Report of November 7, 1951

Interesting as these lines of investigation might be, there are other even more intriguing possibilities indicated by the report of the anonymous witness cited in the document. We note the following items of interest:

1) The facility was apparently under the jurisdiction of the SS, since reference is made to SS guards. Given the time period in view in the document – 1944 – one must conclude that this is yet *another totally unknown* black project inside of Kammler's super-secret SS secret weapons "think tank,: and a very highly classified project, as we shall see in a moment;

2) The facility was apparently a test rig of some sort, *involving a large circular enclosure,* recalling the Henge structure near the Wenceslas Mine in Ludwigsdorff associated with the Bell; the connections and resemblances between the two sites are made even more compelling by the following:

3) The Gut Alt Golssen facility apparently used a great deal of *electricity,* a fact attested to by the distinctive "whine" described by the FBI's witness, but also by the presence of *heavy electrical cabling,* a feature which Igow Witkowski points out was also present at the Henge structure in Ludwigsdorff, a facility that required so *much* electricity, in fact, that it had to have its own power plant built in very close proximity, a fact that we shall consider in more detail in the next chapter;[27]

4) This connection is strengthened even more by the fact that both the Gut Alt Golssen facility and the Henge structure at Ludwigsdorff are both described in similar terms, as being both circular and *columnar and made of concrete*, and by the fact that water was associated with both structures. Witkowski points out that the Ludwigsdorff Henge was actually built in a basin of some sort, apparently for the collection of water or possibly to be filled with some other liquid. Similarly, the Gut Alt Golssen facility was vaguely connected with water by being placed in a swamp, and then later flooded over, apparently in an effort by the SS to conceal its existence from the Russians, which is very

---

[27] See Igor Witkowski, *The Truth About the Wunderwaffe,* pp. 263-268, for a complete discussion of the installations.

similar to what happened to the Bell's underground test facilities in the Wenceslas Mine in Ludwigsdorff: the SS flooded many of its underground galleries.

5) Finally, the Gut Alt Golssen device is observed actually flying – though no speed is given – and this in conjunction with the effect of stalling the engine of the nearby tractor.

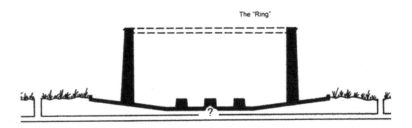

Igor Witkowski's Sketch of the Henge in its Basin at Ludwigsdorff, Courtesy of Igor Witkowski, The Truth About the Wunderwaffe[28]

A number of important questions are raised by this FNBI document and the Gut Alt Golssen facility. Did the witness in fact see what he saw near this small German town in Brandenburg? Or was he perhaps confused or even intentionally lying about the true location of the facility? Might he have perhaps actually seen what he saw taking place not at Gut Alt Golssen at all, but at Ludwigsdorff? By any reckoning, the similarity of the FBI Report's description of the Gut Alt Golssen Facility and those connected with the Bell further south in Silesa are remarkable, and if the report is genuine, it indicates that the Bell project in Silesia was but one component of a project perhaps spread over eastern Germany.

In my opinion, the answers are that the witness saw what he says he saw and where he saw it. He was not confusing Gut Alt Golssen with Ludwigsdorff nor intentionally lying about the location of the site. The similarities between the facilities at the two sites are indeed remarkable, to be sure, but there are differences as well, not the least of which is that Gut Alt Golssen is indeed in a flat, swampy area of Brandenburg, whereas

---

[28] Igor Witkowski, *The Truth About The Wunderwaffe*, p. 271.

Ludwigsdorff is in a comparatively rugged, heavily wooded, and mountainous region of Lower Silesia, and area low in farmland, tractors, and swamps!

We are then dealing with two distinct projects, or perhaps two parts of the same project represented by the Bell, which appear to have other things in common, not the least of which is that they are under SS jurisdiction.

The "Henge" at Ludwigsdorff, Silesia, Modern-Day Ludwicowicze in Poland

3. The Harz Mountain "Time Machine" Rumor

A final clue, and in many ways the most significant if not sensational one, was the persistent rumor of a super-secret Nazi wartime project involving the manipulation of time. Henry Stevens learned of the story through contact with German researcher Friedrich Georg:

> This came to him by an individual he knows and trusts and in-fact (sic) is related to by marriage. As a young person, this man was a soldier in the German Wehrmacht like thousands of others at the time. And like so many others, at the close of the war, in April, 1945, this person found himself in (an) American-run prison detention camp. There, he met a fellow prisoner, a SS soldier, with a strange tale to tell.

> *According to the SS man, Hitler had a hidden facility in the mountains of the Harz region. There, deep under a mountain, Hitler had constructed a time machine. Unfortunately, this machine was no longer accessible (sic) from the surface.*[29]

Stevens, of course, quickly connects the story to the research of Igor Witkowski and Nick Cook on the Bell…

…and with good reason, for as Witkowski points out, one project codename for the Bell was precisely *Projekt Kronos,* or Project Time![30]

Notice also something so extremely significant and so obvious that it might escape attention, as obvious things often do: Friedrich Georg's source indicates that "this machine," which can only be the Bell, "was no longer accessible *from the surface.*" In other words, Stevens and Georg are suggesting that the Bell did not escape Germany at all! It went neither to America, nor to Argentina, but remained buried either in its underground Silesian test site inside the Wenceslas Mine – which would put the Bell in the hands of modern-day Poland – or it was buried beneath some facility in the Harz Mountains in Germany! Indeed, the last possibility is a very likely and little considered third alternative to its mysterious disappearance: Kammler removed the Bell from its site in Ludwigsdorff and, in a masterfully executed operation, misdirected everyone's attention to America and Argentina, but simply moved the device "further up the road" into installations in the Harz of Thuringia, and *buried* it in one of the many underground installations whose tunnels the SS booby-trapped and then sealed prior to the end of the war. If *this* alternative proves to be correct, then the technology of the Bell remained on German soil.[31]

---

[29] Stevens, *Hitler's Suppressed and Still-Secret Weapons,* pp. 248-249, emphasis added.

[30] Q.v. Igor Witkowski, *The Truth About the Wunderwaffe,* pp. 235-236, see also my *SS Brotherhood of the Bell,* pp. 166-167.

[31] Which raises the question, did the "recipe" or even some stocks of the Bell's "fuel", the mysterious "Serum 525" remain in Germany also? It is worth mentioning also that some German researchers maintain that Kammler remained snugly in Czechoslovakia long after the war. If the Bell remained in Germany, then this makes a little more sense. However, I tend to discount this possibility, since an SS General hiding in Czechoslovakia would be in constant fear of

While this author still favors the first two alternatives – flight of the device along with Kammler to America or Argentina – this new alternative possibility does shed a whole new light on why the technology that the Bell represented seemed inexplicably to disappear completely after the war, as if it had fallen off the face of the Earth, for that is indeed, on this view, what may have happened to it. It also sheds further light on the speculative hypothesis that I advanced in *Reich of the Black Sun* and *SS Brotherhood of the Bell*, namely, the possibility that the Bell and/or its project documentation remained in independent Nazi hands after the war.

Is there further corroboration of this possibility?

Indeed there is, for as I pointed out in *The SS Brotherhood of the Bell,* Polish researcher Igow Witkowski reached the conclusion that the United States made every effort *to reassemble as much of the original scientific team that worked on the Bell as possible.*[32] If this be the case, then it is a strong indicator that the U.S. recovered neither the Bell nor its project documentation. But there is a further possibility that must be mentioned in this connection. If the U.S. had learned some vague details about the Bell project, as it surely must have when it interrogated the Bell's project head, Nobel laureate physicist Prof. Dr. Walther Gerlach, for some months after

---

reprisals from Czech citizenry for SS brutality in that country during its Nazi occupation.

The possible presence of the Bell in Germany raises numerous political implications as well, and I outlined some of these in *Reich of the Black Sun* and *The SS Brotherhood of the Bell.* There may be more secretly in play in the post-war West German government's official abjuration of nuclear weapons acquisition than meets the eye. As I argued in those books, there is a substantial body of evidence that this was mere posturing on the part of West Germany, which played a central role and perhaps *the* central role in South Africa's acquisition of nuclear bombs in the late 1970s, and most likely played a similar role in Israel's acquisition of them as well. Beyond this, there are also a number of disquieting circumstantial indicators that the German government may have acquired "scalar" weapons prior to the German reunification. If so, and if the Bell is still sealed in wartime SS installations in Thuringia, then it would constitute the needed missing link to make those weapons even more powerful, and would thus be a high recovery priority for the German government, which would not, of course, ever admit that it was looking for it, much less that it had found it.

[32] *The SS Brotherhood of the Bell,* p. 169, and Igor Witkowski, *The Truth About the Wunderwaffe,* p. 260.

the war, *then possibly one thing the Americans were trying to do was shed any possible light on what had really happened with the unanticipated results of their own Philadelphia Experiment.*

However one views these possibilities, Henry Stevens adds his own new piece of information to this unfolding story, one which adds yet another twist to it. In the winter of 2002 Stevens relates that he had a "chance conversation" with a friend of his named Greg Rowe.

> Once Greg told me that his father had worked for NASA at the Huntsville, Alabama facility. Knowing that some German Paperclip scientists worked there, I asked Greg if any of these worked with his father.
>
> Greg replied with a list of German scientists with whom his father had worked and a few words about each one of them. One of these, Otto Cerny, seemed particularly interesting from Greg's description so I pressed him for more information. What follows is a compilation of several e-mails on the subject of Otto Cerny.
>
> Cerny was Greg's father's boss.... When he was somewhere between 12 and 14 years old, Greg and his family were invited to dinner at the Cerny's house. This would have been between the years 1960-62. Greg sat and listened as the older men talked.
>
> Otto Cerny was an engineer and physicist. He had worked at Peenemünde on a variety of projects. That was why he was in the United States, to work on rockets, and why he was a Paperclip scientist to begin with. But it is his work prior to coming to Peenemünde, which was the subject of discussion that night. *Cerny said that he had worked near Breslau in the early years of the war. It was there that he met his wife who worked in Breslau at a hospital where she was employed doing physical rehabilitation work.*
>
> Cerny continued describing this work that night in Alabama, dismissing it at first as *"weird experiments on the nature of time."* Greg's father must have picked up on this comment because the two men quickly became involved, according to Greg, in a deep discussion concerning the nature of time. Greg told me that it seemed to him now, that, at all times Cerny was a little vague in his statements, choosing his words and being careful of what he said, *almost as if he were under some sort of hidden duress.*[33]

Thus Stevens, like Nick Cook, also ran into that "uneasy feeling" within the American aerospace and defense industries that one

---

[33] Stevens, *Hitler's Suppressed and Still-Secret Weapons,* p. 251, emphasis added.

could talk about such things as antigravity and time manipulations, but only so far, and only with some "discomfort."

The story rings true, however, for Cerny's wife and Cerny himself both worked in Breslau, well-known home within the Nazi flying saucer lore of such advanced projects, and, more importantly, the closest major city to the Bell's actual test site in Ludwigsdorff.

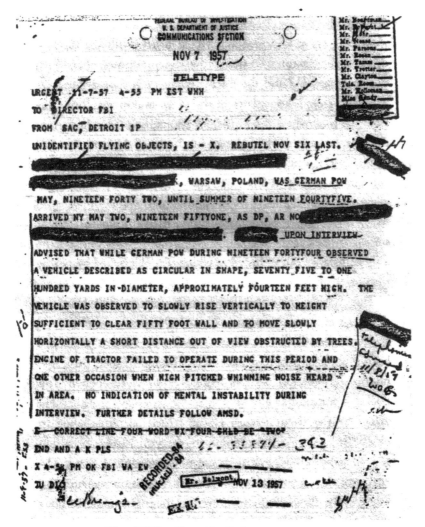

The FBI's Gut Alt Golssen Report

C. A Necessary and Intriguing Tangent

Before summarizing our catalogue of clues that the Allied intelligence teams missed as they scoured Germany for advanced technology and project documentation, let us go back to that FBI Report about the facility at Gut Alt Golssen, and draw the readers' attention to a detail that was probably missed. Look carefully again at the document on the previous page.

Look at the second to the last teletype line which reads:

X A-5B PM OK FBI WA EW.

This designation "X" occurs on many other FBI reports from the first decade or so after the war, reports that concerned an interesting subject matter: UFOs. To put it differently, one is looking at a real life FBI "X File." ·

Their first appearance begins in a series of FBI telexes from field agents in the American northwest in the year 1947, the year that Kenneth Arnold first reported seeing "flying wing" like objects flying in formation near Mount Ranier in Washington. And "one of the men involved in the investigation of UFO reports in the American Northwest that year was none other than FBI Special Agent Guy Bannister,"[34] who was later revealed by New Orleans District Attorney Jim Garrison's JFK assassination investigation to be associated with none other than Lee Harvey Oswald. Bannister's office was in a building – aptly portrayed in Oliver Stone's movie *JFK* which shows the actual building used by Bannister and Oswald – which was also used by Oswald when he was handing out his "Fair Play for Cuba" leaflets.

Occult and esoteric researcher Peter Levenda summarizes this new connection rather cogently:

---

[34] Peter Levenda, *Sinister Forces: A Grimoire of American Political Witchcraft: Book One: The Nine,* (Walterville, Oregon: Trine Day, 2005), p. 173.

Bannister was – during the time of the Arnold sighting, the Maury Island (UFO) affair, and Roswell – an FBI Special Agent assigned to the Butte, Montana field office, which had responsibility for several western states, including Idaho (where Kenneth Arnold resided). A look at recently declassified FBI files for that period in 1947 show a number of telexes from Bannister, some with his initials "WGB", all pertaining to UFO phenomena, as well as other FBI documents with the designation "Security Matter – X" or simply "SM-X," the origin –the author supposes – of the "X Files," which, at least in 1947, *did* exist at the FBI and was concerned with UFOs...[35]

On the following pages I reproduce, courtesy of Mr. Peter Levenda's generosity in sharing them with me, some of these FBI UFO "X Files," including the reports of Guy Bannister.

But what does this mean, in terms of our investigation here? Perhaps it is best to let Mr. Levenda summarize:

> When the powers that be had allowed the Nazi spy and science networks into the United States, it was with the understanding that *they* would control *them,* and not vice versa. As it happened, American hubris probably led to Soviet penetration of American intelligence systems, as Nazi/Soviet double agents found they had unfettered access to US government channels. In addition, by brining over so many Nazis – many of whom were war criminals – they had unknowingly reinstated a Nazi underground in the United States, South America and Australia, not to mention the Middle East.[36]

And there, on the fringes of it all, is Guy Bannister, dutifully filing UFO reports for the FBI's "Security Matter X" files, which, if the Gut Alt Golssen report is any indicator, included monitoring any statements about possible Nazi wartime acquisition of such technology!

Levenda's revelations are disturbing indeed, for they raise to a higher level of credibility a line of speculation concerning the Kennedy assassination conspiracy that was begun decades earlier with the appearance of the so-called "Torbitt Document", which implied that not only were Nazis involved at some level in the

---

[35] Levenda, *Sinister Forces, Book One,* pp. 173-174.
[36] Peter Levenda, *Sinister Forces: A Grimoire of American Political Witchcraft: Book Two: A Warm Gun* (Walterville, Oregon: Trine Day, 2006, p. 88.

planning and execution of the grizzly deed, but that they were involved precisely in order to protect their intelligence and research networks inside the US military industrial complex, which Kennedy, by taking aim at the CIA, had threatened to smash.

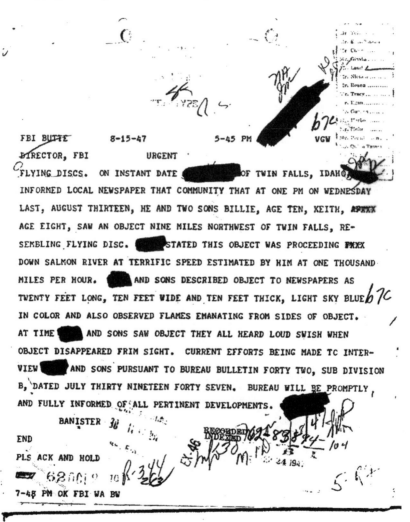

A Bannister UFO FBI "X File"

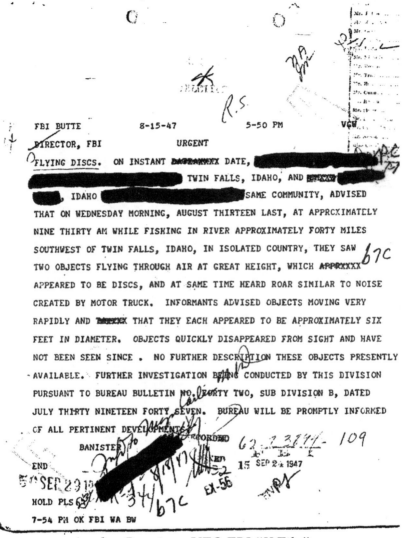

FBI BUTTE   8-15-47   5-50 PM   VCW

DIRECTOR, FBI   URGENT

FLYING DISCS. ON INSTANT ~~XXXXXXXXX~~ DATE, ████████

████████████████████, TWIN FALLS, IDAHO, AND ████████

████, IDAHO ████████████████████████ SAME COMMUNITY, ADVISED

THAT ON WEDNESDAY MORNING, AUGUST THIRTEEN LAST, AT APPROXIMATELY

NINE THIRTY AM WHILE FISHING IN RIVER APPROXIMATELY FORTY MILES

SOUTHWEST OF TWIN FALLS, IDAHO, IN ISOLATED COUNTRY, THEY SAW

TWO OBJECTS FLYING THROUGH AIR AT GREAT HEIGHT, WHICH ~~APPXXXXX~~

APPEARED TO BE DISCS, AND AT SAME TIME HEARD ROAR SIMILAR TO NOISE

CREATED BY MOTOR TRUCK. INFORMANTS ADVISED OBJECTS MOVING VERY

RAPIDLY AND ~~XXXXXX~~ THAT THEY EACH APPEARED TO BE APPROXIMATELY SIX

FEET IN DIAMETER. OBJECTS QUICKLY DISAPPEARED FROM SIGHT AND HAVE

NOT BEEN SEEN SINCE . NO FURTHER DESCRIPTION THESE OBJECTS PRESENTLY

AVAILABLE. FURTHER INVESTIGATION BEING CONDUCTED BY THIS DIVISION

PURSUANT TO BUREAU BULLETIN NO. FORTY TWO, SUB DIVISION B, DATED

JULY THIRTY NINETEEN FORTY SEVEN. BUREAU WILL BE PROMPTLY INFORMED

OF ALL PERTINENT DEVELOPMENTS.

          BANISTER

END

HOLD PLS

7-54 PM OK FBI WA BW

Another Bannister UFO FBI "X File"

Office Memorandum · UNITED STATES GOVERNMENT

TO   : Director, FBI   DATE: September 27, 1947

     SAC, Butte

SUBJECT: FLYING DISCS SIGHTED MAY 5, 1947,
          BETWEEN ELLENSBURG AND SEATTLE, WASHINGTON

          _____ Montana State Prison, Deer Lodge, Montana, has
advised the writer that while driving between Ellensburg and Seattle, Washington, about 3:30 P.M., on May 5, 1947, he sighted a silver object streaking
across the sky. This was also seen by _____, convict chauffeur,
and _____ This object went into a nose dive and they thought it would
crash. However, before reaching the earth it disintegrated, leaving a long
pillar of "gas" hanging in the sky. It was particularly odd because this remained in form and did not blow away. It was observed by these three people
while they drove from twenty to thirty miles.

          This smoky, gaseous pillar was a long ways off and remained high
in the air. _____ said that this silver object was traveling at an
excessively high rate of speed and when it disintegrated it was still a long
way from the earth. _____ said when he first saw it he thought it was
probably a jet propelled plane but that he couldn't tell except that its motions were erratic. He said he had not reported it until he had noticed so
much in the papers about these discs. Although three people saw it, they decided that they must be "seeing things".

          The Seattle Office is requested to advise Mr. _____ 4th
Air Force, S-2, McChord Field, Washington.

          No further action is being taken by the Butte Office due to the
time elapsing between the sighting of this object and the report.

WGB:LB

cc - Seattle

Yet Another Bannister UFO FBI "X File"

PAGE THREE

PART OF ARMY AIR FORCES WHICH MAY EXPLAIN THESE PHENOMENA, ADVICE WOULD
BE GREATLY APPRECIATED. IT IS BELIEVED CONTINUED APPEARANCE OF SUCH
OBJECTS WITHOUT OFFICIAL EXPLANATION MAY RESULT IN HYSTERIA OR PANIC
TWIN FALLS, IDAHO.

    BANISTER

ACK AND HOLD PLS

5-31 PM OK FBI WASH DC WJR

...and another...

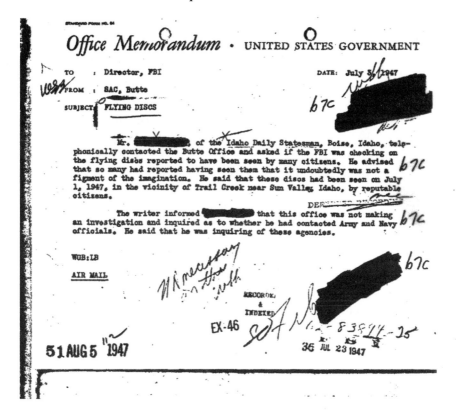

...and yet another.

D. Conclusions

We may now compile our catalogue of clues:

1) First, there are four independent cases and testimonies of secret projects within Nazi Germany or its Fascist Italian ally involving some sort of electromagnetic interference with internal combustion engines, interference which either stops them completely, or causes them to run roughly:
   a) the Italian incident with Benito Mussolini's wife in 1936 as she was driving from Rome to Ostia;[37]

---

[37] For the reader who has been following my presentation of this story as it has been unfolding since *Reich of the Black Sun* and *The SS Brotherhood of the Bell,* the "forgotten" Axis power, Italy, plays a *major* role in the story, a role that

    b) the accounts of strange motor stoppages near the Brocken Mountain in the Harz in 1938;

    c) the account of the tractor engine stoppages near the Gut Alt Golssen facility in Brandenburg in 1944, as reported in the 1957 FBI "X File";

    d) the account of the malfunction of the engines and electrical equipment on Lt. Hitt's P-38 fighter plane over Frankfurt-am-Main in 1945, malfunctions which, moreover, included *compasses spinning wildly though 360 degrees,* a clue to the possible phsyics involved;

2) The need of two of these projects for high electrical consumption: at Gut Alt Golssen and at the Bell's test site in Ludwigsdorff;

---

to this day is shrouded in obscurity. After all, the basic idea of Fermi's graphite moderated reactor – subsequently built by him at the squash court at the University of Chicago – came from a patent from the University of Milan where Fermi had taught in Italy, a patent which *remained* in Fascist Italy's hands throughout its participation in the war. There has also been a persistent rumor approaching almost the status of a legend in certain circles of UFOlogy that the Italian physicist and inventor Guglielmo Marconi headed up a super-secret and independent group of scientists perfecting exotic technologies independently of any government. While absolutely no evidence has ever come forward to substantiate this allegation, it is significant that Italian dictator Mussolini *did* establish a kind of Fascist version of the Majic-12 group in pre-war Italy to study the UFO phenomenon and to compile a database, and that the head of this super-secret brain trust was none other than Marconi.

This allows one to speculate that perhaps the degree of cooperation between this group and Kammler's SS think tank might have been at a very high level, and that perhaps rumors of an independent Marconi group might in fact originate within this wartime cooperation and its post-war continuing independent Nazi research. One may also reasonably speculate that one other likely member of this group would have been the Italian Foreign Minister Gian Galleazo Count Ciano, acting as a liaison. Ciano was, of course, Mussolini's son-in-law, and would have been a logical candidate to oversee liaisons between Italian and German research projects. His inclusion in this role would also place his subsequent execution by Mussolini – at Hitler's insistence – in a very different light, for as Mussolini lost his independence from Nazi Germany and increasingly became a puppet of Hitler, especially after his rescue by SS commando Otto Skorzeny in 1943, Ciano's little-concealed contempt for the Nazis, and his independent spirit, would have made him a risk to the security-obsessed SS.

3) The presence both at Gut Alt Golssen and at Ludwigsdorff of concrete structures in close proximity to water, both of which structures may be described as being henge-like, circular, and columnar, and made of concrete;[38]

4) The presence of one installation associated with engine stoppages in the Harz Mountains at the Brocken, and the stories of "time experiments" in the Harz, the Bell's physical proximity to this area, and its own code name of *Projekt Kronos,* Project Time.

So what clues did the Allies miss? They missed the clues that the Nazis were investigating an area of physics that would yield them vast dividends in many different technological applications: the Nazis were investigating the nature of space-time, and gravity, itself via a variety of high energy rotating electr-magnetic fields. Moreover, they missed the clues that the Nazis were intent on *continuing* to do so after the war.

Accordingly, in the next chapter the Bell's own odd list of operational effects will be added to this list, but not until we have completed another excursion into the odd association of a familiar, ancient, occult, and esoteric symbol with the avante garde notions of theoretical and experimental physics that the Bell represented.

---

[38] The mention of water may also be significant for another reason. Many UFOlogists have noted the high number of UFO sightings over or near fresh water bodies.

11.

THE "SWASTIKA TENSOR," OR:
"HOW EINSTEIN'S TORSION TENSOR MAY HAVE FOUND
A HOME IN THE WAFFEN SS"

*"One finds that distant observers, who measure only the metric field, cannot
distinguish between a (ferromagnetically) polarized source of spinning matter
(which causes torsion locally) and a rotating distribution of matter with the
same total angular momentum (which nowhere causes torsion)."*
Friedrich Hehl[1]

So how do we know that the German quest for advanced field
propulsion technologies, for "limitless energy," and for the
potential planet-busting weapon that torsion represented was
deliberate? This question lies at the heart of this chapter. Our first
approach to an answer to it is simultaneously both an obvious and
a subtle one. It is an answer that has been staring us in the face
with all its naked defiance ever since the black, red, and white
armbands first appeared on the arms of strutting, parade-stepping
Nazis:

The swastika itself.

A. The Swastika as a Simplified Symbol of Rotating Stress in the Medium or Fabric of Space-Time

Along with the Christian Cross, the Communist Hammer and
Sickle, and the Islamic Crescent, the swastika is perhaps one of the
best known and certainly one of the most ancient symbols on the
planet. A symbol of good fortune for many traditions from ancient
American Indian tribes such as the Navaho, to the high mountains
and lamas of Tibet, more recently the swastika has taken on its
much more sinister and notorious association, an association with
which it is and will forever be entangled, having become the

---

[1] Hehl, F.W., P. von der Heyde, and G.D. Kerlich, "General Relativity with
Spin and Tosion: Foundations and Prospects," *Reviews of Modern Physics,* Vol.
48, No. 3, July, 1976, pp. 393-416, cited in Corum, Corum, and Daum, "Tesla's
Egg of Columbus...," p. 37.

chosen symbol, the "corporate logo" so to speak, of one of the most evil, occult, and genocidal ideologies and political parties of human history: the National Socialist German Workers' Party, the NSDAP in its German abbreviation, better known as the Nazis.

But the swastika is also a powerful, and easily understood, symbol of a physics principle, for it is an apt symbol of a rotating stress in the medium itself, and of its enormous potential both for benefit, and also for mass destruction.

To see how, it is only necessary to imagine the swastika as a highly stylized symbol of a rotating vector system of stress that sums to a zero translation vector:

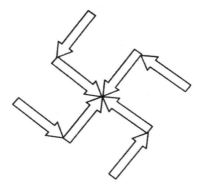

The Counter-Clockwise or "Nazi" Swastika as a Simplified Schematic of Rotating Vectors and Stress

To understand how this ancient symbol functions also as a symbol of *rotational physics*, it is necessary to break it down into the two sub-systems that comprise it: (1) the sub-system of stress:

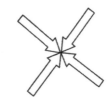

The Sub-System of Stress

And (2) the sub-system of rotation:

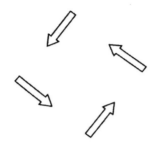

The Sub-System of Rotation

Viewed in this way, the swastika is an *ideogram* for a physical principle, for a rotational stress, for a "shearing" effect in the medium itself.

How?

Notice what was said above: the vectors of force – represented by the arrows in the above diagrams – all sum to a "zero translation vector", which simply means that in spite of the fact that the swastika is *moving, it is not moving linearly, from one point to another.* In fact, the reverse is happening in the diagram: all the vectors of force the ideogram represents are loading into or converging at one point, exactly in the center of the system.

1. A Simplified "Tensor" Analysis of the Swastika (With Apologies to Mathematicians and Physicists)

Before we can proceed with our presentation of how Einstein's torsion tensor may have been "sold" to the Nazi leadership, we must analyze these concepts a bit further. In doing so, we shall present some of the basic concepts of tensor analysis – don't panic, we won't use equations (with apologies to mathematicians and physicists)! Suppose, for the sake of simplicity, that we take the first sub-system of vectors that the swastika contains, the sub-system of rotation, and rotate it just a small amount:

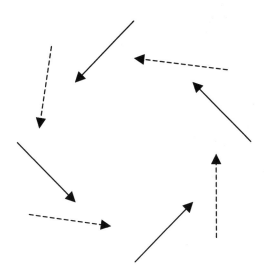

Vectors of Rotation in the Swastika Under Parallel Transport

In above diagram, the dotted arrows represent the new positions of the vectors in the "sub-system of rotation." Each of the vectors in this sub-system has undergone what mathematicians and physicists call a "parallel transport." While the different positions of the solid and dotted arrows may not look at all "parallel" in the normal sense, what "parallel transport" means in tensor analysis is simply to preserve the *magnitude* (the "length") of the vector plus its *angle*. The rotation of the sub-system thus parallel transports the vectors of that system, preserving their magnitude and angles relative to each other.

There is one more basic concept – again with apologies to mathematicians and physicists – to illustrate before we can proceed, and that is torsion itself. If we now take the two systems resulting from parallel transport, the original and the displaced system, the first represented by the solid arrows and the second by the dotted ones, and measure the degree of "displacement" between the two, we have a reasonable, though very simplified, idea of what the torsion tensor does: *it tells how **much** the fabric of space-time has been folded or rotated to produce the degree of* *displacement in evidence.* We could employ a similar technique of analysis for the vectors of the sub-system of *stress*, and obviously, to both sub-systems of stress and rotation taken together. Notice one final, subtle thing: it is the system of rotation that is *producing* the stress or "folding" or "displacement: in the medium.

B. A Hypothetical Scenario: Dr. Gerlach Does a Hard Sell of Torsion to the SS

In my previous book on the Nazi Bell project, *The SS Brotherhood of the Bell,* I indicated that Dr. Walther Gerlach, the Bell project's eventual project head, may have come up with the basic conceptual foundations for the project as early as 1924,[2] just four years prior to Einstein's 1928 Unified Field Theory paper with its torsion tensor. Now let us note one further significant thing about Dr. Walther Gerlach.

The Nazi regime had, of course, ideologically prohibited "Jewish physics" in the Third Reich, thus effectively proscribing any scientific elaboration or experimental research into any of Einstein's ideas. But Dr. Gerlach, in spite of his ideological support and commitment to the Nazi regime never joined the Nazi party, *and never disavowed Einstein nor General Relativity* and in fact on occasion simply ignored the Nazi proscriptions. Nonetheless, Gerlach reached the highest pinnacles of scientific power within Nazi Germany, such that he was placed in charge of its ultimate secret weapon, the Bell, the project that the Nazis had classified higher than any other secret weapons project in the Reich with the classification of *Kriegsendscheidend,* or "War Decisive."

While the case has yet to be argued here that the Bell was conceptually founded to test practical applications of torsion,[3] we assume here for the moment that it was. The problem now becomes, How would Gerlach have sold the Nazi regime to back with serious funding, material, scientific personnel, and labor a project designed to investigate *torsion?*

---

[2] See my *SS Brotherhood of the Bell,* pp. 272-278.
[3] This is in fact the interpretation that British researcher Nick Cook takes in his book *The Hunt for Zero Point,* and that Igor Witkowski maintains in his *The Truth About the Wunderwaffe.*

The answer is as obvious as the swastika on their armbands. Gerlach could easily – and without much recourse to mathematics if he used it at all – have argued that the swastika was a perfect ideogram for the ideas that he wanted to test and develop. Why, the hated Jewish physicist had, with his post-Relativity Unified Field Theory papers, delivered right into the hands of the Reich a mathematical exposition of the Party symbol! For scientific blockheads in the SS such as Reichsführer Himmler, it would have been "obvious," and perhaps even a pleasing irony. For the Nazis, who showed no hesitation in looting and plundering Jewish financial and hard assets, it would have been no different in kind to plunder their intellectual ones as well. And let us remember one more thing about Gerlach: *rotational physics and gravity were his specialties.*

Nor should we forget the other component of this dynamic: the SS itself. Such a "sales pitch" would have intrigued Himmler, with his own kooky interest in the scientific exploration and exploitation of "the occult" for military purposes. What could be a more perfect symbol, with its own deep roots in esotericism and ancient religious systems, than the swastika? And in the much more pragmatic context of Kammler's "think tank," where scientists were basically *freed* from the constraints of party ideology and expected to brainstorm their way to advanced concepts and with them, new weapons, Gerlach would have found an even more eager and accepting audience.

In this hypothetical scenario, the swastika itself became the symbol and ideogram of the torsion tensor; it became a kind of "swastika tensor," the means by which serious scientists such as a Gerlach could investigate the practical engineerable aspects of Einstein's 1928 Unified Field Theory. And they could maintain that they were in full party loyalty while doing so.[4]

Thus viewed the swastika becomes a powerful ideogram for the SS black projects themselves, and for the Bell in particular, for it functions as a symbol of their approach to the manipulation of the fabric of space time for the purposes of exploiting it and

---

[4] A similar approach then, could be taken with the SS' explotation of the implosion notions of Austrian naturalist Viktor Schauberger, whom the SS had actually recruited to work on saucer-like aerodynes.

weaponizing it. It is possible, then, and perhaps even likely, that the Nazi physicists in this project might have even developed their own versions of unified field theories based on, or incorporating, torsion, off the books. It was the perfect ideogram and conceptual key to the apocalyptic power for destruction that their political masters desired.

With these thoughts in hand, on to the Bell itself.

C. The Implications of the Torsion Tensor:
The "Primitive Machine" of the Bell: The Two Counter-Rotating Cylinders in the Bell, and their Probable Configuration

1. A Basic Review of the Dimensions and Operating Parameters of the Bell[5]

The Bell was a device that was shaped like a bell, approximately 12 to 15 feet wide, and approximately 15 to 18 feet tall. Its outer casing was made of a ceramic-metal type material. Around the base of the device were ports for heavy electrical cabling. Additionally, the Bell was cryogenically cooled. Inside the Bell were placed two counter-rotating drums, into which was poured its "fuel," a mysterious compound code-named "IRR Xerum 525," a heavy liquid-gooey substance of violet reddish hue.

As I speculated in *The SS Brotherhood of the Bell,* this substance sounds as if it is based on some isotope of mercury, probably additionally "doped" with some radioactive elements such as thorium or barium or so on.[6] Moreover, as I also outlined in that book, this substance sounds suspiciously like the "Red Mercury" that became the nuclear terrorism scare and fad of the 1990s.[7] Red Mercury was supposedly a compound invented by the

---

[5] For fuller expositions of these, see my *Reich of the Black Sun,* pp. 331-348 , and *SS Brotherhood of the Bell,* pp. 141-308.

[6] With respect to thorium, it should be mentioned that one of the big unsolved mysteries of the war is the fact that the Nazis literally scoured Europe for every last once of thorium, stockpiling it for unknown purposes. Could the reason have been that it was an essential ingredient in this mysterious compound, Xerum 525?

[7] See chapter seven of *The SS Brotherhood of the Bell,* pp. 278-282, 288-296.

Russians for their thermonuclear weapons. Allegedly composed of mercury and antimony, and presumably other materials, the compound was then placed in a reactor to undergo neutron bombardment, a process that made the material an abnormally and unnaturally *dense and heavy liquid,* far beyond the normal density and weight of mercury, since it was allegedly saturated with neutrons, but that also turned it a deep purplish-red color. Over time the material supposedly decayed into a powder and lost its "potency" which could only be recharged by re-immersing it in a nuclear reactor.

According to the Red Mercury legend, the substance was supposedly capable of functioning as an extraordinarily powerful conventional explosive in its own right, an amount the size of a hand grenade allegedly being capable of blowing a large ship out of the water. More importantly, the substance was also allegedly capable of functioning as a trigger for hydrogen bombs *without* the necessity of having an atom bomb as the trigger!

Once inserted into the Bell, this mysterious compound 525 was then rotated in the counter-rotating drums through high electrical potentials. When this happened, the Bell glowed a pale blue glow, and in some accounts that saw it tested outside, levitated. While in operation the Bell buzzed, earned it its nickname among the Germans, *die Bienenstock,* or "the Beehive."

But most unusual about the Bell was that during its initial test, seven of the scientists testing it died. Others who survived complained of vertigo, metallic taste in their mouths, sleeplessness, and other nervous disorders. Organic compounds placed within the field that it generated, such as plants, decayed within a matter of mere hours in some instances into a kind of blackish-gray goo, and did so without putrefaction. So extreme were these effects that the Bell could only be operated safely for approximately two minutes.

The device itself, when tested in its underground facility at the Wenceslas Mine in Ludwigsdorff, was housed in a chamber lined with ceramic bricks, over which rubber matting had to be placed. After each test, these mats had to be removed and burned, and the entire chamber scrubbed down with brine, all of which presumably fell to the concentration camp laborers, thus indicated that this was in all likelihood a hazardous task to perform.

2. The Unified Field Theory, the Torsion Tensor, and Igor Witkowski's Idea of the Plasma Focus

We turn now to a reconsideration of the Bell in the light of all the concepts explored in the previous pages of this book. It is this device which the Nazi regime, and more importantly, the *Kammlerstab* think tank, classified as "war decisive." An important question has now arisen: would it have been so classified if it merely represented a breakthrough in field propulsion, or even "free energy"?

Very possibly.

But if the Bell was a device designed to test *various aspects and implications of torsion,* then it was not only a field propulsion device and "free energy" machine, but also held the potential of leading to a kind of "torsion bomb," for a *reusable* technology capable of "folding and pleating" space-time that manipulate gravity, time, and in effect, can function as a kind of "torsion bomb" would make a hydrogen bomb look like a firecracker. By the nature of the case, it represents a technological and theoretical breakthrough that could lead to not only to revolutionary propulsion and energy systems, but to a weapon of horrendous power and sophistication.

The only question is, *was* the Bell in fact conceived as a device to test the torsion implications of a Unified Field Theory? Here we fall back on the clues of the Bell's operation and its effects and piece them together.

The first and most important of these clues lies in its *counter-rotating cylinders.* These afford the real hint of why the Bell was considered by the Nazis to be a *weapon* and therefore "war decisive."

In my previous book on the Bell, *The SS Brotherhood of the Bell,* I endeavored to show how the Bell could be considered a weapon if one follows the ingenious suggestion of Igor Witkowski that it was a refinement of a standard plasma focus. I did so by explaining some of its effects – particularly the biological effects noted above – as the result of phenomena such as the Mossbauer Effect that it might have accessed. The Mossbauer Effect is simply that certain radioactive materials under certain conditions of stress - usually acoustical – will emit *cohered* X-ray and gamma-ray radiation, that is, that they will act as the lasing cavity for *X-ray and gamma ray lasers,* incredibly powerful and deadly devices in either case. In my most recent book *The Cosmic War,* I expanded upon this concept in the context of plasma cosmology research that uses the plasma focus device. I there reproduced plasma physicist Eric Lerner's diagram of a typical plasma focus device, which clearly shows its two cylinders, one a cathode and the other an anode, nested one inside the other:

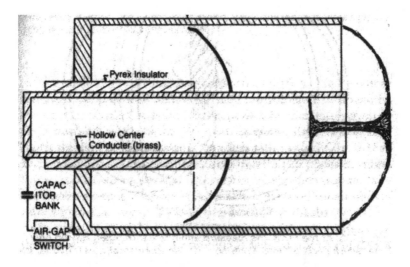

Eric Lerner's Diagram of a Plasma Focus[8]

Now let us recall something little noticed but highly significant. Igor Witkowski, in his *The Truth About the Wunderwaffe,* indicates that the central core of the Bell was stationary and not able to rotate at all, and of course, *neither* cylinder in a typical plasma focus rotates; *both* are stationary.

Thus we are led to an inevitable conclusion as to the arrangement of the counter-rotating cylinders in the Bell, a question I deliberately left unanswered in *The SS Brotherhood of the Bell: the cylinders were **not** nested one inside the other, but*

---

[8] Eric J. Lerner, *The Big Bang Never Happened,* p. 243.

*rather one on **top** of the other. If this is the case, then while it **used** the principles of a plasma focus, the Bell was not a plasma focus in any sense at all, typical or otherwise.*

What would have been the rationale for such an unusual departure from the ordinary arrangement of the drums of a plasma focus? After all, Witkowski makes the insightful observation that by *rotating* the drums contrary to each other, the Nazis hit upon a brilliant and simple modification of the typical focus device.

Now it is necessary to reprise Witkowski's reconstruction of the Bell and its operating principles, to clarify just where we agree, and disagree, with his analysis.

> "The bell" possessed so many characteristic features that finding some kind of unequivocal explanation seemed to be attainable, i.e., there was a basis for verifying different hypotheses. These features were chiefly:
> * *The employment of very high voltages.*
> * *An emphasis of the phenomenon of "magnetic fields separation".*
> * *The occurrence of "vortex compression."*
> * The fact that the device generated very powerful magnetic fields.
> * The spinning of masses/bulky elements as a means to achieve the above effects (directly or indirectly).
> * As a result: the generation of powerful radiation.
> * *The continuous character of "the bell's" operation – i.e. non-pulse.*
> * *The reference about transforming mercury into gold.*[9]

I have highlighted those elements in the above list that are of the greatest interest here. Taking them in the reverse order, the mention of "transforming mercury into gold" is perhaps a reference to an article that Gerlach had written in a 1924 Frankfurt newspaper.[10] In the article, Gerlach mentioned the possibility of such transmutation by subjecting mercury to electromagnetic stress.

As also indicated in Witkowski's comments, he believes the Bell operated in a non-pulsed mode, i.e., in a largely alternating current continuous mode. However, as I outlined in the *SS*

---

[9] Igor Witkowski, *The Truth About the Wunderwaffe*, p. 245, emphasis added.
[10] Ibid., p. 257. See also chapter seven of my *SS Brotherhood of the Bell* for a translation of this article, pp. 272-273.

Brotherhood of the Bell, I believe there are two factors that indicate that the Bell may have in fact utilized two different types of electrical potential, both AC and DC.

The first of my reasons for suggesting a DC component was the characteristic *sound* that the Bell made when in operation: like a "Beehive," and hence its nickname *die Bienenstock.* Such a sound, as I noted there, is characteristic of a high voltage direct current (DC) switch being rapidly opened and closed several thousands of times per minute.

But the second of my reasons I did not disclose in that book. I do so here. One of the unusual features of the installations are Ludwigsdorff that Witkowski mentions is that there as a large electrical power plant that had been specially constructed very near the Henge structure. Heavy duty electrical cables ran from the plant to ports around the basin of the Henge as well as into the underground installations of the mine itself. There are a variety of explanations for why the Nazis would have built a power plant just for these installations, but two are worth mentioning.

The first would be that the project and its installations required a lot of power – and we have already seen that the Bell did. Perhaps, then, the Nazis wished to ensure that power supply for the Ludwigsdorff installations would never be interrupted by Allied or Russian bombing of power relay stations if they had pursued the option of running power lines from somewhere else. But in the final analysis this makes no sense, for if they had wanted to ensure an uninterruptible power supply, they could have buried the power lines in the region. An expensive and time-consuming expedient to be sure, but one far less so than building an entire electrical power plant!

This leads to a second possibility, one connected with my hypothesis that the Bell used two kinds of electricity, alternating, and direct, current. Given that the Bell's power consumption requirements were enormous, as witnessed by the heavy duty electrical cabling that ran from the power plant to the Henge, then this meant its direct current power supply was large. It is a well known fact that direct current, unlike alternating current, dissipates very quickly through a power line. It was for this very reason that Thomas Edison's scheme to electrify America with a large DC power plant every few miles or so finally, and rightly, failed. As a solution to electrification it was simply impractical and environmentally suicidal. Tesla's alternating current won out because it could be easily run over power lines for several hundred miles, and stepped up or down at transforming stations as needed, thereby dramatically reducing the number of power plants needed.

So perhaps the building of an electrical power plant just for the Ludwigsdorff installations is another indicator that *huge amounts* of DC current were needed to operate the Bell. It is the *short distance of the facility from its load end* that is the strongest clue that direct current, in addition to alternating current, of very high voltage was involved with the Bell.

Returning to Witkowski's list, he mentions two final things: "magnetic fields separation" and "vortex compression." To understand these things mean in the context of the Bell in his interpretation, we return to his remarks.

> I reflected upon the whole issue and quite naturally concluded that a high voltage current (as it later proved – over a million volts) could not supply any engine or winding and the like. It must have led to a discharge, and consequently – it must have been a question of plasma physics. As it was to prove, this was the next step forward. At the same time I was reminded...that it is very important for the "active substance" to be characterized by low viscosity...it is possible to "extend" this reasoning and draw the conclusion that gas would have a lower viscosity than liquid, and lower than gas – plasma.
>
> ....
>
> It became evident that under certain conditions plasma created through the flow of electric current, creates in turn a special kind of vortex. Such a vortex is called a plasmoid....
>
> It became evident that such types of plasma vortices are credited with a certain, unique feature – namely the lines of magnetic field force are almost completely closed....Only due to this is a plasmoid of this type extremely stable for a plasma vortex – it is simply almost isolated from its environment. As far as the Theory of Relativity is concerned, the importance of this phenomenon (separation of magnetic fields) is interpreted like this: since the fields are "coupled" with the space-time continuum, the isolation of a field (in this case magnetic), or speaking the language of physics: ensuring the field's locality gives in effect a certain locality of the space-time continuum. In other words: separation of fields is the key to control gravity, because bending of space-time equals the generation of gravity....It is after all a plasma vortex as well as a spinning magnetic field – moreover very strong and spinning very

> quickly. Very quickly – since the magnetic field very strongly compresses the plasma. The compression *is so strong that it is even compared by some to the conditions prevailing during a nuclear explosion.*[11]

But as we have seen, it is not really *General Relativity* that permits this localized manipulation of space-time and gravitational effects at all; it is the 1928 Unified Field Theory, and more specifically, the torsion tensor.

There is, however, a vitally important observation that Witkowski makes that indicates the subtlety and profundity of the German scientists' grasp of the implications of that theory, and that is that magnetic fields had to be isolated or separated, and to do that, means that the spin of atoms that establishes the electric current that in turn establishes the magnetic field had to be cohered, which means that the spin of the atoms all had to be going the same direction and in the same *plane* of spin. This is already a conceptual grasp far beyond what we encountered in the Philadelphia Experiment, and indicates that the Germans were thinking things through with much more deliberateness. Moreover, the choice of a rotating heavy viscuous liquid – a compound probably of mercury and other elements – to create the needed plasma also indicates that their grasp of the materials needed to create the most *efficient and concentrated effect* of torsion was also much more advanced than it was for the Americans who established the conceptual foundations of the Philadelphia Experiment.

And this is an indicator of something else. The American experiment, as was seen, was aiming at radar stealth, and thus was aiming at a low level manipulation of torsion effects. That the results in the full scale test achieved something spectacular and unanticipated is an indicator that deliberate thought had not been taken into achieving anything more from torsion. But with the Bell, the very fact that thought and effort have been expended to *maximize to the highest possible degree* the effects of torsion via the employment of a specially designed compound that will enter a

---

[11] Igor Witkowski, *The Truth About the Wunderwaffe,* p. 249, emphasis added. Thus, the line of research that the Bell represents is also a possible route to the "electromagnetic" initiation and control of fusion.

plasma state means that the recipe to confect the compound – Xerum 525 – had probably been derived over the course of several experiments. Its composition was therefore probably derived, again, in order to maximize the torsion field effects of the Bell. Its recipe was most likely classified as high as the Bell itself. Thus, *its extreme effects on living matter, notwithstanding the deaths of the scientists involved in its first test, were probably expected and sought as confirmations of the presence of torsion fields.* The purpose of the Bell, in other words, was to go far beyond radar stealth.

So then, back to Witkowski, as we approach our explanation of the arrangement of the two counter-rotating cylinders:

> These facts led to some very encouraging conclusions. It seemed that plasma physics was able to ensure a magnetic field strength...and speed of rotation far higher than that of any mechanical system. It would obviously follow from this, that the German "bell" was some kind of "trap for plasma vortex."[12]

There is nothing to dispute here, for Witkowski *has* correctly deduced the basic operating principle behind the Bell.

So, how did it all work, according to him?

> I imagined a large, metal drum, in which a small amount of mercury was present. The drum would then be accelerated to a speed of say tends of thousands of revolutions per minute. Under the influence of the centrifugal force the mercury, as a liquid, would cover the walls of the drum creating a thin layer. After achieving the target speed a high voltage electrical discharge would be created between the circumference of the drum (the mercury layer) – and its axis – the core. Theoretically, this would accelerate the ions of mercury towards the core, with a speed of many kilometers per second. But since the mercury would already possess a certain torque, in due measure of approaching the core its angular velocity would increase... In the case of the drum with mercury this would lead to an overlapping of the two speeds – created by a preservation of the torque and a result of the flow of electric current.[13] From my approximate calculations it followed that by this means it would be possible to achieve a speed of the ultimate

---

[12] Witkowski, *The Truth About the Wunderwaffe,* p. 250.
[13] Remember Kron's rotating machinery and their "slippages" that were only explainable by torsion?

"compressed" vortex of the order of even hundreds of thousands of revolutions per second.[14]

So far so good. But notice that while Witkowski's explanation is quite plausible as far as an accounting of *one* drum goes, it does not really explain why there were *two **counter**-rotating drums, nor does it give a rationalization of what their arrangement might have been.*

It does not account for it, unless one recalls our analogy of wringing an aluminum can from chapter one. This motion involves the counter-rotation of a medium (in this case the aluminum can) *which maximizes the stress in the center of the medium itself, leading ultimately to a maximum "folding" and "pleating" effect – i.e., to maximum torsion – as well as to a potential **shearing effect**, **which would release a violent electro-explosive pulse, a longitudinal pulse in the medium or fabric of space-time itself.***

Thus we arrive at the probable arrangement of the counter-rotating drums inside the Bell: ***their probable arrangement was one on top of the other in order to create and maximize an extreme degree of torsion to create a shearing effect in the medium itself.*** The Bell, in other words, was deliberately *designed* to achieve the bizarre effects that it did: levitation, the quick decay and non-putrefaction of organic matter, and so on. Indeed, we may speculate that organic matter was selected for tests because it was a natural detector of extreme torsion: if the "time" of the affected plants, animals (and presumably humans) was sped up sufficiently so that they decayed into goo within hours of being exposed to the Bell, then this would indeed be one way to test for the presence of torsion.

3. Rationalizations for the Presence of Radioactive Elements in Compound Solution with Mercury in "Xerum 525", and for the Use of Ultra-High Speed Mechanical Rotation in the Bell

---

[14] Witkowski, op. cit., p. 251.

Some within the engineering community think that the mechanical rotation of the drums inside the device would not be as advanced, nor suitable to the Nazi's purposes in exploring torsion field control, as would electrical rotation of the mysterious "IRR Xerum 525" by itself.

While true as far as it goes, I believe there are other alternative, though still speculative, explanations for why mechanical rotation was chosen, and these lie in the putative properties of that compound itself. In my previous book on the Bell, I speculated that this compound was composed of mercury, doped with heavy radioactive isotopes such as thorium or barium, and perhaps other metals with specific chemical properties. In this respect, the Bell's fuel, "IRR Xerum 525" sounded suspiciously like the supposed Russian invention of "Red Mercury." Like the alleged Russian thermonuclear compound, I speculated that the Nazi compound may have been immersed in a functioning nuclear reactor, were it was implanted with other radioactive compounds and subjected to neutron bombardment:

> (Red Mercury) was first produced in the Soviet Union near the high energy physics research institute in Dubna in 1968, which possessed a reactor *"suited to implanting* the material with strontium, caesium and other isotopes." The reactor was suitable, in other words, for *"salting"* or *"doping"* the Red Mercury with other highly radioactive material. At this point, the resemblance of (Red Merucry) – heavy liquid, high radioactivity, deep wine colour – to the Bell's mysterious "Xerum 525" should be obvious.[15]

I then commented as follows:

> Whatever "Red Mercury" may be chemically, certain conclusions about its confection, about its "recipe", may now be drawn:
>
> (1) Mercury itself was most likely involved in whatever compound was actually made – whether that compound was mercury antimony oxide or not[16] - since as a high density liquid metal which can exist

[15] *The SS Brotherhood of the Bell,* p. 292, citing Peter Hounam and Steve McQuillan, *The Mini-Nuke Conspiracy, Mandela's Nuclear Nightmare* (VikingL 1995), p. 64, emphasis added.
[16] Mercury antimony oxide is the chemical formula alleged to be the basis of "Red Mercury."

in its own radioactive isotope forms; it is an ideal vehicle for "salting" or "doping" with other more radioactive materials;

(2) Mercury also has its own peculiar stability properties which manifest themselves when it is highly stressed, as... claimed in ancient texts relating to "mercury vortex engines";

(3) With such a highly "salted" compound, as "Xerum 525" appears to have been, utilized in a device such as the Bell, any number of strange properties may have been discovered by the Germans; and finally and most importantly,

(4) It appears that the essential step in its confection is to subject whatever compound "Red Mercury" represents to exposure in a reactor core. More about this crucial point in a moment.[17]

The crucial point referred to in the previous quotation is that if this line of speculation is true, it would mean, contrary to the Allied Cold War Legend about World War Two German nuclear incompetence, that Nazi Germany actually had a functioning atomic pile somewhere inside the Reich.

While this is not the place to delve into speculations about the possibilities of the Nazi nuclear reactor, it should be noted that I pointed out in *The SS Brotherhood of the Bell,* that Fritz Houtermans had proposed a workable idea for a methane moderated reactor quite early in the war, thus bypassing the problems associated with graphite moderation.[18]

In any case, we are now in a position to speculate why the Bell would have relied on ultra-high speed mechanical rotation in the device. Again, some within the American defense engineering community have made the suggestion that the Bell was nothing more than an outgrowth of German centrifuge isotope enrichment technology, and indeed, I also maintained such a connection

---

[17]Joseph P. Farrell, *The SS Brotherhood of the Bell,* p. 293.

[18] Ibid., pp. 302-303. Of course, once again, the "forgotten Axis partner," Italy, enters the picture here, for as was previously pointed out, Fascist Italy possessed the University of Milan's patent for a graphite moderated reactor, the one subsequently built by Fermi at the University of Chicago. So another speculation presents itself: might this be an indicator, not of Nazi nuclear reactor success, but of *Fascist Italy's* reactor success? Alternatively, it is also known that there was a certain amount of cooperation between the two Axis powers in atomic matters. The plans for the reactor under these circumstances would likely have been shared with Nazi Germany, where they would have disappeared into the bowels of the SS's secret weapons black projects.

probably existed in *The SS Brotherhood of the Bell*. But to maintain that the Bell was nothing more than that is to miss the picture entirely.

Under such high revolutions, the heavy isotopes would indeed begin to separate from lighter atoms, and press towards the wall of the rotating drums. At this point, however, recall Witkowski's prescient analysis based on his speculation that the Bell was a refined version of a plasma focus: the presence of mercury in the compound, subjected to the high voltage stresses, would begin to form a plasma, and this in turn would begin to pinch into plasmoids, vastly increasing the angular momentum of the heavy spnning ions in the plasma.

So *two* effects might in fact have been taking place more or less simultaneously in the Bell: (1) the "plasma pinch" effect of a typical plasma focus, and (2) the pushing of other heavy radioactive atoms toward the walls of the drums by centrifugal force.

But what would the purpose of these two effects be? Once again, it is perhaps explainable if the Nazis *were trying to maximize the shear effecting order to maximize the torsion involved.* If these speculations are correct, then the reason for the Nazis having designed the Bell with electrical and *mechanical* rotation in mind becomes rather obvious. And in turn if this be the case, then the Bell was not designed as any sort of plasma focus device. That principle is involved, to be sure, but as a basis for a machine whose ultimate purposes are far different: to maximize torsion effects through shear.[19]

4. Rationalization for the Use of High Voltage DC Discharge

This quest to maximize shear effects by as many means also lies behind my suggestion in *The SS Brotherhood of the Bell* that two types of electrical potentials, AC and DC, might also have

---

[19] I am indebted to Mr. Tim Ventura of americanantigravity.com for many phone conversations concerning these possibilities, and for his insight that a shear effect may have been involved in the counter-rotation of the Bell's drums. The speculation concerning the heavy elements and the axes of shear is my own.

been involved. As was seen earlier in this chapter, the first rationalization of this speculation is corroborated by the close proximity of an electrical power plant to the Bell's test installations in Ludwigsdorff. Such an expense would hardly be justified from the security standpoint for the project, since underground cabling and transformer stations could have supplied any amount of AC current needed in the installations. The special building of a power plant so close to the installations may thus indicate something else about the parameters of the project, namely, that very high voltage DC may have been needed for the Bell as well.

a. And a Peculiar Connection to the Philadelphia Experiment: A Varo Annotated Edition Commentary

In this connection there is, however, another rationalization, or rather, speculative possibility that should be mentioned, and surprisingly, it comes from peculiar comments in the Varo Annotated Edition of Jessup's *The Case for the UFOs*. The first comment, coming more or less out of the blue and not even really related to anything in Jessup's main text, is this (once again, the peculiar spellings, underlinings, and capitalizations of the annotated will be preserved):

> The Muaneans *Never know What* an atom was & Niether did the Atruscan-Lems. They only know & knew Force-field work as their top accomplishment & found throo inlay work in Metal that the Design had been Hit **by Lightning causing it to have no weight somehow.** THEY WENT ON FROM THAT FLOOR Design or floor pattern which may have been Laid in Lodestone for all I know.[20]

Note the reference to lightning, in other words, to extremely high electrostatic discharge. Note also the reference to lodestone, or magnetism. While no specific connection between the two is made clear by the annotator, it is apparent that he means to draw a connection between them.

But the more interesting comment occurs at the very end of the Varo Edition, a comment that begins a long string of annotations:

---

[20] *Varo Annotated Edition,* p. 56, bold emphasis added, all other emphasis in the original.

WHAT HAPPENS WHEN A **BOLT OF LIGHTNING HITS AT A POINT WHERE THERE IS A "NODE" SUCH AS A "SWIRL" IN THE MAGNETIC SEA** *OR WHERE* A MAG. "DEAD SPOT" caused by the NEUTRALIZATION OF MAG. SEA contra GRAVITY ESPECIALLY, WHAT, WHEN THE NODE & BOLT BOTH ACT OVER BRONZE INLAY. [21]

Interestingly, this annotation seems to hint at some sort of effect achieved by pulsing the center of a magnetic vortex with extremely high voltage electrostatics. It is extremely curious that a similar property, I believe, was at work in the Bell. While it is very unlikely that the annotators of the Varo Edition, whoever they were, knew of the Nazi Bell project, it is an intriguing comment for them to make.

D. A Speculative Solution to the Involvement in the Bell Project of the Mysterious Dr. Elizabeth Adler of the University of Königsberg, And its Relationship to Another Possible Theoretical and Conceptual Foundation for the Bell

One of the persisting mysteries of the Bell is the identity of the mysterious Dr. Elizabeth Adler, and why she was brought into the project. To recall her significance, here is what I wrote about her in *The SS Brotherhood of the Bell:*

> So far, we have encountered in Witkowski's list of Bell personnel two rather well-known scientists, and one very obscure four star SS general. But there is yet another expert involved, and here, one is confronted again with something of a mystery:
> "Within the context of one of the people (involved in the project) the problem of *"a simulation of damping of vibrations towards the center of spherical objects"* appeared. In this case it concerned Dr. Elizabeth

---

[21] *Varo Annotated Edition,* p. 163, bold emphasis added. Curiously, the annotations in the Varo Edition frequently mention the peculiar magnetic and anti-gravitational properties of various metals when "laminated" or "inlaid" with each other, a point that assumes some interest given the strange metal laminations often reported and tested in various laboratories in connection with alleged recovered UFO debris.

Adler, a mathematician from Königsberg University (this name appeared only once)."

Who was Dr. Elizabeth Adler? What was her specialty in mathematics? No one seems to know. My own attempts to find out by contacting the University of Kaliningrad, modern day Königsberg, ended in a wall of stony silence.

But her presence –even if she is only mentioned in connection with the Bell once- is in itself a significant indicator of something. Since Gerlach was himself a capable mathematician and theoretical physicist, Adler's presence must indicate a very *rarefied* form of mathematical expertise was required at some point. This in turn means that the Bell represented no ordinary project. For the SS to have apparently "consulted" a mathematician outside the project must indicate that Elizabeth Adler's mathematical skills were *unique.* Find her area of mathematical expertise, and one will have a *significant* clue into the nature of the physics that the Germans were investigating with the Bell.[22]

Of course, Adler's expertise may have been needed for something as mundane as figuring out how much damping was needed in the Bell's rotating cylinders. But these are not spheres. Or perhaps the nature of her involvement was a cover story put out by the security-obsessed SS to deflect attention away from the real nature of her consultation. Perhaps she was involved in a "math check" for the project.

Or perhaps Witkowski's comments, cited in the quotation above, are actually the truth. From the standpoint of the torsion-based conceptual foundations being explored in this book, they do indeed make sense, for a "damping of vibrations" in the center of a "sphere" would be precisely the sort of expertise needed if one were investigating the kind of extreme shear and torsion effects that counter-rotation of plasmas would involve. But such mathematics was not beyond Gerlach or the scientists involved with the project.

So once again, why involve a mathematician from outside the project, and from the distant University of Königsberg?

Is there any other clue to what Elizabeth Adler may have been doing?

---

[22] Farrell, *The SS Brotherhood of the Bell,* pp. 152-153. The quotation is from Witkowski, *The Truth About the Wunderwaffe,* p. 235, with emphasis there added.

While there is no direct evidence, there is a very significant bit of indirect evidence, and it has already been mentioned, one of those obvious facts that one might overlook unless attention were drawn to it: Elizabeth Adler was a mathematician *from the University of Königsberg*. And of course, the University of Königsberg was home to the very first Unified Field Theory, the "higher-dimensional" unified theory of Theodor Franz Eduard Kaluza, the first theory successfully to unite mathematically the gravitational equations of General Relativity with Maxwell's electromagnetic field equations. It was the very theory that led to the whole Unified Field Theory craze of the 1920s and 1930s in the first place. Dr. Kaluza was, of course, a *Privatdozent* or a kind of "adjunct" in the University's mathematics department, and, after his paper had been published, was certainly a high-profile figure. Dr. Elizabeth Adler could hardly have been present at the University *in the same department* without having heard of his name.

This affords a clue into what the nature of her mathematical involvement in the Bell project might actually have been, for Kaluza's theory required a thorough familiarity and facility with tensor analysis. By being asked by the Nazis to make mathematical studies of damping of "vibrations" in "spherical" objects, it is highly possible that Dr. Adler was, in effect, asked by the Nazis to undertake the same type of higher dimensional tensor analysis of electrical machines as was undertaken in the United States at almost the same time by Gabriel Kron. Something like these speculations, I believe, must lie at the heart of her unique involvement with the Bell.

There are other indicators that connect the Bell with Königsberg and to Kaluza's breathtaking higher-dimensional Unified Field Theory, however, than just the presence of one lone mathematician from the university in the project, and these are the very nature of the Kaluza Theory's geometry itself. Recall that in Kaluza's theory the basic geometry of the universe, of space-time itself, was *cylindrical.*

Thus, with the Bell's two counter-rotating cylinders designed to maximize torsion effects, we have an indicator that perhaps the

Nazis were experimenting with a modified Kaluza-Klein theory, one which incorporated the torsion tensor itself.

Theodor Franz Eduard Kaluza in Later Life

But this is not the only clue that this is precisely what the Nazis were up to. The final clue comes from Witkowski's comment – quoted above – that her involvement in the project concerned the "damping of vibrations" in "spherical objects." What has this to due with torsion?

Recall our earlier analogy of wringing a metal can, and that torsion in effect is the localized spiraling and pleating of the medium of space-time itself. Viewed in the "torsion context", large masses would function as natural resonators of torsion waves. In other words, a planet itself would be a "spherical object", and how to damp vibrations in the planet caused by torsion waves would certainly be a concern to the Nazis! It is a short step from this to the realization that Tesla once boasted that, with proper resonance, waves could be induced in the Earth that would eventually not damp, and cause the planet to break apart.

So Witkowski's clue does, in fact, lead us back to Königsberg, to Kaluza's theory, to torsion, and to the implication that the Nazis had indeed figured out that they were learning to control a physics with the potential to bust the planet itself. The indirect clues are sufficient to conclude as a reasoned circumstantial case that Elizabeth Adler's expertise was in the rarefied and subtle practicalities concerned with tensor analysis of electrical machines and torsion fields applied to "spherical objects." And with this, once again, note that we have also provided yet another chain of reasoning as to why the Nazis classified the Bell as *Kriegsendscheident* or "war decisive." They appreciated its significance not only as a weapons platform, but fully understood the implications of the physics that they were learning to control: it truly had potentially planet busting weapons potential.

Hence the argument that the Nazis could not – and moreover *would* not – have been testing any version of Einstein's Unified Field Theory for ideological reasons falls flat on its face, for it was not the only version of the theory in circulation. The Kaluza-Klein theory had been around longer. All it would have taken was someone with an interest and expertise in spin polarization and gravity to make the connections, via torsion.

Someone like Nobel physics laureate Dr. Walther Gerlach.

E. Gerlach Busies Himself with Bismuth and Ferromagnetism

Gerlach, prominent physicist and scientist, by war's end the ostensible director of Nazi Germany's atom bomb project, and secret director of the Bell project, was a very odd duck indeed to be heading all these sensitive projects. Never a member of the Nazi party, yet a supporter of its regime, Gerlach nonetheless always resisted the "Aryan physics" fanatics within Nazi Germany who wished to proscribe any explorations of Einstein or his "Jewish physics." If nothing else, this is an indicator that, when practical weapons were concerned, the Nazi regime was quick to throw ideology out the window.

But Gerlach represents something else. Besides being a Nobel laureate, Gerlach was a experimental scientist who - after his famous experiment with Stern that earned him his Nobel prize – continued to work in areas concerned with magnetism. It would be safe to say that Gerlach was probably one of the world's foremost experts in magnetism from the years prior to and during the Second World War. He did some work studying the magnetic deflection properties of bismuth,[23] and later designed a series of experiments that demonstrated that the radiometer effect was due to the intensity of light and not its frequency. Later research found him experimenting with ferromagnetism. In short, Gerlach was the perfect man to head a project like the Bell.

The mention of bismuth and Gerlach is important, for perhaps bismuth was one of those elements that was a component of the Bell's fuel, the enigmatic "Xerum 525." And bismuth, with its pinkish appearance, might also account for the violet-reddish hue ascribed to Xerum 525 as well. Given Gerlach's experimental and materials research interest, it also stands to reason that the Bell represented to him a perfect platform on which to test the torsion "absorbing" and "deflecting" properties of various materials. Recall, for example, that the Nazis placed all sorts of organic materials in the presence of the device's field. One may reasonably guess that similar experiments were done on non-organic elements and compounds.

But for what purpose?

Reexamine all the has progressed thus far, and particularly Gerlach's experimental track record. By the time of the Bell, Gerlach's own experiments have provided many of the benchmarks needed to allow such a project to go forward. But why test so many different compounds in the presence of the Bell?

The answer is very simple, but laden with profound implications. If indeed the Bell represents a technology designed to maximize and control torsion fields, then it would appear that the Nazis were in effect trying to measure the electro-magnetic and gravitational coefficients of these materials. In short, they were trying to discover, as an inevitable benchmark of a complete research project, what the torsion-deflecting, and torsion-"resonating," "-amplifying" or "-absorbing" properties of various materials were. All of this, again, would have been an essential experimental benchmark in the project, especially if it had been conceptualized as a test of unified field theory concepts and their "weaponizability."

---

[23] An interesting choice, since bismuth is often said to be a component in the laminated "recovered metals" from UFO crashes.

Learn to control and manipulate torsion in the Unified Field Theory context, and one has learned to control and manipulate gravity, time, electro-magnetism, and space itself. One can manipulate them for energy, for propulsion, and of course, for a horrifyingly powerful weapon of mass destruction, a weapon so powerful that it would make the largest thermonuclear bombs look like child's toys.

No wonder that one British intelligence agent alluded to the fact that Kammler's "think tank" was involved in areas of physics that some would think to be magical, areas that were monstrous, on a daily basis.[24] No wonder, then, that the Nazis gave the Bell a classification higher than their atom bomb project and all of the other wild and sensational projects in the Reich.

Likewide it is also no wonder, with the Bell's disappearance, that someone somewhere is seriously interested in the suppression of the technology, and the "discarded" theory, that it represents.

---

[24] Q.v. my *The SS Brotherhood of the Bell,* pp. 192-241.

12.

THE DISTURBING PARALLELS:
THE BELL, THE SHIP, AND THE SUPPRESSION

"These 'high cabal' fellows make or break nations financially, as is almost being done to Argentina as this is being written. They also have been stopping (coefficient of performance greater than unity) electrical power systems since shortly after the turn of the century, using whatever means are necessary – fair or foul. That is why we are still burning oil, coal, natural gas, and why our automobiles and trucks run off gasoline and diesel, and not off free electrical energy from the vacuum."
Tom Bearden (Lt. Col. US Army, Ret.)[1]

Despite their dissimilarities, both the Philadelphia Experiment and the Nazi Bell project evidence a number of similarities that grow out of their respective conceptual foundations in the torsion tensor and the various Unified Field Theories of the 1920s, whether than of Einstein's 1928 version or some modified Kaluza-Klein theory that incorporated torsion. A catalogue of these is in order.

A. Conceptual and Parameter Similarities

Both projects evidence not only an apparent grounding in these unified field concepts, but more importantly, similarities in their actual execution. For example:

1) Both projects relied on *electrical and magnetic rotation* to achieve their effects. This in turn means that
2) Both projects understood that while the Unified Field Theory or Theories on which they may have been based were incomplete as physical theories, they were nonetheless theories that made specific predictions about the local engineerability of space-time via torsion effects, and that thus, the theory itself was engineerable.
3) Both projects required high electrical power consumption.
4) Both projects achieved fantastic results; and finally,

---

[1] Tom Bearden, *Energy from the Vacuum: Concepts and Principles,* p. 211.

5) In both projects, *some* of these results were unanticipated, and in both projects, many of these were biological and physiological effects.

B. Similarities of Biological Effects

1) Both projects, when first tested at full scale, exhibited unanticipated biological and physiological effects. Some of the Bell's scientists were killed accidentally in the first tests, and many of its other participants experienced lingering physiological effects for some time afterward, such as vertigo, sleeplessness, and metallic tastes in their mouths. Similarly, the Philadelphia Experiment's test ship's crew experienced extreme disorientation similar to Purkinji effects, and, if Allende's allegations are correct – as they have every appearance of being – in some cases spontaneous combustion, or simple disappearance resulted, often when re-exposed to weak magnetic fields.

2) In the case of the Bell, it would appear that subsequent testing on organic materials was done in part to understand the torsion effects on various materials, and in part to learn how to mitigate these effects on living beings. The accidental deaths resulting from its initial tests were thus perhaps viewed as being confirmations of the Bell's original design parameters, rather than as failures of the experiments as such.

3) In the case of the Philadelphia Experiment, however, it would appear – judging from the U.S. Navy's reaction to the Varo Edition – that no further testing was done, or if so, that it was done under some other entity. The extreme physiological effects appeared to be viewed by the U.S. Navy as failures in the total design concept of the experiment, which would explain why further testing was suspended, or as is more likely, handed over to some other agency.

C. The Most Disturbing Similarity: Their Disappearance

But in spite of all these parallels and similarities, there is a much more disturbing similarity that unites both projects. Both projects, like the U.S.S. *Eldridge* herself, appeared to have completely disappeared. In the case of the Bell, there are now three possible avenues that it traversed:

1) It went – pace Nick Cook and Igor Witkowski – into some super-secret post-war American black project;
2) It disappeared – pace British researcher Geoffrey Brooks – into a post-war independent and ongoing Nazi project in Argentina; or,
3) As outlined in this book, it may have remained in Germany itself, buried in the tunnels and galleries of Kammler's SS facilities in the Harz Mountains. In the latter instance, the question becomes *where did its project documentation go?* In this instance the trail is even thinner than with the Bell itself. It is unlikely that the SS would have buried it as well. So where did the documentation go?

And what about the Philadelphia Experiment? Where did *it* go?

In our speculations we have argued that the U.S. Navy at some point may either have lost control of the experiment when some other entity wrested control over it from the Navy, or that the Navy may have turned it over to some other entity for continued experimentation. In either case, the result is the same. The project, its technology and project documentation, simply disappeared. All that remains are, as was seen in part two, suggestive log books and doctored entries.

And this is the point: *both* projects disappeared. They are entirely and completely *gone.*

And therewith we discover the disturbing implication. It would, perhaps, be possible to dismiss the evidence in favor of one or the other project as being entirely circumstantial and conjectural in spite of the wealth of details surrounding each, and thereby to dismiss one or the other project's disappearance as an accident or coincidence of history. However, it becomes much more difficult, if not implausible and irrational, to do so when a reasonable case can be made that both projects were experimentally rationalized on the basis of some form of Unified Field Theory and the torsion tensor. It becomes even more problematical when one adds to these considerations that each project represents a different side in the world's most terrible and destructive war to date. Nor is the possibility that their respective disappearances were coordinated from some central point here in view nor is it an issue, for whether or not there is such an entity, the fact of their mutual disappearance can hardly be accidental.

D. Two Curious Things

There are, in fact, two curious things that not only would tend to corroborate the view that their disappearance was not coincidental, but that give some slight indication that their disappearance might somehow be related. The first of these is a photograph of the very ONR committee that led to the Varo Annotated Edition, a photograph in which none other than Dr. Werner Von Braun sits front and center. The second of these is an incident revealed in a set of documents that this author discovered in the U.S. National Archives and Records Administration in College Park, Maryland. Of the two, the latter is much more significant, and it will be dealt with last.

1. The ONR Photo with Von Braun

Charles Berlitz and William Moore included a photograph in their book which, upon closer examination in the context of the foregoing considerations, might be a symbolic indicator that much more was afoot in the ONR in the post-war period than would meet the eye. The photograph is of the Project Orbiter Committee, which, as their own caption indicates, was the very same "group that contacted Dr. Jessup).["2] As they indicate, the photograph was taken on March 17, 1955, at approximately the same period as the ONR's initial contact with Jessup. Seated at the far left of the table

---

[2] Berlitz and Moore, *The Philadelphia Experiment,* first page of photographic section.

is Commander George W. Hoover, one of the officers involved in the Varo-Jessup affair. In the row of men standing behind him, fifth from the right hand side of the picture, and almost dead center in the photo, is none other than Austin W. Stanton, at that time President of Varo Inc. And seated opposite all these men, slightly to the right of center in the picture, is none other than Dr. Wernher Von Braun, isolated at the table as if he is holding court.

The Project Orbiter Committee, March 17, 1955. Commander Hoover is seated on the far left. Austin Stanton, President of Varo, Inc., stands in the center of the row behind him. Dr. Von Braun is Seated toward the center of the table in the grey suit.

The presence of Von Braun on the ONR Project Orbiter Committee raises certain disturbing questions in relationship to the Philadelphia Experiment. As the Varo Edition itself stated, the ONR's interest in the marked up annotations in Jessup's UFO book – at least *officially* – was because no clue into the nature of UFO propulsion and gravity control should be overlooked. After all, the space race was on! Given that the Varo Edition was printed and circulated among the Navy's "top people", it stands to reason that Wernher Von Braun was likely to have been one of those "top people" that received a copy of the Varo Edition! If so, then it means that at least one ex-Nazi had significant insight into one of America's most sensitive wartime projects. But this is not the only super-secret research pie he had his formerly SS fingers in!

The *other* pie is indicated by asking the following question: is there any evidence, direct or otherwise, that might corroborate the possibility that he did know about the Philadelphia Experiment?

Indeed there is, and it is *strange* evidence.

In my first book on wartime Nazi secret weapons, *Reich of the Black Sun,* I pointed out that in the so-called Cooper-Cantwheel series of the famous (or depending on one's lights, infamous) MAJIC-12 documents, there is a document entitled "White Hot Intelligence Estimate." As I pointed out in that book, the document purports to be a preliminary technological evaluation of whatever craft had crashed at Roswell, New Mexico in July of 1947. And as I also point out, the document itself indicates that after the American examiners were suitably mystified as to what they now had in their possession, they called in the Paperclip scientists to take a look and render their opinion as well![3] Viewed in the context of this discussion, what this indicates is that the U.S. military was sharing some of its most sensitive secrets with some of the top Nazi scientists in the country. Since Von Braun was in New Mexico during the time period of the Roswell crash, this would mean – if indeed the document proves to be genuine – that he had his hands in the UFO pie, and the Philadelphia Experiment pie as well!

As I also pointed out in *Reich of the Black Sun,* it is *highly unlikely* that the U.S. military would have shared its Roswell UFO secret with the Paperclip Nazis *if it had reasonably convinced itself that the technology that they now possessed was extra-terrestrial and therefore decades or hundreds of years in advance of any terrestrial technology.* The presence of the Paperclip Nazis

---

[3] See my *Reich of the Black Sun,* pp. 287-291.

examining the craft means something different: the military was "fishing."

And the presence of Von Braun on the Project Orbiter Committee, and his possible receipt of a copy of the Varo Edition, means that he was a highly placed individual in the U.S. effort to study UFOs and any assumed or related technology. His presence in the Orbiter ONR Committee, in other words, *lends credence to my earlier interpretation of the "White Hot Intelligence Estimate" in* **Reich of the Black Sun:** *His presence there tends to support the idea, based on the internal evidence of the "White Hot Intelligence Estimate," that at least that document within the Cooper-Cantwheel collection of* Majic-12 *documents is genuine.* At the minimum, it argues that if the documents are *not* genuine but a fabrication, then they are an extremely well-conceived fabrication, for who would reasonably assume, if fabricating a document, that the U.S. military would expose extra-terrestrial technology to its former and only-recently-defeated enemies? For someone to have fabricated the suggestion that the Roswell craft was revealed to the Paperclip scientists implies, by the very nature of the case, inside knowledge that at least *some* of these "ex"-Nazis were privy to the most sensitive areas of American military research and intelligence.

If this line of reasoning is true, then it means that at least Von Braun had extensive, if not full, knowledge not only of the US UFO effort, but of its experiments in radar stealth and absorption, and all the unanticipated effects; it means that Von Braun knew of its efforts to render practical military use of Einstein's 1928 Unified Field Theory. Von Braun, in other words, likely knew the salient details of the Philadelphia Experiment.

Bottom line: there is a connection – whatever its exact nature may be - between (1) these two famous events, (2) their subsequent suppression by the U.S. military and (3) one very highly placed Nazi within the American military-industrial complex. And given the close knit nature of the relationships between the Paperclip Nazis inside NASA and elsewhere, we may reasonably assume that whatever Von Braun knew, they also knew.

But while the U.S. and its highest secrets were apparently an open book at least to some Paperclip Nazis, they themselves apparently managed to keep some secrets to themselves. Moreover, these secret were apparently so important that the U.S. risked a major incident with the Eastern bloc less than a year after the European War's end.

2. The Czech Incident, 1946

And this brings us to what I call "the Czech Incident."

I first learned about this incident when some remarkable documents came into my hands as the result of searches in the U.S. National Archives. To my knowledge, these documents are publicly revealed here for the first time.

In the early months of 1946, as Europe was still locked in the grip of winter, the French and American press in Europe broke a small story, which dropped off the radar screen almost as soon as it had appeared.

It seemed that sometime in February of that year, a small team of American commandos belonging to units of the U.S. Third Army slipped across the German-Czech border into Soviet occupied Czechoslovakia on a "raid." The Czechs of course raised a furor (at the behest of their Soviet masters, no doubt), and then the incident died down and was totally forgotten.

But this "minor" incident has what I believe to be truly significant implications and portents. To understand what they are, we need to turn to the declassified documents themselves and how they came to my attention.

While researching my previous book on the Bell, *The SS Brotherhood of the Bell* I came across the fact that it was a combat command of the Third American Armored Division that had first entered SS General Kammler's "think tank" headquarters at the Skoda Works in Pilsen, Czechoslovakia. So, naturally enough, I began searching for that unit's combat reports and intelligence reports in the Archives.

I didn't find them, but what I did find was equally if not more important, as it turned out. What I had found was a set of War and State Department documents all relating to what they themselves referred to as "the Czech Incident." The documents, as catalogued in the National Archives, were as follows:

Item Number	Description
REP0006C: RG 319, P & OTS Decimal File 1946-1948 270/15/32/7, box 75 350.05 Case 7-8,	Czech Incident
REP0006C: RG 319, P & O Decimal File 1946-1948 270/15/25/7, box 465 580 ATC Case 25,	ATC in Czechoslovakia
REP0006C RG 319, Plans and Operations Decimal File 1946-1948 270/15/24/6, Box 405 286.3 case 19,	1 March 1946, Removal of Documents

Needless to say, I was intrigued. What were we doing in Czechoslovakia, well within the Eastern Soviet bloc, in 1946? According to the file descriptions, we were "removing documents." What *sort* of documents, I wondered? And why was the U.S. *Army* doing this? Why risk a major international incident just to remove some documents?

Naturally, I ordered the set, and was stunned.

I received a small sheaf of papers about ¼" thick, but they told quite a story if one read between the lies….er….lines. The first document that I read was a letter from Congressman A.J. Sabath (D, Ill.), then Chairman of the House Rules Committee, to Robert P. Patterson, President Truman's Secretary of War:

House of Representatives U.S.
Committee on Rules
Washington, D.C.
March 1, 1946

Honorable Robert P. Patterson
Secretary of War
War Department
Washington 25, D.C.

Dear Mr. Secretary:

    I was indeed surprised to read that some officers of the U.S. Army *have removed certain documents from a certain place in Czechslovakia.*

    May I inquire who has issued such orders, and the underlying reason for issuing the orders or authorizing such act. I have been informed that these papers and documents *have been returned to the Czechoslovak government;* nevertheless, I am interested in who has issued such order and the reason for issuing same.

Respectfully yours,

A.J. Sabath

I was stupefied by this letter. In it, three sensational assertions were made regarding a military operation inside Soviet occupied Czechoslovakia in 1946:

1) Sabath states that U.S. Army *officers* were inside Czechoslovakia in 1946;
2) That they "removed certain documents from a certain place" inside that country; and what was the most incredible of them all,
3) That these documents were subsequently returned to the Czechoslovakian government!

So in other words, officers of the U.S. Army had entered Czechoslovakia, and removed documents. An international incident occurred as, quite naturally, the Czech government had protested. The documents were then returned!

    So why, I asked myself, had the U.S. Army risked a major international incident to remove documents, only to return them again? Something, obviously, was wrong with this picture.

SEVENTY-NINTH CONGRESS

A. J. SABATH, ILL., CHAIRMAN

E. E. COX, GA.   LEO E. ALLEN, ILL.
HOWARD W. SMITH, VA.   EARL C. MICHENER, MICH.
J. BAYARD CLARK, N. C.   CHARLES A. HALLECK, IND.
JOHN J. DELANEY, N. Y.   CLARENCE J. BROWN, OHIO
WILLIAM M. COLMER, MISS.
JOE B. BATES, KY.
ROGER C. SLAUGHTER, MO.

House of Representatives U. S.

Committee on Rules

Washington, D. C.
March 1, 1946

Honorable Robert P. Patterson
Secretary of War
War Department
Washington 25, D. C.

Dear Mr. Secretary:

I was indeed surprised to read that some officers
of the U. S. Army have removed certain documents from
a certain place in Czechoslovakia.

May I inquire who has issued such orders, and
the underlying reason for issuing the orders or authorizing
such act. I have been informed that these papers and
documents have been returned to the Czechoslovak government;
nevertheless, I am interested in who has issued such
order and the reason for issuing same.

Respectfully yours,

A. J. Sabath

*Congressman Sabath's Inquiry to the War
Department Concerning the Czech Incident*

I became even more intrigued when I read the document that
accompanied the Congressman's letter, which hardly clarified the
matter.

TO: WDOPD   FROM: A.C. of S., G-2   date: 7 Mar 46 COMMENT NO. 2
Col Lovell/71497/mnr

1. Letter was received by Secretary of War from Congressman A.J. Sabath of Illinois expressing surprise that U.S. Army officers had removed certain documents from Czechoslovakia. The Congressman wanted to know who issued such orders and the underlying reason therefore.

2. Recommend a letter substantially as follows be prepared for signature of Secretary of War.

> "Please refer to your letter of 1 March 1946 concerning the recent incident involving members of the U.S. Army engaged in the recovery of hidden German documents in Czechoslovakia. An exhaustive investigation has been made by the War Department and I am satisfied that our representatives in Germany, as well as those in the U.S. Embassy in Prague, acted in good faith.
>
> *Captured German documents are one of the basic sources of information essential to the occupation of Germany and the prosecution of Nazi war criminals.* The party which entered Czechoslovakia for the purpose of recovering these documents did not proceed arbitrarily into Czechoslovakia *but obtained prior border clearance from the Czechoslovakian mission in Regensburg, Germany.* It appears that the misunderstanding which arose was due to a failure to follow established protocol and that such clearance as had been obtained was not on a sufficiently high level within the Czechoslovakian government, once the importance of the documents became known.
>
> *The Czechoslovakian Government as well as Czech officials in Germany appear to be completely satisfied by United States explanations and the return of the documents.*

Besides the fact that the letter never answered the real question in Congressman Sabath's letter, namely, who had issued the orders for the mission in the first place, the response itself appeared to me to be, on close examination, a deliberate obfuscation. Consider its assertions:

1) U.S. Army Officers had indeed crossed into Czechoslovakia;
2) They obtained- so the letter maintains – their border passes from the Czech mission in Regensburg, Germany;

3) The purpose of the mission had been to recover documents necessary to the War Crimes Trials then in progress in Nuremburg.
4) The obtained border passes did not come from a sufficiently high level of the Czech government, and hence, an international incident had occurred, which blew over with American "explanations" and the "return of the documents."

But there is something quite wrong with this easy picture. Why had permission not been sought from a sufficiently high level within the Czech government to begin with? Why *risk* an international incident, with U.S. army personnel deep inside the Soviet zone of occupation, to begin with, especially if the mission were simply to recover documents necessary to the War Crimes trials? Why risk a *military* operation, when a simple request to the Czech government – just as anxious to see Nazi war criminals punished as any other European nation – probably would have procured the necessary documents? And finally, why would the Czech mission in Regensburg not have known that the border passes would have to have come from "a high level" of their government?

In short, the U.S. army appeared to be complicating matters no end simply to recover incriminating documents. And that meant that the documents which were being sought probably had nothing whatsoever to do with the war crimes trials at all. Some *other* types of documents were being sought.

It looked to me as if the "Czech Incident" was beginning to take on all the trappings of a covert intelligence operation. Even the mention of passes from the Czech mission in Regensburg was a bit too much information, and, as I was to discover, it appeared in none of the other documents. Perhaps, I thought, if it was an intelligence operation, fake border passes had been prepared. The presence of the Czech mission in Regensburg would have given intelligence operatives easy access to Czech forms, inks, papers, and seals, and it would have been a relatively easy thing to accomplish.

No. The U.S. Army would not have risked an international incident merely to recover documents of historical or judiciary interest.

TO: WDOPD   FROM: A. C. of S., G-2   DATE: 7 Mar 46 COMMENT NO. 2
                                                       Col Lovell/71497/mnr

1. Letter was received by Secretary of War from Congressman A. J. Sabath of Illinois expressing surprise that U. S. Army officers had removed certain documents from Czechoslovakia. The Congressman wanted to know who issued such orders and the underlying reason therefore.

2. Recommend a letter substantially as follows be prepared for signature of Secretary of War.

"Please refer to your letter of 1 March 1946 concerning the recent incident involving members of the U. S. Army engaged in the recovery of hidden German documents in Czechoslovakia. An exhaustive investigation has been made by the War Department and I am satisfied that our representatives in Germany, as well as those in the U. S. Embassy in Prague, acted in good faith.

Captured German documents are one of the basic sources of information essential to the occupation of Germany and the prosecution of Nazi war criminals. The party which entered Czechoslovakia for the purpose of recovering these documents did not proceed arbitrarily into Czechoslovakia but obtained prior border clearance from the Czechoslovakian mission in Regensburg, Germany. It appears that the misunderstanding which arose was due to a failure to follow established protocol and that such clearance as had been obtained was not on a sufficiently high level within the Czechoslovakian government, once the importance of the documents became known.

The Czechoslovakian Government as well as Czech officials in Germany appear to be completely satisfied by United States explanations and the return of the documents.

War Department Memo Suggesting a Draft of a Letter in Reply to Congressman Sabath

Then I turned to the other documents in the sheaf from the National Archives, and these did indeed tell the "rest of the story," for they consisted of a series of Top Secret War Department letters and communiqués, none of which seemed to be able to get their story right.

The first letter was dated 19 February, 1946, and read as follows:

§§§

TOP SECRET

War Department
War Department General Staff
Operations Division
Washington, D.C.
Washington 25, D.C.

MEMORANDUM FOR LIEUTENANT GENERAL HULL: 19 February 1946
(THROUGH: Theater Group, OPD)
SUBJECT: Seizure of Documents by American Soldiers in Czechoslovakia

1. *As a result of a series of cables between State Department officials in Czechoslovakia and the State Department* as well as between USFET G-2, Military Attache, Czechoslovakia and War Department, G-2, *a conference was held at the State Department this date at which representatives of G-2, OPD, and the State Department were present. Purpose of the conference was to determine the course of action in the affair,* involving American soldiers allegedly violating Czechoslovak sovereignty *by a "raid" into Czechoslovak territory to procure 12,000 pounds of highly classified German documents.*

2. **The "raid", of which G-2 in Washington knew nothing prior to its completion, was successful in that the documents were removed into Germany** although 3 American soldiers engaged in the enterprise were apprehended by the Czechs and are now being held by Czech authorities.

3. *The exact contents of the cases removed are unknown, but it is believed that they consist of personal official files of Hitler and Himmler.* **The Czechs, however, seem to hold the opinion that the material was related to the most highly developed radar equipment and data.**

4. *The State Department feels that the Czechoslovak government could very well claim the raid to be in the nature of an act of war.* To placate the Czechs,

303

State Department has instructed their ambassador to say that an investigation of the matter is being made.

5. As a result of the conference, G-2 is holding a teleconference with General Sibert, G-2, USFET, on 20 February 1946. A copy of the proposed War Department transmission is attached.

Incl   /s/ ALFRED D. STARBIRD
Copy of proposed telecom   Colonel, GSC
With ETO, G-2   Chief, European Section
                                              Theater Group, OPD

§§§

This was truly stunning stuff! Even a surface reading will leaves one with the indelible impression that the "minor incident" was anything but minor! But closer reading reveals even more discrepancies and disturbing implications:

1) Note first of all that the document header is the General Staff's Operations division. This is highly significant, since later on in the memorandum it is revealed that "G-2" in Washington knew nothing of what was, by that very admission, a covert intelligence operation in the first place! Just who *may* have known in Washington D.C. is not revealed, if indeed anyone did. This means that the "raid" was a "deep black" operation, and therefore, that the documents that were being sought were hardly of merely historical importance. Something else entirely was at stake.

2) The memorandum also reveals how many documents were sought: 12,000 *pounds*, or 6 *tons* of papers! This would have required that the "raiding party" include several soldiers, and most definitely at least one large heavy load bearing truck, if not more. This means that the "raid" had to have been a well-planned affair. Given that I now knew that it *was* a covert intelligence operation involving U.S. military personnel, my earlier speculation about forged border papers began to look much more plausible.

304

3)   The memorandum also makes another astonishing admission, namely, that not only were the documents successfully removed to Germany - and that meant to the American zone of occupation in Bavaria – but also that their exact contents were unknown; they were believed "to consist of personal official files of Hitler and

WAR DEPARTMENT
WAR DEPARTMENT GENERAL STAFF
OPERATIONS DIVISION
WASHINGTON 25, D. C.

MEMORANDUM FOR LIEUTENANT GENERAL HULL: 19 February 1946
(THROUGH: Theater Group, OPD)

SUBJECT: Seizure of Documents by American Soldiers in Czechoslovakia.

    1.   As a result of a series of cables between State Department officials in Czechoslovakia and the State Department as well as between USFET G-2, Military Attache, Czechoslovakia and War Department, G-2, a conference was held at the State Department this date at which representatives of G-2, OPD, and the State Department were present. Purpose of the conference was to determine the course of action in the affair, involving American soldiers allegedly violating Czechoslovak sovereignty by a "raid" into Czechoslovak territory to procure 12,000 pounds of highly classified German documents.

    2.   The "raid", of which G-2 in Washington knew nothing prior to its completion, was successful in that the documents were removed into Germany although 3 American soldiers engaged in the enterprise were apprehended by the Czechs and are now being held by Czech authorities.

    3.   The exact contents of the cases removed are unknown, but it is believed that they consist of personal official files of Hitler and Himmler. The Czechs, however, seem to hold the opinion that the material was related to the most highly developed radar equipment and data. The Czechs have demanded that the material be turned back to Czechoslovakia immediately in return for the release of the 3 American military personnel now being held by them.

    4.   The State Department feels that the Czechoslovak government could very well claim the raid to be in the nature of an act of war. To placate the Czechs, State Department has instructed their ambassador to say that an investigation of the matter is being made.

    5.   As a result of the conference, G-2 is holding a teleconference with General Sibert, G-2, USFET, on 20 February 1946. A copy of the proposed War Department transmission is attached.

Incl
  Copy of proposed telecon
   with ETO, G-2

ALFRED D. STARBIRD
Colonel, GSC
Chief, European Section
Theater Group, OPD

DECLASSIFIED
Authority NND 770016
By W NARA, Date

War Department Memorandum of Feb. 19, 1946

Himmler." This was preposterous on the face of it. Either Washington was lying and *did* know the contents, or it did not, and *someone else* authorized the operation, and *did* know, or at least had a strong suspicion, of what they contained. And if someone *else* had authorized the operation, that would explain why the War Department's response to Congressman Sabath never was able to answer Sabath's question regarding who had issued the orders for the operation to begin with.

4) The memorandum then gives out its "best guess" or even "cover story" as to what the documents may have been: personal official files of Hitler and Himmler themselves. But this again raises the nasty question once again: why risk a covert military operation simply to recover documents of merely historical interest, even if they *were* the private papers of Hitler and Himmler? If the documents really *were* their private papers, what about their contents would have warranted such a risky operation? It appeared to me as if a cover story were being privately circulated within the upper echelons of the American command structure, and that meant disinformation was occurring on a very high level. Moreover, the memorandum itself confirmed my analysis of the "risk" factor involved, for it states unequivocally that the State Department representatives at the inter-agency conference were very concerned that the Czech government – and by implication its Soviet masters – could regard the incursion as an act of war, which by any recognized standard of international law it clearly was. So again, what about the documents merited such a risk? Clearly, they had to contain something of supreme importance to assume this risk.

5) What that something may have been was also stated clearly in the memorandum, for as far as the Czech government was concerned, the documents had nothing whatsoever to do with Hitler or Himmler, and everything to do with some very advanced *technology,* with "the most highly developed radar equipment and *data.*"

With that admission, I began to smell the distinct odor of a connection between the raid and the super-secret SS secret weapons think-tank of *Obergruppenführer* Kammler, which was based, after all, in Czechoslovakia.

It was the mention of *radar equipment and data* that made the connection, for as I had outlined in *The SS Brotherhood of the Bell,* late war German radar experiments with wave-mixing on their Radar Absorbent Materials (RAM) had actually discovered the principles of *phase conjugation,*[4] a principle that could be turned into a horrendously powerful weapon,[5] and a principle that was also conceptually related both to the Bell, and more importantly, to some of the principles behind the Philadelphia Experiment.[6] Indeed, from Bearden's research into scalar physics, I knew at least one of the names of the Nazi scientists involved with this project: Dr. Hellmann. Pay attention to that name, for it will appear again before we're through. Like every other secret weapon project in Nazi Germany, Hellmann's radar project would have fallen under the direct aegis of Kammler's "think-tank."

This last fact was what convinced me that I was reading the carefully contrived documentation concerning a deep black covert military operation. But the nagging question remained: *Whose operation was it? Who gave the order for it?*

These new considerations also raised another series of questions, revealed by the *first* two documents already examined; these stated that the documents were *returned* to Czechoslovakia. Was it likely that the U.S. military would have risked a major international incident to recover documents that were merely Hitler's and Himmler's secret papers, only to *return* them to Czechoslovakia?

Bestimmt nicht!

It is far more likely that the documents that were retrieved were one thing, and that the documents that were returned were quite another. After all, the U.S. had no shortage of secret Nazi papers

---

[4] See my *The SS Brotherhood of the Bell,* pp. 222-236.
[5] See my *The Cosmic War: Interplanetary Warfare, Modern Physics and Ancient Texts,* pp. 100-135; 234-274.
[6] See the present work, pp. 171-174.

that could have been turned over to the Czechs without really relinquishing anything genuinely sensitive or valuable.

Was there any confirmation of the basic outlines of this scenario that had emerged? Indeed there was.

§§§

TOP SECRET

WAR DEPARTMENT
WAR DEPARTMENT GENERAL STAFF
OPERATIONS DIVISION
WASHINGTON 25, D.C.

20 February 1946

MEMORANDUM FOR: General Hull (Through Theater Grp.)
SUBJECT: *Intelligence Forray* into Czechoslovakia

1. From tele-conference this morning on the subject of the raid by American military personnel into Czechoslovakia, it was determined that the documents removed consisted of:

    a. *German counter-intelligence correspondence relating to Bohemia-Moravia,* papers belonging to Himmler, Von Ribbentrop, Frank and Funk and among the documents,
    b. *Gestapo and German intelligence papers relating to Bohemia-Moravia,*
    c. President Benes files from 1918 to 1938,
    d. *Locations of treasures spotted in caves in Czechoslovakia.*

2. G-2, War Department, has been informed that the Herald Tribune, Paris, has complete story on the affair except for contents of documents. The theater, this morning, indicated that it would be impossible to retain control of the press in this matter because of the actions by Czechoslovakia in closing their border to all American travellers(sic).

3. The State Department is dispatching a cable to its Embassy at Prague authorizing the Ambassador to apologize for his affair.

                      /s/ ALFRED D. STARBIRD
                      Colonel, G.S.C.
                      Chied, European Section
                      Theater Group, OPD

This document was the clincher that connected the "raid" to the *Kammlerstab,* for notice the first two items: "German counter-intelligence correspondence relating to Bohemia-Moravia" and "Gestapo and German intelligence papers relating to Bohemia-Moravia." Recall that Bohemia-Moravia was a Reich Protectorate

TOP SECRET

WAR DEPARTMENT
WAR DEPARTMENT GENERAL STAFF
OPERATIONS DIVISION
WASHINGTON 25, D. C.

20 February 1946

MEMORANDUM FOR: General Hull *(Through Theater Grp)*.

SUBJECT: Intelligence Forray into Czechoslovakia

    1. From tele-conference this morning on the subject of the raid by American military personnel into Czechoslovakia, it was determined that the documents removed consisted of:

        a. German counter-intelligence correspondence relating to Bohemia-Moravia, papers belonging to Himmler, Von Ribbentrop, Frank and Funk, and among the documents,

        b. Gestapo and German intelligence papers relating to Bohemia-Moravia,

        c. President Benes files from 1918 to 1938,

        d. Locations of treasures spotted in caves in Czechoslovakia.

    2. G-2, War Department, has been informed that the Herald Tribune, Paris, has complete story on the affair except for contents of documents. The theater, this morning, indicated that it would be impossible to retain control of the press in this matter because of the actions by Czechoslovakia in closing their border to all American travellers.

    3. The State Department is dispatching a cable to its Embassy at Prague authorizing the Ambassador to apologize for this affair.

ALFRED D. STARBIRD
Colonel, G.S.C.
Chief, European Section
Theater Group, OPD

BEST COPY AVAILABLE

TOP SECRET

War Department Memorandum of Feb 20, 1946, Indicating Real Contents of Documents

under the direct jurisdiction of the SS, and that the triple belt of counter-intelligence security surrounding Kammler's "think tank" was headed by none other than "Gestapo Müller." Given that this belt of security would have infested literally all of Bohemia with Gestapo agents sniffing out potential breaches, this cache of counter-intelligence documents doubtless included a great deal of information on the Kammler Group, its personnel, its projects, and their locations. Hence, even the last reference to "treasure hidden in caves" may be an oblique reference to the Kammler Group's numerous underground installations in the Harz and in the German-Czech Sudetenland.

This interpretation put the whole operation in an entirely new light, for it appeared that someone, somewhere in the U.S. military and/or intelligence community was trying to gain as much information as possible about the Group and its projects, and this implies that the U.S. military, to some extent, was in the dark on some aspects of Kammler's "think tank."

By now knowing that I had discovered some truly significant documentation that had hitherto not been known, I decided to share them with my colleague and fellow-Bell-researcher, Igor Witkowski. I copied the documents and wrote a short letter, mailing them to him in Warsaw. His response, dated 10 April, 2006, was not long in coming, and I cite the main body of his letter below:

> As to the documents on the foray into Czechoslovakia, I fully share your view. It's not self-consistent, I mean I will never believe that Patton's army has taken such a risk (at least political) and has gone so deep into the other party's territory for something that didn't have really concrete value. What is presented in the documents is a version that they have found something purely historical.
>
> It contradicts the other sources, as you mentioned....In other words, you may quote me in your book if you want, that in my view, on the basis of numerous materials and testimonies I am absolutely sure that the released story is incomplete and false.[7]

---

[7] Igor Witkowski, personal communication with the author, April 10, 2006.

But this was not to be the end of our correspondence on the matter, for I replied to Witkowski's letter with an email outlining the connection to Dr. Hellmann and the late-war German radar wave-mixing on non-linear materials, the experiments that led to the German discovery of phase conjugation.[8] Witkowski's response was even more provocative, for it revealed another, more sinister, connection:

> That's very interesting. If it's the same Hellmann that I think about, that's making the story even more intriguing. (A) certain Hellmann from the AEG was mentioned in the context of the Chronos project and I tried to "find" him. It had turned out that such a person played a leading role in the Argentine Huemul (sic) Project (nuclear) in the 40s/50s – the full purpose of which wasn't clear even to one of the directors of today's research center that I talked with.[9]

If it was the same Hellmann, and there is little reason to doubt it, since the *physics principles are related,* then there are two clear connections to the Bell project: (1) through AEG, or the *Allgemeine Elektricitäts Gemeinschaft*, the corporation that was contracted to build the power supply for the Bell; and (2) through his connection with the Bell directly through "Project Chronos", the Bell's code-name. Notably, Witkowski also mentions a connection to the post-war Nazi fusion and plasma research conducted in Argentina! And there is one final connection. The documents that I had uncovered indicated approximately where the "raid" was seeking the cache of hidden Nazi papers: near a river bed approximately 30 miles south of Prague!

So what does all of this mean? Who might have issued the orders?

As Witkowski points out, the U.S. Army personnel involved in the raid were most likely from the U.S. Third Army in Bavaria, General George S. Patton's command. And it was Patton, after all, who was in command of the forces that ultimately entered and occupied Pilsen, Czechoslovakia, headquarters of the Kammler Group. The Third Army thus apparently continued its hunt for

---

[8] Email of the author to Igor Witkowski, April 19, 2006.
[9] Email of Igor Witkowski to the author, April 20, 2006.

information of the "think tank" for some period after the famous general's untimely and suspicious death.

But there is another entirely different possibility suggested by the documents' apparent confusion over the contents of the cache of Nazi papers, and their inability to come up with a clear indication of where the order for the operation had actually come from. Throughout the documents cited here, one senses a certain *genuine* mystification on the part of the War Department, as it scrambles to learn as much about the operation as it could.

So....

....what if the orders did not come from within the American command structure at all?

What if the emerging Nazi International, in the form of its many "assistance" organizations like *Die Spinne* (The Spider), the *Kammeradenwerk* or ODESSA (*Organization der ehemahlige SS Angehörigen*, Organizaition of Former SS Members), had actually run the operation as a "false flag" operation, using American uniforms, American-English speaking SS commandos, American papers and so on? It is a possibility, and given the inability of the War Department's own G-2 intelligence to come up with anything like a consistent explanation of the contents of the documents, it is a reasonable possibility.[10] Nonetheless, my personal opinion inclines to the idea that it was an American conceived and executed operation, though most likely one emanating from the OSS, and not the military directly.

§§§

So what do we have?

The same conceptual foundations, secret experiments by the war's two most powerful and opposed combatants, similarly fantastic results in each case, and a theory that was "incomplete"

---

[10] Against this speculation, the documents do refer to three captured American soldiers taken by the Czechs during the course of the operation. These were held prisoner until the documents were returned and an apology made. However, the documents nowhere mention these soldiers' names (possibly for reasons of security). It would not have been too difficult for the SS to capture or "plant" prisoners for the Czechs, solidifying the false flag deception.

but engineerable: all these things taken together do not spell coincidence but suppression. The fact that both projects along with their science, technology, and documentation *continue* to be suppressed *does* raise the possibility of a central coordinating mechanism. There are very few agencies in the world with the means, resources, and methods of surveillance and suppression to do so. If there was indeed a continuing post-war Nazi International operating inside and along side of the various victorious powers' black projects, then the suppression of the Philadelphia Experiment, and if the possibility that control of its documentation and technology were either wrested from the U.S. Navy, or that control of it was inadvertently handed over to it, then the possibility is disturbing indeed. It means that two conceptual branches of that discarded theory were reunited in the "peace" that followed.

But it need not be a Nazi International. Other entities may have worked in cooperation with it.

In either case, we know what they are.

We know their think tanks by name.

We know their family surnames and histories.

We know their politics and policies.

We know their memberships and affiliations.

We know their goals.

We know their avaricious hording of all means of power: financial, technological, political, and cultural.

We know who owns them...

...and whom they really serve.

BIBLIOGRAPHY

Berlitz, Charles, and Moore, William. *The Philadelphia Experiment: Project Invisibility.* London: Souvenir Press. 1979. ISBN 0 285 62400 8.

Berlitz, Charles. *The Bermuda Triangle.* New York: Avon Books. 1974. ISBN 0-389-00465-8.

Cook, Nick. *The Hunt for Zero Point: One Man's Journey to Discover the Biggest Secret Since the Invention of the Atom Bomb.* London: Century. 2001. ISBN 0 7126 69531.

Corum, K.L., Corum, J.F., Ph.D., and Daum, J.F.X., Ph.D., "Tesla's Egg of Columbus, Radar Stealth, The Torsion Tensor, and the 'Philadelphia Experiment'." Colorado Springs: 1994 Tesla Symposium. 1994.

"Dru (a.k.a. Howard A. Strom), and Cunningham, Debra J. *Special Investigative Report #1: Carlos Miguel Allende's Witness Account of "The Philadelphia Experiment."* Oceanside, CA: (No Publisher Listed), 2003.

Einstein, Albert. "Unified Field Theory of Gravitation and Electricity," trans. A. Unzicker and T. Case, *Session Report of the Prussian Academy of Sciences,* July 25th, 1925, pp. 414-419.

-----. "New Possibility for a Unified Field Theory of Gravitation and Electricity," trans. A. Unzicker and T. Case, *Session Report of the Prussian Academy of Sciences,* June 14, 1928, pp. 224-227.

-----. "Riemannian Geometry with Maintaining the Notion of Distant Parallelism," trans. A. Unzicker and T. Case, *Session Report of the Prussian Academy of Sciences,* June 7, 1928, pp. 217-221.

-----. "Unified Field Theory Based on Riemannian Metrics and Distant Parallelism," trans. A. Unzicker and T. Case, *Mathematische Annalen,* 102 (1930), pp. 685-697.

Farrell, Joseph P. *The SS Brotherhood of the Bell: NASA's Nazis, JFK, and Majic-12.* Kempton, Illinois: Adventures Unlimited Press. 2006.

315

Jessup, Morris K. *The Case for the UFO: Unidentified Flying Object, "Varo Edition."* Castelnau-Barbarens, France: The Quantum Future Group. 2003.

Kaku, Michio. *Hyperspace: A Scientific Odyssey Through Parallel Universes, Time Warps, and the 10th Dimension.* Oxford University Press. 1994. ISBN 0-19-508514-0.

Kaku, Michio, and Thompson, Jennifer. *Beyond Einstein: The Cosmic Quest for the Theory of the Universe.* New York: Anchor Doubleday. 1987. ISBN 0-385-47781-3.

Kron, Gabriel. *Tensors for Circuits.* Dover. 1959. No ISBN.

Kron, Gabriel. "Tensor Analysis of Rotating Machinery: The Transient Performance of Asymmetrical Machines under Unbalanced Conditions." 1933.

Levenda, Peter. *Sinister Forces: A Grimoire of American Political Witchcraft, Book One: The Nine.* Walterville, Oregon: TrineDay. 2005. ISBN 0-9752906-2-2.

Levenda, Peter. *Sinister Forces: A Grimoire of American Political Witchcraft, Book Two: A Warm Gun.* Walterville, Oregon: TrineDay. 2005. ISBN 0-9752906-3-0.

Levenda, Peter. *Sinister Forces: A Grimoire of American Political Witchcraft, Book Three: The Manson Secret.* Walterville, Oregon: TrineDay. 2005. ISBN 0-9752906-4-9.

Redfern, Nicholas. *The F.B.I. Files: The FBI's UFO Top Secrets Exposed.* London: Simon and Schuster. 1998. ISBN 0-684-81938-4.

Stevens, Henry. *Hitler's Suppressed and Still-Secret Weapons, Science, and Technology.* Kempton, Illinois: Adventures Unlimited Press. 2007.

SECRETS OF THE MYSTERIOUS VALLEY
by Christopher O'Brien
No other region in North America features the variety and intensity of unusual phenomena found in the world's largest alpine valley, the San Luis Valley of Colorado and New Mexico. Since 1989, Christopher O'Brien has documented thousands of high-strange accounts that report UFOs, ghosts, crypto-creatures, cattle mutilations, skinwalkers and sorcerers, along with portal areas, secret underground bases and covert military activity. This mysterious region at the top of North America has a higher incidence of UFO reports than any other area of the continent and is the publicized birthplace of the "cattle mutilation" mystery. Hundreds of animals have been found strangely slain during waves of anomalous aerial craft sightings. Is the government directly involved? Are there underground bases here? Does the military fly exotic aerial craft in this valley that are radar-invisible below 18,000 feet? These and many other questions are addressed in this all-new, work by one of America's top paranormal investigators. Take a fantastic journey through one of the world's most enigmatic locales!
460 pages. 6x9 Paperback. Illustrated. Bibliography. $19.95. Code: SOMV

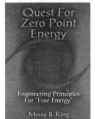

QUEST FOR ZERO-POINT ENERGY
Engineering Principles for "Free Energy"
by Moray B. King
King expands, with diagrams, on how free energy and anti-gravity are possible. The theories of zero point energy maintain there are tremendous fluctuations of electrical field energy embedded within the fabric of space. King explains the following topics: Tapping the Zero-Point Energy as an Energy Source; Fundamentals of a Zero-Point Energy Technology; Vacuum Energy Vortices; The Super Tube; Charge Clusters: The Basis of Zero-Point Energy Inventions; Vortex Filaments, Torsion Fields and the Zero-Point Energy; Transforming the Planet with a Zero-Point Energy Experiment; Dual Vortex Forms: The Key to a Large Zero-Point Energy Coherence. Packed with diagrams, patents and photos. With power shortages now a daily reality in many parts of the world, this book offers a fresh approach very rarely mentioned in the mainstream media.
224 PAGES. 6x9 PAPERBACK. ILLUSTRATED. $14.95. CODE: QZPE

TAPPING THE ZERO POINT ENERGY
Free Energy & Anti-Gravity in Today's Physics
by Moray B. King
King explains how free energy and anti-gravity are possible. The theories of the zero point energy maintain there are tremendous fluctuations of electrical field energy imbedded within the fabric of space. This book tells how, in the 1930s, inventor T. Henry Moray could produce a fifty kilowatt "free energy" machine; how an electrified plasma vortex creates anti-gravity; how the Pons/Fleischmann "cold fusion" experiment could produce tremendous heat without fusion; and how certain experiments might produce a gravitational anomaly.
180 PAGES. 5x8 PAPERBACK. ILLUSTRATED. $12.95. CODE: TAP

THE FREE-ENERGY DEVICE HANDBOOK
A Compilation of Patents and Reports
by David Hatcher Childress
A large-format compilation of various patents, papers, descriptions and diagrams concerning free-energy devices and systems. *The Free-Energy Device Handbook* is a visual tool for experimenters and researchers into magnetic motors and other "overunity" devices. With chapters on the Adams Motor, the Hans Coler Generator, cold fusion, superconductors, "N" machines, space-energy generators, Nikola Tesla, T. Townsend Brown, and the latest in free-energy devices. Packed with photos, technical diagrams, patents and fascinating information, this book belongs on every science shelf. With energy and profit being a major political reason for fighting various wars, free-energy devices, if ever allowed to be mass distributed to consumers, could change the world! Get your copy now before the Department of Energy bans this book!
292 PAGES. 8x10 PAPERBACK. ILLUSTRATED. BIBLIOGRAPHY. $16.95. CODE: FEH

THE TIME TRAVEL HANDBOOK
A Manual of Practical Teleportation & Time Travel
edited by David Hatcher Childress
In the tradition of *The Anti-Gravity Handbook* and *The Free-Energy Device Handbook*, science and UFO author David Hatcher Childress takes us into the weird world of time travel and teleportation. Not just a whacked-out look at science fiction, this book is an authoritative chronicling of real-life time travel experiments, teleportation devices and more. *The Time Travel Handbook* takes the reader beyond the government experiments and deep into the uncharted territory of early time travellers such as Nikola Tesla and Guglielmo Marconi and their alleged time travel experiments, as well as the Wilson Brothers of EMI and their connection to the Philadelphia Experiment—the U.S. Navy's forays into invisibility, time travel, and teleportation. Childress looks into the claims of time travelling individuals, and investigates the unusual claim that the pyramids on Mars were built in the future and sent back in time. A highly visual, large format book, with patents, photos and schematics. Be the first on your block to build your own time travel device!
316 PAGES. 7x10 PAPERBACK. ILLUSTRATED. $16.95. CODE: TTH

ETHER TECHNOLOGY
A Rational Approach to Gravity Control
by Rho Sigma
This classic book on anti-gravity and free energy is back in print and back in stock. Written by a well-known American scientist under the pseudonym of "Rho Sigma," this book delves into international efforts at gravity control and discoid craft propulsion. Before the Quantum Field, there was "Ether." This small, but informative book has chapters on John Searle and "Searle discs;" T. Townsend Brown and his work on anti-gravity and ether-vortex turbines. Includes a forward by former NASA astronaut Edgar Mitchell.
108 PAGES. 6x9 PAPERBACK. ILLUSTRATED. $12.95. CODE: ETT

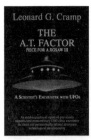

THE A.T. FACTOR
A Scientists Encounter with UFOs: Piece For A Jigsaw Part 3
by Leonard Cramp
British aerospace engineer Cramp began much of the scientific anti-gravity and UFO propulsion analysis back in 1955 with his landmark book *Space, Gravity & the Flying Saucer* (out-of-print and rare). His next books (available from Adventures Unlimited) *UFOs & Anti-Gravity: Piece for a Jig-Saw* and *The Cosmic Matrix: Piece for a Jig-Saw Part 2* began Cramp's in depth look into gravity control, free-energy, and the interlocking web of energy that pervades the universe. In this final book, Cramp brings to a close his detailed and controversial study of UFOs and Anti-Gravity.
324 PAGES. 6x9 PAPERBACK. ILLUSTRATED. BIBLIOGRAPHY. INDEX. $16.95. CODE: ATF

COSMIC MATRIX
Piece for a Jig-Saw, Part Two
by Leonard G. Cramp
Leonard G. Cramp, a British aerospace engineer, wrote his first book *Space Gravity and the Flying Saucer* in 1954. Cosmic Matrix is the long-awaited sequel to his 1966 book *UFOs & Anti-Gravity: Piece for a Jig-Saw.* Cramp has had a long history of examining UFO phenomena and has concluded that UFOs use the highest possible aeronautic science to move in the way they do. Cramp examines anti-gravity effects and theorizes that this super-science used by the craft—described in detail in the book—can lift mankind into a new level of technology, transportation and understanding of the universe. The book takes a close look at gravity control, time travel, and the interlocking web of energy between all planets in our solar system with Leonard's unique technical diagrams. A fantastic voyage into the present and future!
364 PAGES. 6x9 PAPERBACK. ILLUSTRATED. BIBLIOGRAPHY. $16.00. CODE: CMX

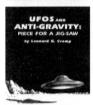

UFOS AND ANTI-GRAVITY
Piece For A Jig-Saw
by Leonard G. Cramp
Leonard G. Cramp's 1966 classic book on flying saucer propulsion and suppressed technology is a highly technical look at the UFO phenomena by a trained scientist. Cramp first introduces the idea of 'anti-gravity' and introduces us to the various theories of gravitation. He then examines the technology necessary to build a flying saucer and examines in great detail the technical aspects of such a craft. Cramp's book is a wealth of material and diagrams on flying saucers, anti-gravity, suppressed technology, G-fields and UFOs. Chapters include Crossroads of Aerodymanics, Aerodynamic Saucers, Limitations of Rocketry, Gravitation and the Ether, Gravitational Spaceships, G-Field Lift Effects, The Bi-Field Theory, VTOL and Hovercraft, Analysis of UFO photos, more.
388 PAGES. 6x9 PAPERBACK. ILLUSTRATED. $16.95. CODE: UAG

THE TESLA PAPERS
Nikola Tesla on Free Energy & Wireless Transmission of Power
by Nikola Tesla, edited by David Hatcher Childress
David Hatcher Childress takes us into the incredible world of Nikola Tesla and his amazing inventions. Tesla's rare article "The Problem of Increasing Human Energy with Special Reference to the Harnessing of the Sun's Energy" is included. This lengthy article was originally published in the June 1900 issue of *The Century Illustrated Monthly Magazine* and it was the outline for Tesla's master blueprint for the world. Tesla's fantastic vision of the future, including wireless power, anti-gravity, free energy and highly advanced solar power. Also included are some of the papers, patents and material collected on Tesla at the Colorado Springs Tesla Symposiums, including papers on: •The Secret History of Wireless Transmission •Tesla and the Magnifying Transmitter •Design and Construction of a Half-Wave Tesla Coil •Electrostatics: A Key to Free Energy •Progress in Zero-Point Energy Research •Electromagnetic Energy from Antennas to Atoms •Tesla's Particle Beam Technology •Fundamental Excitatory Modes of the Earth-Ionosphere Cavity
325 PAGES. 8x10 PAPERBACK. ILLUSTRATED. $16.95. CODE: TTP

THE FANTASTIC INVENTIONS OF NIKOLA TESLA
by Nikola Tesla with additional material by David Hatcher Childress
This book is a readable compendium of patents, diagrams, photos and explanations of the many incredible inventions of the originator of the modern era of electrification. In Tesla's own words are such topics as wireless transmission of power, death rays, and radio-controlled airships. In addition, rare material on German bases in Antarctica and South America, and a secret city built at a remote jungle site in South America by one of Tesla's students, Guglielmo Marconi. Marconi's secret group claims to have built flying saucers in the 1940s and to have gone to Mars in the early 1950s! Incredible photos of these Tesla craft are included. The Ancient Atlantean system of broadcasting energy through a grid system of obelisks and pyramids is discussed, and a fascinating concept comes out of one chapter: that Egyptian engineers had to wear protective metal head-shields while in these power plants, hence the Egyptian Pharoah's head covering as well as the Face on Mars! •His plan to transmit free electricity into the atmosphere. •How electrical devices would work using only small antennas. •Why unlimited power could be utilized anywhere on earth. •How radio and radar technology can be used as death-ray weapons in Star Wars.
342 PAGES. 6x9 PAPERBACK. ILLUSTRATED. $16.95. CODE: FINT

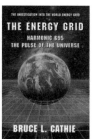

THE ENERGY GRID
Harmonic 695, The Pulse of the Universe
by Captain Bruce Cathie.
This is the breakthrough book that explores the incredible potential of the Energy Grid and the Earth's Unified Field all around us. Cathie's first book, *Harmonic 33*, was published in 1968 when he was a commercial pilot in New Zealand. Since then, Captain Bruce Cathie has been the premier investigator into the amazing potential of the infinite energy that surrounds our planet every microsecond. Cathie investigates the Harmonics of Light and how the Energy Grid is created. In this amazing book are chapters on UFO Propulsion, Nikola Tesla, Unified Equations, the Mysterious Aerials, Pythagoras & the Grid, Nuclear Detonation and the Grid, Maps of the Ancients, an Australian Stonehenge examined, more.
255 PAGES. 6x9 TRADEPAPER. ILLUSTRATED. $15.95. CODE: TEG

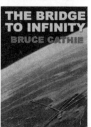

THE BRIDGE TO INFINITY
Harmonic 371244
by Captain Bruce Cathie
Cathie has popularized the concept that the earth is crisscrossed by an electromagnetic grid system that can be used for anti-gravity, free energy, levitation and more. The book includes a new analysis of the harmonic nature of reality, acoustic levitation, pyramid power, harmonic receiver towers and UFO propulsion. It concludes that today's scientists have at their command a fantastic store of knowledge with which to advance the welfare of the human race.
204 PAGES. 6x9 TRADEPAPER. ILLUSTRATED. $14.95. CODE: BTF

THE HARMONIC CONQUEST OF SPACE
by Captain Bruce Cathie
Chapters include: Mathematics of the World Grid; the Harmonics of Hiroshima and Nagasaki; Harmonic Transmission and Receiving; the Link Between Human Brain Waves; the Cavity Resonance between the Earth; the Ionosphere and Gravity; Edgar Cayce—the Harmonics of the Subconscious; Stonehenge; the Harmonics of the Moon; the Pyramids of Mars; Nikola Tesla's Electric Car; the Robert Adams Pulsed Electric Motor Generator; Harmonic Clues to the Unified Field; and more. Also included are tables showing the harmonic relations between the earth's magnetic field, the speed of light, and anti-gravity/gravity acceleration at different points on the earth's surface. New chapters in this edition on the giant stone spheres of Costa Rica, Atomic Tests and Volcanic Activity, and a chapter on Ayers Rock analysed with Stone Mountain, Georgia.
248 PAGES. 6x9. PAPERBACK. ILLUSTRATED. BIBLIOGRAPHY. $16.95. CODE: HCS

LEY LINE & EARTH ENERGIES
An Extraordinary Journey into the Earth's Natural Energy System
by David Cowan & Chris Arnold
The mysterious standing stones, burial grounds and stone circles that lace Europe, the British Isles and other areas have intrigued scientists, writers, artists and travellers through the centuries. How do ley lines work? How did our ancestors use Earth energy to map their sacred sites and burial grounds? How do ghosts and poltergeists interact with Earth energy? How can Earth spirals and black spots affect our health? This exploration shows how natural forces affect our behavior, how they can be used to enhance our health and well being. A fascinating and visual book about subtle Earth energies and how they affect us and the world around them.
368 PAGES. 6x9 PAPERBACK. ILLUSTRATED. BIBLIOGRAPHY. INDEX. $18.95. CODE: LLEE

DARK MOON
Apollo and the Whistleblowers
by Mary Bennett and David Percy
•Was Neil Armstrong really the first man on the Moon?
•Did you know a second craft was going to the Moon at the same time as Apollo 11?
•Do you know that potentially lethal radiation is prevalent throughout deep space?
•Do you know there are serious discrepancies in the account of the Apollo 13 'accident'?
•Did you know that 'live' color TV from the Moon was not actually live at all?
•Did you know that the Lunar Surface Camera had no viewfinder?
•Do you know that lighting was used in the Apollo photographs—yet no lighting equipment was taken to the Moon?
All these questions, and more, are discussed in great detail by British researchers Bennett and Percy in *Dark Moon*, the definitive book (nearly 600 pages) on the possible faking of the Apollo Moon missions. Bennett and Percy delve into every possible aspect of this beguiling theory, one that rocks the very foundation of our beliefs concerning NASA and the space program. Tons of NASA photos analyzed for possible deceptions.
568 PAGES. 6x9 PAPERBACK. ILLUSTRATED. BIBLIOGRAPHY. INDEX. $25.00. CODE: DMO

THE ANTI-GRAVITY HANDBOOK
edited by David Hatcher Childress, with Nikola Tesla, T.B. Paulicki, Bruce Cathie, Albert Einstein and others
The new expanded compilation of material on Anti-Gravity, Free Energy, Flying Saucer Propulsion, UFOs, Suppressed Technology, NASA Cover-ups and more. Highly illustrated with patents, technical illustrations and photos. This revised and expanded edition has more material, including photos of Area 51, Nevada, the government's secret testing facility. This classic on weird science is back in a 90s format!
- **How to build a flying saucer.**
- **Arthur C. Clarke on Anti-Gravity.**
- **Crystals and their role in levitation.**
- **Secret government research and development.**
230 PAGES. 7x10 PAPERBACK. ILLUSTRATED. $16.95. CODE: AGH

ANTI–GRAVITY & THE WORLD GRID
Is the earth surrounded by an intricate electromagnetic grid network offering free energy? This compilation of material on ley lines and world power points contains chapters on the geography, mathematics, and light harmonics of the earth grid. Learn the purpose of ley lines and ancient megalithic structures located on the grid. Discover how the grid made the Philadelphia Experiment possible. Explore the Coral Castle and many other mysteries, including acoustic levitation, Tesla Shields and scalar wave weaponry. Browse through the section on anti-gravity patents, and research resources.
274 PAGES. 7x10 PAPERBACK. ILLUSTRATED. $14.95. CODE: AGW

ANTI–GRAVITY & THE UNIFIED FIELD
edited by David Hatcher Childress
Is Einstein's Unified Field Theory the answer to all of our energy problems? Explored in this compilation of material is how gravity, electricity and magnetism manifest from a unified field around us. Why artificial gravity is possible; secrets of UFO propulsion; free energy; Nikola Tesla and anti-gravity airships of the 20s and 30s; flying saucers as superconducting whirls of plasma; anti-mass generators; vortex propulsion; suppressed technology; government cover-ups; gravitational pulse drive; spacecraft & more.
240 PAGES. 7x10 PAPERBACK. ILLUSTRATED. $14.95. CODE: AGU

THE MYSTERY OF THE OLMECS
by David Hatcher Childress

Lost Cities author Childress takes us deep into Mexico and Central America in search of the mysterious Olmecs, North America's early, advanced civilization. The Olmecs, now sometimes called Proto-Mayans, were not acknowledged to have existed as a civilization until an international archeological meeting in Mexico City in 1942. At this time, the megalithic statues, large structures, ceramics and other artifacts were acknowledged to come from this hitherto unknown culture that pre-dated all other cultures of Central America. But who were the Olmecs? Where did they come from? What happened to them? How sophisticated was their culture? How far back in time did it go? Why are many Olmec statues and figurines seemingly of foreign peoples such as Africans, Europeans and Chinese? Is there a link with Atlantis? In this heavily illustrated book, join Childress in search of the lost cites of the Olmecs!
432 Pages. 6x9 Paperback. Illustrated. Bibliography. $20.00. Code: MOLM

PATH OF THE POLE
Cataclysmic Pole Shift Geology
by Charles H. Hapgood
Maps of the Ancient Sea Kings author Hapgood's classic book *Path of the Pole* is back in print! Hapgood researched Antarctica, ancient maps and the geological record to conclude that the Earth's crust has slipped on the inner core many times in the past, changing the position of the pole. *Path of the Pole* discusses the various "pole shifts" in Earth's past, giving evidence for each one, and moves on to possible future pole shifts. Packed with illustrations, this is the sourcebook for many other books on cataclysms and pole shifts.
356 PAGES. 6x9 PAPERBACK. ILLUSTRATED. $16.95. CODE: POP

MAPS OF THE ANCIENT SEA KINGS
Evidence of Advanced Civilization in the Ice Age
by Charles H. Hapgood
Charles Hapgood's classic 1966 book on ancient maps produces concrete evidence of an advanced world-wide civilization existing many thousands of years before ancient Egypt. He has found the evidence in the Piri Reis Map that shows Antarctica, the Hadji Ahmed map, the Oronteus Finaeus and other amazing maps. Hapgood concluded that these maps were made from more ancient maps from the various ancient archives around the world, now lost. Not only were these unknown people more advanced in mapmaking than any people prior to the 18th century, it appears they mapped all the continents. The Americas were mapped thousands of years before Columbus. Antarctica was mapped when its coasts were free of ice!
316 PAGES. 7x10 PAPERBACK. ILLUSTRATED. BIBLIOGRAPHY & INDEX. $19.95. CODE: MASK

REICH OF THE BLACK SUN
Nazi Secret Weapons and the Cold War Allied Legend
by Joseph P. Farrell

Why were the Allies worried about an atom bomb attack by the Germans in 1944? Why did the Soviets threaten to use poison gas against the Germans? Why did Hitler in 1945 insist that holding Prague could win the war for the Third Reich? Why did US General George Patton's Third Army race for the Skoda works at Pilsen in Czechoslovakia instead of Berlin? Why did the US Army not test the uranium atom bomb it dropped on Hiroshima? Why did the Luftwaffe fly a non-stop round trip mission to within twenty miles of New York City in 1944? *Reich of the Black Sun* takes the reader on a scientific-historical journey in order to answer these questions. Arguing that Nazi Germany actually won the race for the atom bomb in late 1944, *Reich of the Black Sun* then goes on to explore the even more secretive research the Nazis were conducting into the occult, alternative physics and new energy sources. The book concludes with a fresh look at the "Nazi Legend" of the UFO mystery by examining the Roswell Majestic-12 documents and the Kecksburg crash in the light of parallels with some of the super-secret black projects being run by the SS. *Reich of the Black Sun* is must-reading for the researcher interested in alternative history, science, or UFOs!

352 PAGES. 6x9 PAPERBACK. ILLUSTRATED. BIBLIOGRAPHY. $16.95. CODE: ROBS

THE GIZA DEATH STAR DEPLOYED
The Physics & Engineering of the Great Pyramid
by Joseph P. Farrell

Farrell expands on his thesis that the Great Pyramid was a chemical maser, designed as a weapon and eventually deployed—with disastrous results to the solar system. Includes: Exploding Planets: The Movie, the Mirror, and the Model; Dating the Catastrophe and the Compound; A Brief History of the Exoteric and Esoteric Investigations of the Great Pyramid; No Machines, Please!; The Stargate Conspiracy; The Scalar Weapons; Message or Machine?; A Tesla Analysis of the Putative Physics and Engineering of the Giza Death Star; Cohering the Zero Point, Vacuum Energy, Flux: Synopsis of Scalar Physics and Paleophysics; Configuring the Scalar Pulse Wave; Inferred Applications in the Great Pyramid; Quantum Numerology, Feedback Loops and Tetrahedral Physics; and more.

290 PAGES. 6x9 PAPERBACK. ILLUSTRATED. BIBLIOGRAPHY. $16.95. CODE: GDSD

THE GIZA DEATH STAR
The Paleophysics of the Great Pyramid & the Military Complex at Giza
by Joseph P. Farrell

Physicist Joseph Farrell's amazing book on the secrets of Great Pyramid of Giza. *The Giza Death Star* starts where British engineer Christopher Dunn leaves off in his 1998 book, *The Giza Power Plant*. Was the Giza complex part of a military installation over 10,000 years ago? Chapters include: An Archaeology of Mass Destruction, Thoth and Theories; The Machine Hypothesis; Pythagoras, Plato, Planck, and the Pyramid; The Weapon Hypothesis; Encoded Harmonics of the Planck Units in the Great Pyramid; High Frequency Direct Current "Impulse" Technology; The Grand Gallery and its Crystals: Gravito-acoustic Resonators; The Other Two Large Pyramids; the "Causeways," and the "Temples"; A Phase Conjugate Howitzer; Evidence of the Use of Weapons of Mass Destruction in Ancient Times; more.

290 PAGES. 6x9 PAPERBACK. ILLUSTRATED. $16.95. CODE: GDS

THE LAND OF OSIRIS
An Introduction to Khemitology
by Stephen S. Mehler

Was there an advanced prehistoric civilization in ancient Egypt who built the great pyramids and carved the Great Sphinx? Did the pyramids serve as energy devices and not as tombs for kings? Mehler has uncovered an indigenous oral tradition that still exists in Egypt, and has been fortunate to have studied with a living master of this tradition, Abd'El Hakim Awyan. Mehler has also been given permission to present these teachings to the Western world, teachings that unfold a whole new understanding of ancient Egypt . Chapters include: Egyptology and Its Paradigms; Asgat Nefer—The Harmony of Water; Khemit and the Myth of Atlantis; The Extraterrestrial Question; more.

272 PAGES. 6x9 PAPERBACK. ILLUSTRATED. COLOR SECTION. BIBLIOGRAPHY. $18.00 CODE: LOOS

EDEN IN EGYPT
by Ralph Ellis

The story of Adam and Eve from the Book of Genesis is perhaps one of the best-known stories in circulation, even today, and yet nobody really knows where this tale came from or what it means. But even a cursory glance at the text will demonstrate the origins of this tale, for the river of Eden is described as having four branches. There is only one river in this part of the world that fits this description, and that is the Nile, with the four branches forming the Nile Delta. According to Ellis, Judaism was based upon the reign of the pharaoh Akhenaton, because the solitary Judaic god was known as Adhon while this pharaoh's solitary god was called Aton or Adjon. But what of the identities of Adam and Eve? The Israelites were once the leaders of Egypt and would originally have spoken Egyptian (Joseph, according to the Bible, was prime minister of all Egypt). This discovery allows us to translate the Genesis story with more confidence, and the result is that it seems that Adam and Eve were actually Pharaoh Akhenaton and his famous wife Queen Nefertiti. Includes 16 page color section.

320 PAGES. 6x9 PAPERBACK. ILLUSTRATED. BIBLIOGRAPHY. INDEX. $20.00. CODE: EIE

GUARDIANS OF THE HOLY GRAIL
by Mark Amaru Pinkham
This book presents this extremely ancient Holy Grail lineage from Asia and how the Knights Templar were initiated into it. It also reveals how the ancient Asian wisdom regarding the Holy Grail became the foundation for the Holy Grail legends of the west while also serving as the bedrock of the European Secret Societies, which included the Freemasons, Rosicrucians, and the Illuminati. Also: The Fisher Kings; The Middle Eastern mystery schools, such as the Assassins and Yezidhi; The ancient Holy Grail lineage from Sri Lanka and the Templar Knights' initiation into it; The head of John the Baptist and its importance to the Templars; The secret Templar initiation with grotesque Baphomet, the infamous Head of Wisdom; more.
248 PAGES. 6x9 PAPERBACK. ILLUSTRATED. BIBLIOGRAPHY. $16.95. CODE: GOHG

SECRETS OF THE HOLY LANCE
The Spear of Destiny in History & Legend
by Jerry E. Smith
As Jesus Christ hung on the cross a Roman centurion pieced the Savior's side with his spear. A legend has arisen that "whosoever possesses this Holy Lance and understands the powers it serves, holds in his hand the destiny of the world for good or evil." *Secrets of the Holy Lance* traces the Spear from its possession by Constantine, Rome's first Christian Caesar, to Charlemagne's claim that with it he ruled the Holy Roman Empire by Divine Right, and on through two thousand years of kings and emperors, until it came within Hitler's grasp—and beyond! Did it rest for a while in Antarctic ice? Is it now hidden in Europe, awaiting the next person to claim its awesome power? Neither debunking nor worshiping, *Secrets of the Holy Lance* seeks to pierce the veil of myth and mystery around the Spear. Mere belief that it was infused with magic by virtue of its shedding the Savior's blood has made men kings. But what if it's more? What are "the powers it serves"?
312 PAGES. 6x9 PAPERBACK. ILLUSTRATED. BIBLIOGRAPHY. $16.95. CODE: SOHL

SUNS OF GOD
Krishna, Buddha and Christ Unveiled
by Acharya S
From the author of the controversial and best-selling book *The Christ Conspiracy: The Greatest Story Ever Sold* comes this electrifying journey into the origins and meaning of the world's religions and popular gods. Over the past several centuries, the Big Three spiritual leaders have been the Lords Christ, Krishna and Buddha, whose stories and teachings are so remarkably similar as to confound and amaze those who encounter them. As classically educated archaeologist, historian, mythologist and linguist Acharya S thoroughly reveals, these striking parallels exist not because these godmen were "historical" personages who "walked the earth" but because they are personifications of the central focus of the famous and scandalous "mysteries." These mysteries date back thousands of years and are found globally, reflecting an ancient tradition steeped in awe and intrigue. In unveiling the reasons for this highly significant development, the author presents an in-depth analysis that includes fascinating and original research based on evidence both modern and ancient—captivating information kept secret and hidden for ages.
428 PAGES. 6x9 PAPERBACK. ILLUSTRATED. BIBLIOGRAPHY. INDEX. $18.95. CODE: SUNG

THE ORION PROPHECY
Egyptian and Mayan Prophecies on the Cataclysm of 2012
by Patrick Geryl and Gino Ratinckx
In the year 2012 the Earth awaits a super catastrophe: its magnetic field will reverse in one go. Phenomenal earthquakes and tidal waves will completely destroy our civilization. These dire predictions stem from the Mayans and Egyptians—descendants of the legendary Atlantis. The Atlanteans had highly evolved astronomical knowledge and were able to exactly predict the previous world-wide flood in 9792 BC. They built tens of thousands of boats and escaped to South America and Egypt. In the year 2012 Venus, Orion and several others stars will take the same 'code-positions' as in 9792 BC! For thousands of years historical sources have told of a forgotten time capsule of ancient wisdom located in a labyrinth of secret chambers filled with artifacts and documents from the previous flood.
324 PAGES. 6x9 PAPERBACK. ILLUSTRATED. BIBLIOGRAPHY. $16.95. CODE: ORP

HOW TO SURVIVE 2012
by Patrick Geryl
In his previous books, *The Orion Prophecy* and *The World Cataclysm in 2012*, Patrick Geryl presented in great detail the scenario set to take place in the year 2012, a scenario of complete and utter destruction which has occurred in Earth's past and will occur again. Due to a recurring pattern of activity in the sun's magnetic fields, the magnetic poles of the sun reverse from time to time. This, in turn, causes the release of massive solar flares that lash out into the solar system. These cause havoc with the Earth's magnetic field, resulting in the reversal of the Earth's magnetic poles, hence a reversal of its very rotation! The Earth's outer crust is thrown into chaos, with planet-wide earthquakes, volcanoes and tidal waves reshaping landmasses and seas in a matter of hours. Civilization as we know it will end. Billions of casualties will occur worldwide; very few humans will survive. In the face of this immense cataclysm, Geryl urges mankind to prepare and endure. The outlook is bleak, but the obstacles are not insurmountable. In this book, Geryl provides the blueprint for those wishing to survive the disaster to prepare themselves and prevail. He explains in detail the myriad problems survivors will encounter, and the precautions that need to be taken to overcome them. It is his hope that with this information in hand, enough people will live on to reestablish civilization and continue human life on Earth.
294 Pages. 6x9 Paperback. Illustrated. Bibliography. Index. $16.95. Code: HS20